AQA History

A New Roman Empire? Mussolini and Italy 1922–1945

Chris Rowe
Series editor
Sally Waller

Nelson Thornes

Published in 2010 by:
Nelson Thornes Ltd
Delta Place
27 Bath Road
CHELTENHAM
GL53 7TH
United Kingdom

13 14 15 16 / 10 9 8 7 6 5 4 3

A catalogue record for this book is available from the British Library

ISBN 978 1 4085 0312 6

Cover photograph courtesy of Topfoto

Illustrations by David Russell Illustration

Page make-up by Thomson Digital

Printed in China by 1010 Printing International Ltd

Contents

Introduction

Nelson Thornes

Nelson Thornes has worked hard to ensure this book offers you excellent support for your AS or A Level course. You can be confident that the range of learning, teaching and practice materials has been checked and is matched to the requirements of your specification.

How to use this book

The features in this book include:

Timeline

Key events are outlined at the beginning of the book. The events are colour-coded so you can clearly see the categories of change.

Learning objectives

At the beginning of each section you will find a list of learning objectives that contain targets linked to the requirements of the specification.

Key chronology

A short list of dates usually with a focus on a specific event or legislation.

Key profile

The profile of a key person you should be aware of to fully understand the period in question.

Key terms

A term that you will need to be able to define and understand.

Did you know?

Interesting information to bring the subject under discussion to life.

Exploring the detail

Information to put further context around the subject under discussion.

A closer look

An in-depth look at a theme, person or event to deepen your understanding. Activities around the extra information may be included.

Sources

Sources to reinforce topics or themes and may provide fact or opinion. They may be quotations from historical works, contemporaries of the period or photographs.

Cross-reference

Links to related content within the book which may offer more detail on the subject in question.

Activity

Various activity types to provide you with different challenges and opportunities to demonstrate both the content and skills you are learning. Some can be worked on individually, some as part of group work and some are designed to specifically 'stretch and challenge'.

Question

Questions to prompt further discussion on the topic under consideration and are an aid to revision.

Summary questions

Summary questions at the end of each chapter to test your knowledge and allow you to demonstrate your understanding.

Study tip

Hints to help you with your study and to prepare for your exam.

Practice questions

Questions at the end of each section in the style that you may encounter in your exam.

Learning outcomes

Learning outcomes at the end of each section remind you what you should know having completed the chapters in that section.

Web links in the book

Because Nelson Thornes is not responsible for third party content online, there may be some changes to this material that are beyond our control. In order for us to ensure that the links referred to in the book are as up-to-date and stable as possible, the web sites provided are usually homepages with supporting instructions on how to reach the relevant pages if necessary.

Please let us know at **kerboodle@nelsonthornes.com** if you find a link that doesn't work and we will do our best to correct this at reprint, or to list an alternative site.

Introduction to the History series

When Bruce Bogtrotter in Roald Dahl's *Matilda* was challenged to eat a huge chocolate cake, he just opened his mouth and ploughed in, taking bite after bite and lump after lump until the cake was gone and he was feeling decidedly sick. The picture is not dissimilar to that of some A Level history students. They are attracted to history because of its inherent appeal but, when faced with a bulging file and a forthcoming examination, their enjoyment evaporates. They try desperately to cram their brains with an assortment of random facts and subsequently prove unable to control the outpouring of their ill-digested material in the examination.

The books in this series are designed to help students and teachers avoid this feeling of overload and examination panic by breaking down the AQA History specification in such a way that it is easily absorbed. Above all, they are designed to retain and promote students' enthusiasm for history by avoiding a dreary rehash of dates and events. Each book is divided into sections, matched to those given in the specification, and the content is further broken down into chapters that present the historical material in a lively and attractive form, offering guidance on the key terms, events and issues, and blending thought-provoking activities and questions in a way designed to advance students' understanding. By encouraging students to think for themselves and to share their ideas with others, as well as helping them to develop the knowledge and skills needed for this course, this book should ensure that students' learning remains a pleasure rather than an endurance test.

To make the most of what this book provides, students will need to develop efficient study skills from the start and it is worth spending some time considering what these involve:

- Good organisation of material in a subject-specific file. Organised notes help develop an organised brain and sensible filing ensures time is not wasted hunting for misplaced material. This book uses cross-references to indicate where material in one chapter has relevance to material in another. Students are advised to adopt the same technique.
- A sensible approach to note-making. Students are often too ready to copy large chunks of material from printed books or to download sheaves of printouts from the internet. This series is designed to encourage students to think about the notes they collect and to undertake research with a particular purpose in mind. The activities encourage students to pick out information that is relevant to the issue being addressed and to avoid making notes on material that is not properly understood.
- Taking time to think is by far the most important component of study. By encouraging students to think before they write or speak, be it for a written answer, presentation or class debate, students should learn to form opinions and make judgements based on the accumulation of evidence. The beauty of history is that there is rarely a right or wrong answer so, with sufficient evidence, one student's view will count for as much as the next.

Unit 2

Unit 2 promotes the study of significant periods of history in depth. Although the span of years may appear short, the chosen topics are centred on periods of change that raise specific historical issues and they therefore provide an opportunity for students to study in some depth the interrelationships between ideas, individuals, circumstances and other factors that lead to major developments. Appreciating the dynamics of change, and balancing the degree of change against elements of continuity, make for a fascinating and worthwhile study. Students are also required to analyse consequences and draw conclusions about the issues these studies raise. Such themes are, of course, relevant to an understanding of the present and, through such an historical investigation, students will be guided towards a greater appreciation of the world around them today, as well as develop their understanding of the past.

Unit 2 is tested by a 1 hour 30 minute paper containing three questions. The first question is compulsory and based on sources, while the remaining two, of which students will need to choose one, are two-part questions as described in Table 1. Plentiful sources are included throughout this book to give students some familiarity with contemporary and historiographical material, and activities and suggestions are provided to enable students to develop the required skills. Students should familiarise themselves with the question breakdown, additional hints and marking criteria given below before attempting any of the practice questions at the end of each section.

Answers will be marked according to a scheme based on 'levels of response'. This means that the answer will be assessed according to which level best matches the historical skills displayed, taking both knowledge and understanding into account. All students should have a copy of these criteria and need to use them wisely.

Table 1 *Unit 2: style of questions and marks available*

Unit 2	Question	Marks	Question type	Question stem	Additional notes for students
Question 1 based on three sources of *c*.300 – 500 words in total	(a)	12	This question involves the comparison of two sources	Explain how far the views in Source B differ from those in Source A in relation to ...	Take pains to avoid simply writing out what each source says with limited direct comment. Instead, you should try to find two or three points of comparison and illustrate these with reference to the sources. You should also look for any underlying similarities. In your conclusion, you will need to make it clear exactly 'how far' the views differ
Question 1	(b)	24	This requires use of the sources and own knowledge and asks for an explanation that shows awareness that issues and events can provoke differing views and explanations	How far ... How important was ... How successful ...	This answer needs to be planned as you will need to develop an argument in your answer and show balanced judgement. Try to set out your argument in the introduction and, as you develop your ideas through your paragraphs, support your opinions with detailed evidence. Your conclusion should flow naturally and provide supported judgement. The sources should be used as 'evidence' throughout your answer. Do ensure you refer to them all
Question 2 and 3	(a)	12	This question is focused on a narrow issue within the period studied and requires an explanation	Explain why ...	Make sure you explain 'why', not 'how', and try to order your answer in a way that shows you understand the inter-linkage of factors and which were the more important. You should try to reach an overall judgement/conclusion
Question 2 and 3	(b)	24	This question is broader and asks for analysis and explanation with appropriate judgement. The question requires an awareness of debate over issues	A quotation in the form of a judgement on a key development or issue will be given and candidates asked: Explain why you agree or disagree with this view (of ... in the years ...)	This answer needs to be planned as you will need to show balanced judgement in your answer. Try to think of points that agree and disagree and decide which way you will argue. Set out your argument in the introduction and support it through your paragraphs, giving the alternative picture too but showing why your view is the more convincing. Your conclusion should flow naturally from what you have written

Marking criteria

Question 1(a)

Level 1 Answers either briefly paraphrase/describe the content of the two sources or identify simple comparison(s) between the sources. Skills of written communication are weak. *(0–2 marks)*

Level 2 Responses compare the views expressed in the two sources and identify some differences and/or similarities. There may be some limited own knowledge. Answers are coherent but weakly expressed. *(3–6 marks)*

Level 3 Responses compare the views expressed in the two sources, identifying differences and similarities and using own knowledge to explain and evaluate these. For the most part, answers are clearly expressed. *(7–9 marks)*

Level 4 Responses make a developed comparison between the views expressed in the two sources and own knowledge is applied to evaluate these and to demonstrate a good contextual understanding. For the most part, answers show good skills of written communication. *(10–12 marks)*

Question 1(b)

Level 1 Answers may be based on sources or on own knowledge alone, or they may comprise an undeveloped mixture of the two. They may contain some descriptive material that is only loosely linked to the focus of the question or they may address only a part of the question. Alternatively, there may be some explicit comment with little, if any, appropriate support. Answers are likely to be generalised and assertive. There is little, if any, awareness of different historical interpretations. The response is limited in development and skills of written communication are weak. *(0–6 marks)*

Level 2 Answers may be based on sources or on own knowledge alone, or they may contain a mixture of the two. They may be almost entirely descriptive with few explicit links to the focus of the question. Alternatively, they may contain some explicit comment with relevant but limited support. They display limited understanding of different historical interpretations. Answers are coherent but weakly expressed and/or poorly structured. *(7–11 marks)*

Level 3 Answers show a developed understanding of the demands of the question using evidence from both the sources and own knowledge. They provide some assessment backed by relevant and appropriately selected evidence, but they lack depth and/or balance. There is some understanding of varying historical interpretations. For the most part, answers are clearly expressed and show some organisation in the presentation of material. *(12 –16 marks)*

Level 4 Answers show explicit understanding of the demands of the question. They develop a balanced argument backed by a good range of appropriately selected evidence from the sources and own knowledge, and a good understanding of historical interpretations. For the most part, answers show organisation and good skills of written communication. *(17–21 marks)*

Level 5 Answers are well focused and closely argued. The arguments are supported by precisely selected evidence from the sources and own knowledge, incorporating well-developed understanding of historical interpretations and debate. For the most part, answers are carefully organised and fluently written, using appropriate vocabulary. *(22–24 marks)*

Question 2(a) and 3(a)

Level 1 Answers contain either some descriptive material that is only loosely linked to the focus of the question or some explicit comment with little, if any, appropriate support. Answers are likely to be generalised and assertive. The response is limited in development and skills of written communication will be weak. *(0–2 marks)*

Level 2 Answers demonstrate some knowledge and understanding of the demands of the question. Either they are almost entirely descriptive with few explicit links to the question or they provide some explanations backed by evidence that is limited in range and/or depth. Answers are coherent but weakly expressed and/or poorly structured. *(3–6 marks)*

Level 3 Answers demonstrate good understanding of the demands of the question providing relevant explanations backed by appropriately selected information, although this may not be full or comprehensive. For the most part, answers are clearly expressed and show some organisation in the presentation of material. *(7–9 marks)*

Level 4 Answers are well focused, identifying a range of specific explanations backed by precise evidence and demonstrating good understanding of the connections and links between events/issues. For the most part, answers are well written and organised. *(10–12 marks)*

Question 2(b) and 3(b)

Level 1 Answers either contain some descriptive material that is only loosely linked to the focus of the question or address only a limited part of the period of the question. Alternatively, there may be some explicit comment with little, if any, appropriate support. Answers are likely to be generalised and assertive. There will be little, if any, awareness of different historical interpretations. The response is limited in development and skills of written communication are weak. *(0–6 marks)*

Level 2 Answers show some understanding of the demands of the question. Either they are almost entirely descriptive with few explicit links to the question or they contain some explicit comment with relevant but limited support. They display limited understanding of different historical interpretations. Answers are coherent but weakly expressed and/or poorly structured. *(7–11 marks)*

Level 3 Answers show a developed understanding of the demands of the question. They provide some assessment, backed by relevant and appropriately selected evidence, but they lack depth and/or balance. There is some understanding of varying historical interpretations. For the most part, answers are clearly expressed and show some organisation in the presentation of material. *(12–16 marks)*

Level 4 Answers show explicit understanding of the demands of the question. They develop a balanced argument backed by a good range of appropriately selected evidence and a good understanding of historical interpretations. For the most part, answers show organisation and good skills of written communication. *(17–21 marks)*

Level 5 Answers are well focused and closely argued. The arguments are supported by precisely selected evidence leading to a relevant conclusion/judgement, incorporating well-developed understanding of historical interpretations and debate. For the most part, answers are carefully organised and fluently written, using appropriate vocabulary. *(22–24 marks)*

Introduction to this book

Mussolini's Italy was shaped by war and the idea of war. Fascism was born out of Italy's experience in the First World War and the social and political upheavals of 1919–22. Fascism eventually collapsed (twice – once in 1943 and again in 1945) because of the military defeats that resulted from Mussolini's fatal decision to enter the Second World War in 1940. In between, Mussolini first established a fascist dictatorship and then attempted to transform Italians into Fascists through totalitarian ideology, and to establish a New Roman Empire in Africa and the Mediterranean. In the end, Mussolini left Italy in a rather worse situation than he found it and his imperial ambitions led to disastrous defeats. Whether Mussolini was a failure throughout his rule, or only failed because he ruined his own early successes by making a wrong decision in June 1940, is the key question at the heart of this book.

The legacy of the past

Benito Mussolini came to power in 1922, promising to rescue Italy from the economic and political crisis that followed the First World War and from the long-term failures of **Liberal Italy** since unification. The rise of Fascism after the First World War was rooted in the legacy of Italy's past, both in the development of the united Italy from 1870 and in the situation of Italy at the end of the First World War.

Key terms

Liberal Italy: the name commonly given to the new united Italy from 1870 to 1922. Liberal Italy was a parliamentary democracy, ruled by a constitutional monarchy.

Oligarchy: the monopolisation of political power by social and political groups. In an oligarchy, power is rotated or shared (and there may be the outward trappings of democracy) but is actually controlled by a narrow group for their own interests.

The political system

Italian unification was a long and complicated process from 1848 to 1870, involving many different groups with different aims. Before unification, Italy consisted of several disparate states and regions. Even after unification was completed, there were deep differences between republicans and monarchists, between revolutionaries and moderates, between Catholics and anti-clerical Liberals, between northerners and southerners. The Liberal Italy that emerged by 1870 did not satisfy the hopes and expectations of all Italians.

Democratic and republican idealists felt that their ideals had been betrayed and that the process of unification had been hijacked by the north-western kingdom of Piedmont, led by the cunning and manipulative Count Cavour. The new Italy was dominated by the northern elites – the educated middle-class professionals and the prosperous business interests of cities such as Turin and Milan. People in the South had little loyalty to the new political system. Political power after 1870 was almost permanently in the hands of the narrow liberal **oligarchy** that dominated governments on behalf of the northern elites. This system has been described as 'managed democracy' – an outwardly democratic system that was actually manipulated by a powerful minority.

In the 'Crispi era', until 1893, power was in the hands of Francesco Crispi and his political allies. From 1903, the key political leader was Giovanni Giolitti, a protégé of Crispi, who continued to operate the same oligarchic system but faced growing challenges from new political forces, especially due to the rise of Socialism and trade union power as a result of industrialisation. The First World War intensified these challenges but, in 1919, the leaders of the old liberal oligarchy still pulled the strings of government.

There were many Italians who felt that this 'Giolittianism' did not represent their interests. Socialists and trade unionists objected to its 'favouritism' to businessmen and industrialists. The peasants, especially in the South, felt neglected and marginalised. Republican idealists felt cheated and let down because unification had only gone halfway. The Catholic Church was deeply hostile to the **anti-clericalism** of the State. In the years after the First World War, new political parties were beginning to challenge the existing political ruling class.

Key terms

Anti-clericalism: opposition to the Church having influence on politics and society outside the religious sphere.

The monarchy

After unification was achieved, Italy became a constitutional monarchy. The King of Piedmont, Victor Emmanuel I, became King of Italy in 1861. This resulted in a long-term lack of legitimacy for the Italian monarchy. Piedmont, a kingdom in the north-west corner of Italy, did not represent the whole nation. Emmanuel I was succeeded by his son Umberto I in 1878. In 1900, King Umberto I was assassinated by an anarchist, leaving his only son, Victor Emmanuel III, to become king – a small, rather unimpressive man, who sometimes found it hard to exert his authority. In 1919, there were rumours that Victor Emmanuel III might be forced to abdicate in favour of his cousin, the militaristic Duke of Aosta.

Church and society

The gulf between Liberal Italy and the Catholic Church was deep and wide. In the process of unification, French troops had occupied Rome and the papacy had been deprived of territorial control over the Papal States. The ultra-conservative Pope, Pius IX, denounced the united Italian State as 'un-Christian'. From 1870, the papacy refused to recognise the legitimacy of the State and insisted that true Catholics should not even vote in elections. The political parties who dominated Liberal Italy believed in anti-clericalism. There were frequent clashes between Church and State on education and other social issues. This divide continued to exist until 1929. The clash between Church and State deepened the social divisions in Italy, especially between urban and rural societies (and thus between north and south).

The crisis of the economy

Liberal Italy experienced significant economic growth, but this was very patchy and was not on the same scale as other expanding economies like Britain and Germany. The Italian economy was also notable for its 'dualism' – the virtually complete economic separation between north and south.

In the 'northern triangle' between Milan, Turin and Genoa, there was rapid industrialisation and economic development. Big agricultural producers in the Po valley adopted modern farming techniques. There was a boom in railway construction and shipping. New heavy industries emerged in the years before 1915, producing iron and steel, glass, electric power, chemicals and motor cars.

Southern Italy, however, remained desperately poor. In the years between 1890 and 1914, 3 million emigrants left Italy for the Americas.

The South was a backward agricultural society, tightly controlled by the landowners of huge estates. There was little economic development. The biggest single source of income for southern peasants was money sent home from relatives who had gone to the United States or Argentina.

In 1915, Italy entered the First World War in a mood of patriotic optimism, confident of gaining prestige and new territories through a short, victorious war. In reality, three years of war achieved much less than had been hoped and put massive strain on the Italian economy. When the war ended in 1918, the country was faced with huge debts, by the dislocation of the pre-war economy and by high inflation. There was extreme poverty in the South and violence and industrial unrest in the North. The post-war economic crisis put the government under pressure. These pressures were intensified by the mood of dissatisfaction in Italy following the peace settlement.

The dream of empire

In the years after unification, Italy's hopes of becoming a Great Power were not fulfilled. Efforts at colonial expansion had only limited success. Italy managed to gain territory in North Africa with the seizure of Libya in 1911–12, but this did not really compensate for the humiliating defeat of Italian forces by native armies at Adowa, in Ethiopia, in 1896. During the Age of Imperialism, Italy was always overshadowed by the military and economic power of Britain, France and Germany.

The sense of frustrated Nationalism and the need to assert national pride was behind the decision to enter the First World War in 1915. The eventual victory by 1918 was seen by Italians as a great national achievement won by huge sacrifices. There were hopes of Italy being recognised as an equal partner by Britain, France and the United States. There were unrealistic expectations that Italy would gain even more from the peace settlement than had been promised in the secret clauses of the Treaty of London that had tempted Italy into war in 1915.

Key chronology

The legacy of the past

1861 Kings of Piedmont become Kings of Italy

1870 Occupation of Rome
Completion of unification

1895 Formation of PSI

1896 Defeat at Adowa

1911 Conquest of Libya

1915 Italian entry into First World War

1917 Defeat at Caporetto

1919 Paris peace settlement

The birth of Fascism, 1919–21

The post-war crisis

During 1919–21, Italy was gripped by a major political and economic crisis. There was rocketing inflation (rising prices) and also widespread food shortages. Integrating hundreds of thousands of ex-soldiers back into the peacetime economy was a difficult task that was often mishandled. Industrial relations were very poor, with frequent strikes, factories being occupied by workers and lockouts by the employers; often accompanied by outbreaks of violence. In the countryside, there were several instances of peasants seizing land illegally. The middle classes were fearful that there would be economic and political breakdown, leaving Italy open to 'Bolshevism', revolution and civil war.

In the crisis conditions that followed the First World War, the political elites of Liberal Italy found themselves struggling to maintain their traditional dominance. On the left, there was a surge in support for the PSI, the Socialist Party founded in 1895. In the first post-war elections, in May 1919, the PSI gained 32 per cent of the

Fig. 1 *Italy, c.1922*

vote and 156 seats. By 1921, trade union membership reached 2 million. The government came under attack from conservative nationalists on the right, demanding a crackdown against the 'socialist threat'.

The government also faced challenges from the three new political forces that were emerging in 1919:

- The extreme left-wing socialists who broke away to form the communist PCI in January 1921.
- The Catholic activists who responded to the Pope's decision to permit Catholics to take part in politics and formed the PPI, or *Popolari*, led by a Sicilian priest, Don Luigi Sturzo.
- The new fascist movement, the *Fasci di Combattimento*, formed in March 1919 and led by Benito Mussolini.

Rising support for these new parties took votes away from the centrist liberal parties that supported the government.

Cross-reference

The PCI, the PPI and the fascist movement are covered in more depth in Chapter 1 on page 19.

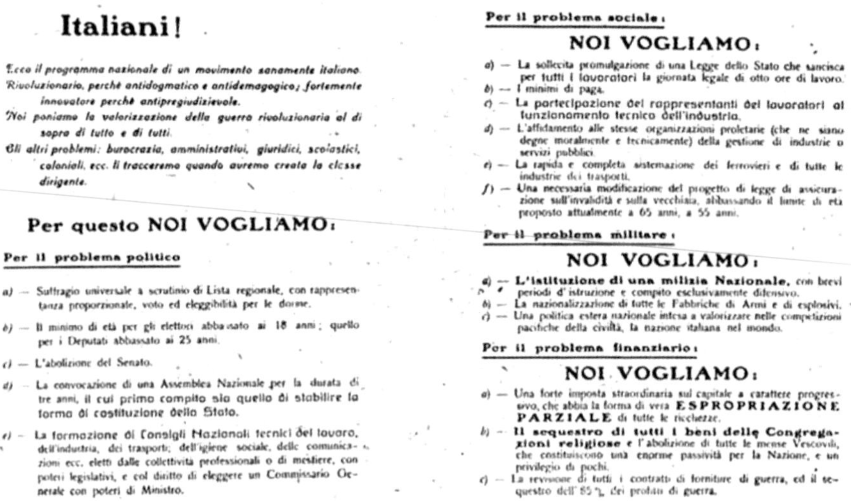

FASCI ITALIANI DI COMBATTIMENTO - Comitato Centrale

MILANO - Via Paolo da Cannobbio, 37 - Telefono 7156

Italiani!

Ecco il programma nazionale di un movimento sanamente italiano.
Rivoluzionario, perchè antidogmatico e antidemagogico; fortemente innovatore perchè antipregiudizievole.
Noi poniamo la valorizzazione della guerra rivoluzionaria al di sopra di tutto e di tutti.
Gli altri problemi: burocrazia, amministrativi, giuridici, scolastici, coloniali, ecc. li tracceremo quando avremo creata la classe dirigente.

Per questo NOI VOGLIAMO:

Per il problema politico

a) — Suffragio universale a scrutinio di Lista regionale, con rappresentanza proporzionale, voto ed eleggibilità per le donne.

b) — Il minimo di età per gli elettori abbassato ai 18 anni; quello per i Deputati abbassato ai 25 anni.

c) — L'abolizione del Senato.

d) — La convocazione di una Assemblea Nazionale per la durata di tre anni, il cui primo compito sia quello di stabilire la forma di costituzione dello Stato.

e) — La formazione di Consigli Nazionali tecnici del lavoro, dell'industria, dei trasporti, dell'igiene sociale, delle comunicazioni ecc. eletti dalle collettività professionali o di mestiere, con poteri legislativi, e col diritto di eleggere un Commissario Generale con poteri di Ministro.

Per il problema sociale:

NOI VOGLIAMO:

a) — La sollecita promulgazione di una Legge dello Stato che sancisca per tutti i lavoratori la giornata legale di otto ore di lavoro.
b) — I minimi di paga.
c) — La partecipazione dei rappresentanti dei lavoratori al funzionamento tecnico dell'industria.
d) — L'affidamento alle stesse organizzazioni proletarie (che ne siano degne moralmente e tecnicamente) della gestione di industrie o servizi pubblici.
e) — La rapida e completa sistemazione dei ferrovieri e di tutte le industrie dei trasporti.
f) — Una necessaria modificazione del progetto di legge di assicurazione sull'invalidità e sulla vecchiaia, abbassando il limite di età proposto attualmente a 65 anni, a 55 anni.

Per il problema militare:

NOI VOGLIAMO:

a) — **L'istituzione di una milizia Nazionale,** con brevi periodi d'istruzione e compito esclusivamente difensivo.
b) — La nazionalizzazione di tutte le Fabbriche di Armi e di esplosivi.
c) — Una politica estera nazionale intesa a valorizzare nelle competizioni pacifiche della civiltà, la nazione italiana nel mondo.

Per il problema finanziario:

NOI VOGLIAMO:

a) — Una forte imposta straordinaria sul capitale a carattere progressivo, che abbia la forma di vera **ESPROPRIAZIONE PARZIALE** di tutte le ricchezze.
b) — **Il sequestro di tutti i beni delle Congregazioni religiose** e l'abolizione di tutte le mense Vescovili, che costituiscono una enorme passività per la Nazione, e un privilegio di pochi.
c) — La revisione di tutti i contratti di forniture di guerra, ed il sequestro dell'85 % dei profitti di guerra.

Fig. 2 *The first manifesto of the Fasci di Combattimento, 1919*

The position of the government was further weakened by the impact on public opinion of the post-war peace settlement. Italy made some substantial gains, including the German-speaking southern Tyrol, Trieste, Istria and Slav-speaking areas in Dalmatia, but this was not enough to satisfy Italian nationalists who insisted that Italy should have received more reward for the great sacrifices in the war. The nationalists claimed Italy should also have received the sea port of Fiume (Rijeka in Croatia) and a share of the former German colonies in Africa. Nationalist anger was not only directed at Britain and France for 'mutilating' Italy's victory; they bitterly attacked their own liberal government for being 'too weak'.

Cross-reference

The question of Fiume and the 'Mutilated Victory' is discussed further in Chapter 7 on pages 88–9.

The nationalist campaign culminated in the occupation of Fiume by 2,000 Italian volunteers (*arditi*), led by the flamboyant nationalist poet Gabriele D'Annunzio in September 1919. The occupation of Fiume was humiliating and damaging for the Italian government, who agreed with D'Annunzio about Fiume but were under international pressure to take action against the illegal occupation. In November 1920, Italy and Yugoslavia agreed the Treaty of Rapallo to settle the status of Fiume and, in December, the Italian government finally forced D'Annunzio and his amateur army to pull out of the city.

Key profile

Gabriele D'Annunzio (1863–1938)

D'Annunzio was a poet, novelist and journalist from a very wealthy background. He became famous as a fighter pilot in the First World War, especially for his daring 'Flight over Vienna'. He was a fanatical nationalist. During 1919–20, D'Annunzio led 2,000 volunteers in the occupation of the port of Fiume, which was disputed between Italy and Yugoslavia. D'Annunzio is often regarded as a forerunner of Mussolini and influenced the style and ideology of the fascist movement, though he had no active role in the regime. Mussolini gave him a lavish State funeral in 1938.

The occupation of Fiume was a disaster for the government and a boost to its enemies. One prime minister, Vittorio Orlando, had to resign in 1919 after the reaction against the Treaty of Versailles. His successor, Francesco Nitti, resigned in June 1920, mostly because of the Fiume affair. This brought Giovanni Giolitti back as prime minister, but he was in a weaker position than ever before. Gabriele D'Annunzio, meanwhile, had shown what might be achieved by violence and direct action. In many ways, D'Annunzio opened the way for the rise of Benito Mussolini.

The rise of Mussolini

Mussolini was a radical Socialist who turned away from Socialism because of his fanatical Nationalism. He was a journalist with a flair for self-publicity, but the movement he founded in Milan in March 1919 was tiny, with only around 50 followers. There was little ideological unity in this little group of troublemakers, who had wildly different attitudes, including monarchists, radical left-wingers and anti-Catholics and other extreme views. In 1919, Mussolini was only on the fringes of Italian politics, virtually unknown compared with Gabriele D'Annunzio. In the elections in November, Mussolini won only 2 per cent of the vote in Milan. The Socialists out-polled the Fascists by seven to one. By the end of 1919, there were no more than 4,000 fascist supporters in total.

From these unpromising beginnings, however, Mussolini was able to mould his fascist movement into a significant political force. This was achieved mostly by presenting the Fascists as Italy's 'last defence' against the threat of socialist revolution. In the summer of 1920, about 500,000 workers took part in a mass occupation of factories in northern Italy after a dispute in the metallurgical industry boiled over. This sparked fears of revolution. Fascist membership increased sharply and Mussolini was able to claim that fascist violence was the only way to counter the socialist threat.

Fascist *squadre d'azione* (action squads) carried out an organised campaign of violence that established the reputations of the *ras* (the important squad leaders), such as Italo Balbo in Ferrare and Dino Grandi in Bologna. Between December 1920 and May 1921, fascist squads killed about 200 Socialists and injured almost a thousand. Many people, including those in government, approved of the fascist actions, at least privately. There was little interference from the police.

The elections of May 1921 revealed the growing strength of the Fascists and the success of their violent tactics. Desperate to prop up his government, Giolitti invited Mussolini to join his National Bloc to fight the election together. This electoral pact with Giolitti gave the Fascists a lot more political respectability and they won 35 seats in the election. Mussolini and the Fascists had arrived on the political scene.

Giolitti's attempt to use the 35 Fascists in the Chamber of Deputies to keep his coalition government going did not work. He was forced to resign in June 1921. Parliamentary government almost broke down because the outcome of the election had left politics in Italy virtually deadlocked between three groupings (the government bloc, the centrist opposition and the left opposition) of equal size.

Between 1917 and 1919, Mussolini had shifted from a socialist journalist to become a violent revolutionary, but from May 1921 he decided it was tactically necessary to act like a respectable politician in order to maximise his influence in parliament. In July 1921, Mussolini even made a truce with the Socialists, the so-called Pact of Pacification, to stop the violence between them. This caused fierce protests from the leaders of the fascist squadre d'azione, who were not interested in political compromises but wanted to be let loose. In November 1921, the Fascists reorganised as the PNF (National Fascist Party). Mussolini gave in to pressure from the radicals and cancelled the Pact of Pacification. Fascist violence started up again on an even bigger scale than before.

By the end of 1921, Italian politics was in a permanent state of crisis. At that time, there was little likelihood of the Fascists coming to power, but there seemed no prospect of political stability being achieved by anyone else. During 1922, the fascist movement was able to exploit the sense of complete breakdown in Italy and move closer to achieving power.

Timeline

The colours represent different types of events as follows: Social, Political, Foreign (policy), Economic

1922	1923	1924	1925	1926	1927
Election of Pope Pius XI March on Rome Mussolini appointed prime minister	Fascist Grand Council founded Gentile school reforms introduced Acerbo Law Corfu crisis	Acquisition of Fiume Election victory of fascist-led National List The Matteotti Affair Start of press censorship	Battle for Grain launched Italian mediation at Locarno Treaties Attempt to assassinate Mussolini by Zaniboni First autostrada built	Rocco's Syndical Law National Fascist Confederation of Workers Unions Formation of ONB (the Balilla) Ministry of Corporations established	Police state established Battle for Births launched Battle for the Lira

1928	1929	1930	1931	1932	1933	1934
One-party State established Battle for Land launched	Concordat between Mussolini and the papacy Fascists win 99 per cent of votes in single-list elections	Friendship Treaty with Austria First effects of Great Depression in Italy First Italian 'talkie' *La canzone dell'amore*	Formation of IMI Oath of loyalty required from all university teachers Clashes between Church and State over Catholic youth groups	Mussolini's first meeting with Clara Petacci Opening of new cities reclaimed from Pontine marshes	Formation of IRI Mussolini's meeting with Dollfuss to support Austria First official 'Mother and Child Day'	Italian forces mobilised after murder of Dollfuss First signs of openly anti-British line in the press Wal Wal incident on Somalia-Abyssinia border

1935	1936	1937	1938	1939	1940
Stresa Front Italian invasion of Abyssinia Policy of 'autarchia' launched	Completion of conquest of Abyssinia Italian intervention in Spanish Civil War Rome-Berlin Axis Drop of 40 per cent in value of the lira	Italian forces defeated at Guadalajara in Spain Ministry of Popular Culture (minculpop) formed Italian withdrawal from League of Nations	Race laws introduced 40,000 Italian troops on Ebro offensive in Spain Italian mediation at Munich Conference	Pact of Steel Italian invasion of Albania Italian non-belligerence at outbreak of war in Europe	Italian entry into Hitler's war Italian invasions of North Africa and Greece

1941	1942	1943	1944	1945	1946
Defeats of Italian armies in North Africa Bread rationing introduced Italian declarations of war against USSR and United States	Failure of attempts to seize Malta Allied daylight bombing raids on Milan	Allied invasion of Sicily Mussolini dismissed from power Armistice between allies and new Italian government Salo Republic established in northern Italy	Execution of Count Ciano Massacre at Ardeatine caves Liberation of Rome by allied forces Last meeting between Mussolini and Hitler	Partisan uprising in Milan Capture and death of Mussolini End of Second World War	Secret burial to hide Mussolini's body Establishment of the Italian Republic

1 Establishing the fascist regime, 1922–29

1 The rise to power

In this chapter you will learn about:

- the political situation in Italy at the time Mussolini came to power
- the impact of the March on Rome and the threat of violence, including the Matteotti Affair
- the reasons why the traditional elites were willing to collaborate with Mussolini
- the nature of the fascist movement and of Mussolini's leadership cult
- the extent to which Mussolini had consolidated his regime by 1927.

Fig. 1 *King Victor Emmanuel III and Mussolini (right) in 1922*

16 May, 1922:

In the morning of 12 May 63 000 people are at the gates of Ferrara. At 10 am precisely, I rapidly review the columns and put myself at their head. The whole city greets our progress. The windows are full. The discipline of our poor peasants with their ragged clothes is splendid. The spectators are visibly moved and applaud. The castle is blockaded. At a given signal, while I pass the gateway, the crowd roars; roars that shake the glass of the surrounding buildings: *Down with the government! Long live Italy!*

Italo Balbo's diary, 16 May 1922. Quoted in J. Whittam, ***Fascist Italy****, 1995*

The process of establishing a fascist dictatorship went through several distinct phases. In the first phase, from March 1919 to the end of 1921, the fascist movement grew from a small group of violent misfits to a powerful force in national politics. In the second phase, from December 1921 to October 1922, Mussolini exploited the crisis conditions in Italy and the weakness of the political system so effectively that the ruling elites were panicked into handing him power as the legally appointed prime minister. In the third phase, from October 1922 to 1925,

Mussolini consolidated his political power by changing the constitution and suppressing the anti-fascist opposition. In the final phase, from 1925 to 1929, Mussolini completed the process of neutralising potential rivals and began to put in place the structures of a permanent dictatorship.

At times, Mussolini found himself in danger of being toppled from power, or so constrained by other politicians that he would have had no freedom of action. That he survived these dangers and eventually established a secure dictatorship was due to many factors, including charismatic leadership, compromises with untrustworthy allies, extensive violence and intimidation, skilful use of propaganda and a lot of low political cunning.

Key chronology

The consolidation of power, 1922–29

1922 October	March on Rome Mussolini becomes prime minister
1923 May	Acerbo Law passed
1924 April	Election victory of fascist list
1924 June	Matteotti Affair and Aventine Secession
1925 May	Palazzo Vidoni Pact
1926 April	Rocco Law
1927 January	Establishment of police state
1929 February	Lateran Treaties with the papacy

Table 1 *Prime ministers of Italy, 1914–22*

March 1914	Antonio Salandra
June 1916	Paolo Boselli
October 1917	Vittorio Orlando
June 1919	Francesco Nitti
June 1920	Giovanni Giolitti
July 1921	Ivanoe Bonomi
February 1922	Luigi Facta

The coming to power of the Fascists

At the beginning of 1922, Italy was in a state of permanent political instability. Fascist violence was increasing in intensity. Parliamentary government could only function through patched-up coalition government by political parties who were incapable of united action. The government headed by Ivanoe Bonomi since July 1921 depended on an alliance between the anti-clerical Radical Party and the PPI (*Partito Popolare Italiano – Popolari* – or Italian Popular Party), a party specifically representing Catholic interests. In February 1922, the PPI withdrew its support and Bonomi was forced to resign. This was the fourth government collapse since 1919 and it was difficult for anyone to form a government capable of maintaining a majority in parliament. After weeks of discussions, King Victor Emmanuel III appointed as prime minister an experienced politician widely regarded as a nonentity, Luigi Facta.

Key profiles

Ivanoe Bonomi (1873–1951)

Bonomi was a moderate Socialist who became prime minister of Italy in 1921. In February 1922, he was forced to resign because of a split in his coalition government. Bonomi withdrew from politics after Mussolini came to power and stayed on the sidelines until 1940, when he joined the anti-fascist opposition. He was made prime minister of the new Italian Republic in 1944, replacing Marshal Badoglio. Bonomi stayed in power until 1945. After the war, he played a key role in Italy's transition to democracy.

Luigi Facta (1861–1930)

Facta was a Liberal Party politician who entered politics in 1892. He held various minor posts in government before becoming finance minister in 1910. According to the historian Denis Mack Smith, in *Mussolini & Italy* (1984), Facta was 'a timid, ignorant provincial lawyer who had risen in politics through seniority alone. His appointment as prime minister was at first taken as a joke.' In July 1922, Facta was dismissed but was then re-appointed because there was nobody else. When faced with the March on Rome, Facta declared martial law but the King refused to sign the decree into law. Facta resigned and was replaced by Mussolini.

Luigi Facta did not have the force of personality or the political strength to carry an effective government and his coalition soon broke up. In July 1922, the King dismissed him but could not find anyone else able to form a government; on 1 August he re-appointed Facta. By then, social

Fig. 2 *Mussolini and Blackshirt leaders, 1922*

unrest and political violence were running out of control. Fascist Party membership had reached 300,000. Fascist leaders had seized control in one city after another; in May 1922 they forcibly removed the elected communist town council in Bologna. In the countryside, local landlords were financing the Fascists to intimidate their rebellious labourers. The government and the police did little to interfere.

The rise of the Fascists was assisted by the mistakes of their opponents. On 1 August 1922, the day Luigi Facta formed his new government, the Socialists organised a general strike. They hoped it would push the government into taking action against the Fascists, but it had the opposite effect. It gave the Fascists an excuse to launch violent attacks against the strikers and it exposed the divisions in Facta's coalition. Some wanted firm action to suppress the Fascists, others wanted to include them in the government.

By September 1922, three rival political groupings were preparing to take decisive action to resolve the political crisis:

- The first was the traditional political establishment. They expected Facta to resign and a new government to be formed under one of the old guard, either Giolitti or Salandra. A congress of liberal politicians was held at Bologna early in October to plan for such a government, which would try to 'tame' Mussolini by including fascist ministers.
- The second was the group around Luigi Facta, who started making military preparations and ordered more troops to be stationed in Rome. Facta also wanted to use the prestige of Gabriele D'Annunzio, the 'hero' of Fiume, who had a strong following among ex-soldiers and was potentially a powerful rival to Mussolini. Facta and D'Annunzio made plans for a mass rally of national unity to be held on 4 November (the anniversary of Italy's victory in 1918). It was clear that this was intended to be a 'Stop Mussolini' rally.
- The third group was the Fascists, who now controlled so many local governments in Italy that Mussolini was ready to make a bid for power. The fascist radicals were straining at the leash and Mussolini knew he had to act before the 4 November rally, which might have been a serious threat to him. The only question was how? Would it be through violence in the streets, or by peaceful means?

Activity

Talking point

Working in three groups, analyse the strengths and weaknesses of the three political groupings competing for power in 1922.

Key chronology

The decisive year: 1922

February	Resignation of Bonomi
March	Facta appointed prime minister
July	Breakdown of Facta's coalition
August	Re-appointment of Facta
	Socialist General Strike
	Fascist attacks in Milan
September	Mussolini's tour of northern cities
October	Liberal congress at Bologna
	March on Rome

The fascist movement

Key profiles – fascist leaders

Italo Balbo (1896–1940)

Italo Balbo was seen as a war hero for his exploits on the Alpine front in the First World War. He was ras of the fascist squads in Ferrara and was one of the key leaders of the March on Rome. Balbo became famous as an aviator, leading two mass flights across the Atlantic Ocean in 1930 and 1933; after which he was made Marshal of the Italian Air Force. Balbo was appointed Governor of Libya, partly to reduce his ability to rival Mussolini. In 1940, he was killed when Italian forces shot down his plane at Tobruk, apparently by mistake.

Roberto Farinacci (1892–1945)

Farinacci was a leader of the violent right-wing elements in the fascist movement and played a key role in the use of intimidation by the fascist squads. He became Secretary of the Fascist Party in 1925, but his influence declined because he was seen as too extreme. Farinacci made a comeback during the Abyssinian War and was appointed to the Fascist Grand Council in 1937. He was very pro-German and anti-Semitic. He was responsible for enforcing the Race Laws from 1938 and strongly supported the war in alliance with Germany. He was executed by Italian partisans in 1945.

Achille Starace (1889–1945)

Starace was a fanatical nationalist who led fascist squads in the March on Rome and was the leader of the volunteer Blackshirt militia, the MVSN. Starace then became Secretary of the PNF (National Fascist Party) in 1931. Although he was regarded as a war hero for his actions in the Abyssinian War, he gradually lost favour with Mussolini and was replaced as Party Secretary in 1939. Starace was sacked as leader of the MVSN for military incompetence in 1941. His political career ended in 1943 when he was arrested after the fall of Mussolini. In 1945, he was captured by partisans and executed in Milan.

Leandro Arpinati (1892–1945)

Arpinati was a friend of Mussolini before 1914. In 1920, Arpinati was one of the leaders of the fascist *squadristi* and a vice-secretary in the PNF. From 1926 to 1929, he was *podesta* of Bologna. In 1930, he was accused of involvement in an attempt to assassinate Mussolini that had taken place in 1926 – he spent several years in prison or under house arrest. In 1943, Mussolini invited Arpinati to join the government of the Salo Republic, but he refused. He was killed by partisans in April 1945.

Dino Grandi (1895–1968)

Grandi was ras of Bologna and a leading figure on the radical and violent wing of the fascist movement from 1919. He was elected to parliament in 1921 and later held several government posts, including Foreign Minister from 1929 and Ambassador to Great Britain from 1932 to 1939. Grandi opposed Mussolini over entering the war in 1940 and over his management of the war effort. In July 1943, Grandi proposed the motion to the Fascist Grand Council that led to Mussolini's dismissal. He was sentenced to death by the Salo Republic, but had already escaped to safety in Spain.

Emilio De Bono (1866–1944)

De Bono was an army general who became a committed Fascist after the war. He was one of the ***Quadrumvirs*** who organised and led the March on Rome and later was commander of the fascist militia. In 1935, De Bono was Supreme Commander of the invasion of Ethiopia and promoted Marshal of the army – but was sacked soon afterwards for being too cautious. In July 1943, De Bono was one of the 17 members of the Fascist Grand Council who voted against Mussolini. Because of this, the Salo Republic executed him for 'treason' in January 1944.

By the beginning of 1922, the fascist movement had swelled to about 240,000 members. The majority of them were from the lower middle classes in the North, where the movement had originated in 1919.

Key terms

Quadrumvirs: the leaders of the four columns of the March on Rome: Italo Balbo; Michele Bianchi; Emilio De Bono; and Cesare Maria De Vecchi. The term was taken from the *Quadrumvirate* who had been joint leaders of the Republic in Ancient Rome.

Did you know?

One of the striking features of the leaders of the fascist movement in 1922 was how young they were. They were almost all in their thirties, much the same age as Mussolini, and they all remained key players in the fascist regime throughout the 20 years of Mussolini's rule. Apart from Italo Balbo, who was killed in an air crash in 1940, they were all present at the dramatic Fascist Grand Council meeting on 25 July 1943.

Cross-reference

Mussolini's dismissal after the Fascist Grand Council meeting in July 1943 is covered in Chapter 10 on pages 123–7.

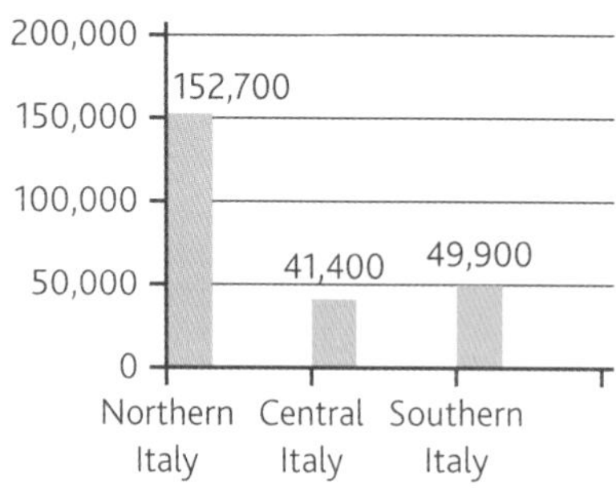

Fig. 3 *Fascist membership, January 1922*

During 1920 and 1921, however, the fascist movement had gained many new recruits from central Italy and the rural South. These men were generally young, restless and attracted to violence.

Fig. 4 *Fascist squadristi in the village of Montevergine, c.1925*

People joined the fascist movement for a variety of motives. There were monarchists and republicans; there were Catholics and fanatical anti-Catholics. Many were more concerned with local issues than national ones. Many were students – it is estimated that more than 10 per cent of all university students joined the Fascists in the early 1920s. Even more were ex-soldiers, who fitted easily into the militaristic, street-fighting style of the paramilitary fascist squadre d'azione. There was little unity or coherence of ideas and it was difficult for Mussolini to control the disparate groups. Local fascist leaders, the ras, such as Dino Grandi in Bologna and Italo Balbo in Ferrara, had great power and influence in their regions, rather like medieval barons.

The Fascist squads consisted of young men from the bourgeoisie and petty bourgeoisie of the countryside and of provincial towns. Many were students, but some were socially humbler and there were working-class youngsters among them as well: a mixture of spoilt brats, misfits and hooligans. Some of them were demobilised officers or else sons or younger brothers of demobilised officers. They were all young, some very young, proud of their youth and of the war they had fought in, or merely dreamed about, and in their violence they employed methods used by the shock troops in the war. The life and dignity of others mattered little to them; indeed it might even seem right and credible to humiliate them.

 **2**

G. Carocci, ***Italian Fascism****, 1972. Quoted in J. Pollard,* ***The Fascist Experience in Italy****, 1998*

Activity

Source analysis

Read Sources 2 and 3. Using these sources and the other evidence in this chapter, make a list of the different social groups who provided recruits for Fascism in 1922. For each group, try to identify the key motives for joining the PNF.

Outside the major cities of northern Italy, Fascism spread into the countryside and small towns of a specifically defined area. It never managed to move beyond this 'ghetto' until after the March on Rome, when seizure of the centralised Italian system of government gave Mussolini and the Fascists control over local government too. Through the prefects, Fascism was able to impose itself on local councils in many areas outside its classic heartlands, especially in the South.

 **3**

J. Pollard, ***The Fascist Experience in Italy****, 1998*

From May 1921, when he made his electoral pact with Giolitti, Mussolini tried to make the movement more disciplined and more respectable in the eyes of the elites and the middle classes, but this often caused resentment from local fascist leaders who wanted to be let loose. If Mussolini seemed too revolutionary, he would alienate the politicians and influential social groups he wanted to win over; if he did not sound revolutionary enough, he would infuriate the impatient and violent elements on the radical wing of Fascism, who dreamed of actually seizing power in the streets. Mussolini was not opposed to violence, but he wanted to be able to turn fascist violence on and off, like a tap, in order to frighten the old elites into giving him power legally (Source 4).

> It is necessary to form a party, well-organised and disciplined, so that it is able, when required, to transform itself into an army capable of using power defensively as well as offensively. This party must have a mind, that is, a programme. Theoretical assumptions must be reviewed, changed and, if necessary, abandoned.
>
> **4** *Mussolini in **Il Popolo d'Italia**, August 1921. Quoted in D. Sassoon, **Mussolini and the Rise of Fascism**, 2007*

Mussolini's efforts to control fascist extremism only partially succeeded. He was able to reorganise the movement into the PNF (*Partito Nationale Fascista* or National Fascist Party) in 1921, but he had to call off his truce with the Socialists, the so-called Pact of Pacification, and leave fascist local leaders free to use violent methods in their own areas.

In the summer of 1922, fascist violence enhanced Mussolini's chances of coming to power. The decision of the reformist Socialists to call a general strike on 31 July gave an ideal excuse for fascist squads to attack strikers in several cities across Italy. On 3 August, Fascists stormed into Milan, fought running battles against socialist supporters in the streets and burned down the building of the socialist newspaper, *Avanti*. They then attacked the town hall and took over running the trains to break the strike by the transport workers.

Fascist actions made the government appear weak and ineffective in dealing with the 'socialist threat'. Mussolini looked strong and decisive by comparison. The idea of using the strength of the Fascists to support the government, rather than trying to suppress the Fascists by using the army, became more attractive. In the autumn of 1922, the way was open for Mussolini to launch his bid for power. The stage was set for the March on Rome.

Activity

Thinking point

Put yourself in the position of a British journalist reporting from Rome in October 1922. Write a brief news report assessing the chances of Mussolini coming to power during the next few weeks.

Fig. 5 *The Fasces, the emblem of the PNF*

Mussolini's March on Rome

From 1922, until the fall of Mussolini, the anniversary of the March on Rome was commemorated in every corner of Italy as a day of national celebration. What was being commemorated was the legend of how the massed marching columns of Blackshirts (a reference to the black uniform worn by the fascist squads) converged on Rome from all over Italy, sweeping aside the old political system by fascist discipline, military strength and the popular will of the people. The legend was simple, heroic and decisive. The truth was messy, not very heroic and sometimes farcical.

The Fascist Party congress, due to start on 24 October, was to be the launch-pad for Mussolini's bid for power. On 16 October, the fascist leaders made their plans for the March on Rome to take place on 28 October, just after the PNF congress. The march looked (and was meant to look) like a military **coup d'état** – four columns of squadristi who would start from different fascist strongholds and march towards Rome, gathering size and strength as they progressed across Italy. It was a direct challenge to the power of the State, but it was a staged theatrical performance based on bluff and blackmail, not on force of arms.

Key terms

Coup d'état: overturning a government and seizing power by the use of force.

Four fascist leaders, the Quadrumvirs, were placed at the head of the March:

- Italo Balbo, the Fascist Party boss of Ferrara.
- Emilio De Bono, a senior general in the Italian army.
- Michele Bianchi, a revolutionary syndicalist on the left wing of the PNF.
- Cesare Maria De Vecchi, on the monarchist wing of the PNF.

Key profiles

Cesare Maria De Vecchi (1884–1969)

De Vecchi was on the monarchist wing of the PNF. His power base was Turin. In 1922, he was one of the Quadrumvirs, leading the March on Rome. In 1929, Mussolini chose him to be ambassador to the papacy. From 1935, De Vecchi was Minister of Education. In July 1943, De Vecchi voted against Mussolini in the Fascist Grand Council. As a result, the Salo Republic sentenced him to death in 1944 but the Catholic Church helped him to escape to Argentina. He returned to Italy after the war and was a founder of the neo-fascist MSI (Italian Social Movement).

Michele Bianchi (1883–1930)

Bianchi was a revolutionary syndicalist and trade union organiser. His power base was Milan. Bianchi was originally a Socialist, but joined the Fascists in 1919 and was one of the founders of the PNF. He was one of the Quadrumvirs leading the March on Rome. Bianchi became Party Secretary in 1923 and played a key role in organising the fascist list for the elections in 1924. He was appointed to the Fascist Grand Council, but lost influence in the party due to ill health. He died of TB in 1930.

On 16 October, the day of his meeting with the Quadrumvirate, Mussolini also held talks with Gabriele D'Annunzio to try to overcome the disputes between them. Although the two men had similar nationalist and anti-democratic ideologies, they were rivals rather than allies. In August 1921, for example, when the fascist ras were furious with Mussolini over his Pact of Pacification with the Socialists, Balbo had proposed that D'Annunzio should replace Mussolini as *Duce* (leader). D'Annunzio finally said no to the offer and Mussolini survived the challenge from the ras, but the episode deepened the bad feeling between him and D'Annunzio.

In the autumn of 1922, just before the March on Rome, it was known that D'Annunzio was talking to liberal politicians like Facta and Giolitti – and that D'Annunzio had agreed to take part in a mass rally of national unity in Rome, scheduled for 4 November. The clear intention of the rally was to stop Mussolini's rise to power. The March on Rome happened a week before the rally could take place and the challenge fizzled out.

On 24 October, the Fascist Party congress opened and Mussolini made his demands clear – five cabinet posts for Fascists in the next government, or else. On 26 October, Mussolini made a rousing speech to announce that it was time to seize power. On the night of 27 October, fascist squads seized the town halls and the railway stations in Florence and Milan. On 28 October, the March on Rome began. If the government gave orders for the army to crush the Fascists, and if the army obeyed the order, it was certain that the marchers, who numbered 20,000 at the most, would be crushed. Mussolini was fairly certain this would not happen and that Facta would crumble.

Mussolini joined the marchers just long enough for an impressive photograph to be taken, and then went back to his hotel room in Milan to conduct his political negotiations over the telephone, while the marchers straggled along the road towards Rome, mostly in pouring rain. Many were stopped at police checkpoints. On the morning of 28 October, Facta declared martial law. It was now up to the King to sign the decree bringing in a

Exploring the detail

There were other reasons why Mussolini was able to neutralise the threat from D'Annunzio. Mussolini sent several pleading letters to him, together with lavish gifts of money to pay off his debts. Another key factor was that D'Annunzio was badly injured when he was pushed out of a window after a fight with his mistress. By the time D'Annunzio recovered from his injuries, Mussolini was established in power. After D'Annunzio's death in 1938, the fascist regime awarded him a huge State funeral and his home on Lake Garda, the *Vittoriale*, became a sort of fascist shrine.

Activity

Talking point

Working in four groups, assemble evidence under each of the following headings to show why Mussolini faced major obstacles when attempting to achieve power on the eve of the March on Rome:

- Historical.
- Ideological.
- Political.
- Personal.

state of emergency. He did not do so, partly because he was unsure of the army's loyalty. He preferred to see the negotiations between Mussolini and Salandra produce a compromise government including fascist ministers.

On 29 October, Mussolini turned up the pressure on Salandra and the King. He refused the offer of a share in government and demanded full authority for himself. The King caved in. On 30 October, he appointed Mussolini as prime minister. At last, the March on Rome could be allowed to have its triumphant ending. Swelled by many late arrivals, the Fascists paraded through Rome while Mussolini watched from his balcony in the Hotel Savoy. This was not a seizure of power; Mussolini was appointed legally, according to the constitution, although it was also revolutionary, accompanied by the whiff of violence.

Political changes and compromises

After his appointment as prime minister in October 1922, Mussolini quickly set up a 'national government' – a coalition much like the one Salandra had proposed, including three Fascists, two Democrats, one Liberal, one Nationalist, two from the Popolari and two senior army officers. The only difference from Salandra's scheme was that Mussolini was in charge, not one of the old guard.

The make-up of the new government showed how much Mussolini depended on political compromises, especially with the army. Until October 1922, the economic and political crisis had worked in Mussolini's favour – the worse things were (or, more especially, the worse people thought they were) the easier it was for Mussolini to offer himself as the radical solution to the country's problems. Once he was prime minister, his situation was completely changed. He had to achieve success quickly, or his government would be blamed.

Mussolini had several political advantages at the end of 1922. He could put the key ministries in fascist hands. He could transform the squads into an organised fascist militia, the MVSN. Local government in many towns and cities was already in fascist hands and now Mussolini could extend this control by appointing Fascists to positions of authority. Mussolini also needed the ability to pass laws swiftly, without endless parliamentary debates. He was able to achieve this, at least temporarily, by playing on the fear of revolution in Italy to persuade the other parties to rush through a law granting his government temporary emergency powers for 12 months.

Mussolini then moved to tighten his control over his own movement by setting up the Fascist Grand Council. Despite its imposing name, the Fascist Grand Council existed simply to rubber-stamp Mussolini's decisions. It had no real power – at least not until 25 July 1943.

It might seem surprising that Mussolini was able to obtain his right to rule by decree as easily as he did, but there were in fact several important factors running in his favour:

- The King had his opportunity to block Mussolini in October 1922, but failed to act. After that, it was too late for him to make a stand against Mussolini, even if he wanted to. Without the King's backing, it was very difficult for other politicians to oppose Mussolini.
- The sense of a power vacuum during the autumn of 1922 meant a lot of people wanted a 'strong government', even if they did not like Mussolini's methods.
- The sense of growing impatience with the old 'establishment' led to a desire for generational change.

Activity

Talking point

Working in two groups, prepare evidence and arguments for the following class debate: 'History is always written by the winning side.'

Key chronology

The March on Rome, October 1922

16 October	Mussolini's meeting with the Quadrumvirate
24 October	Start of PNF congress
27 October	Seizure of public buildings in Florence and Milan
28 October	Start of March on Rome
	Martial law proposed
	Refusal by the King to sign martial law decree
	Resignation of Luigi Facta
	Mussolini offered a share of power
29 October	Mussolini refuses to join Salandra's coalition
30 October	Mussolini appointed prime minister
	March on Rome ends in triumphant parade

Cross-reference

The actions of the Fascist Grand Council in July 1943 are covered in Chapter 10 on page 126.

Activity

Thinking point

Using the evidence in this chapter, assemble **five** main reasons why Mussolini's rise to power was crowned with success in October 1922, despite the fact that less than two years before he had been leader of an insignificant fringe party. Rank your reasons in order of importance.

- The fears of violence and civil war. The so-called 'Bolshevik threat' was not really likely to overthrow the social order, but many Italians genuinely believed that it was. They were even more afraid of violent revolution by the Fascists and believed it was essential to give Mussolini real political power because he was the only one who could keep the Fascists under control.

Mussolini's position was not yet fully secure, however. He needed political respectability and legitimacy. He needed, as soon as possible, to win an election. He needed to show he could control the wilder elements in the fascist movement. It was essential for him to win support, or at least passive acceptance, from the ruling elites.

The old elites

Mussolini had already gone a long way towards reassuring the old elites before he came to power. He had moved away from the anti-Catholic and anti-monarchist ideology that characterised the early fascist movement in 1919. He had tried hard to convince the ruling elites that the PNF was a disciplined, organised party, firmly under his control. This process continued after he became prime minister as he set about consolidating his power. The most important groupings Mussolini had to win over or neutralise included conservative and nationalist political leaders, the armed forces, the large landowners, big industrialists, the Catholic Church and the monarchy.

The political establishment had been willing to compromise with Mussolini for some time before October 1922. Actually, they wanted to manipulate him, using fascist political strength for their own purposes. Mussolini knew this and outmanoeuvred them. Once in power, he kept their support. Giolitti and Salandra, for example, both voted in favour of Mussolini's temporary powers to rule by decree. The nationalist politicians liked Mussolini's anti-Communism and also his promises in foreign policy.

Key profiles

Giovanni Giolitti (1842–1928)

Giolitti was a dominant personality in the politics of Liberal Italy. Together with his rival, Antonio Salandra, Giolitti was later blamed for compromising with Mussolini and so failing to prevent the rise of Fascism. Giolitti was prime minister three times, but was always influential even when not actually in power. In 1921, Giolitti made an electoral pact with Mussolini that enabled the Fascists to participate in the parliamentary elections. The tactic failed and Giolitti resigned in 1921. He remained an influential figure in parliament during Mussolini's consolidation of power.

Antonio Salandra (1853–1931)

Salandra was a conservative politician who was Italy's prime minister from 1914 to 1916 and was an important part of the political elite in post-war Italy. Salandra enthusiastically supported Italian intervention in the First World War but his views became more conservative and nationalist after the war. In 1922, he supported the idea of bringing Mussolini into the government; though later changed his mind and tried to oppose Fascism.

The armed forces were also ready to cooperate with Mussolini. The army had been very divided in 1922, with many officers who were fascist sympathisers, or actually active fascist leaders such as General De Bono, but also many anti-fascist officers who regarded the squadre d'azione as a dangerous rabble. These negative attitudes dwindled after Mussolini gained power and showed he could control his movement. Senior officers also liked Mussolini's promises to modernise and expand the armed forces.

The big landowners had mixed feelings about Fascism. They feared that the regime would encourage illegal land grabbing and the breaking up of the large estates, but they also made deals with fascist leaders to suppress trouble in agricultural districts. Mussolini moved quickly to reassure the landowners that they would be left alone. Later policies such as ruralisation and the Battle for Grain provided further reassurance to landowners.

Cross-reference

Ruralisation is covered in Chapter 3 on page 43 and the Battle for Grain is covered on pages 43–4.

Reassuring the industrialists was more difficult. The revolutionary syndicalist wing of the PNF led by men such as Michele Bianchi and Edmondo Rossoni was very powerful. The fascist trade unions, or syndicates, had ambitious plans to take control of key industries and force employers to accept radical changes in industrial relations. When the fascist regime began talking about reorganising industry into 'corporations', the employers were really alarmed. Mussolini did much to win them over, however, by appointing Alberto De Stefani as Finance Minister and by restricting the bargaining rights of trade unions.

The Catholic Church was the most difficult of all. Mussolini had toned down his anti-Catholic attacks, but the Church was hostile to the new fascist regime over many issues, including youth groups and education. Mussolini tailored some of his social policies to suit the wishes of the Church, for example, promising to ban contraception and to introduce religious education into secondary schools. Relations with the papacy improved, but the divide between Church and State was still there. Mussolini avoided open confrontation, but it was not until 1929 that he finally achieved a complete reconciliation.

Over and above all the other elites was the monarchy. Victor Emmanuel III had made Mussolini prime minister and it was the King who could dismiss him under the constitution.

The King

In his reign of 46 years, King Victor Emmanuel III proved to be an unremarkable ruler who achieved little. On three occasions, his actions did have a significant political impact on Italy. The first was when he backed Italy's entry into the First World War in 1915, even though public opinion was against it. The second was when he appointed Mussolini prime minister on 30 October 1922. The third was when he dismissed Mussolini on 25 July 1943. Otherwise, Victor Emmanuel's reign was mostly noteworthy for the actions he did not take to curb Mussolini.

Victor Emmanuel was a very small man physically, not much more than five feet tall. Many Italians, including members of the royal family, thought that his political stature was very small, too. In many ways, he lived up to the advice his father Umberto I had given him while he was still a Crown Prince: 'Remember: To be a king all you need to know is how to sign your name, how to read a newspaper and how to sit on a horse.'

Key profile

King Victor Emmanuel III of Italy (1869–1947)

Victor Emmanuel III became king in 1900, after his father, Umberto I, was assassinated. In 1922, Victor Emmanuel refused to authorise the use of martial law against the March on Rome, thus handing power to Mussolini. The King had little importance during the years of fascist rule until July 1943, when he suddenly dismissed Mussolini, replaced him with Marshal Badoglio and tried to negotiate an end to the war. In April 1944, the King gave most of his royal authority to Crown Prince Umberto. In May 1946, Italy became a republic and the King went into exile.

During the post-war political crisis, Victor Emmanuel became disillusioned with the ruling political class. In the summer of 1922, unrest in Italy, especially the general strike called by the Socialists, presented the King with two difficult choices: who would be the best prime minister to bring a return to stability? What was the best way to deal with Mussolini and the rise of the Fascists? In the end, the King decided that there was one solution to both of these problems – make Mussolini prime minister. This was, however, only a last-minute decision, not one he planned in advance. What made him do it?

There were several pressures on the King in 1922:

The royal family

The King's mother, Queen Margherita, had pro-fascist sympathies and was all in favour of a 'strong man' to save Italy from revolution. Just before the March on Rome, Margherita publicly showed her approval of the fascist cause by inviting the Quadrumvirs to her palace. The King's cousin, the Second Duke of Aosta, was even more pro-fascist than Queen Margherita. Aosta was a handsome war hero, greatly admired by ex-soldiers, and his influence over the army was an important factor. Even more important from Victor Emmanuel's point of view was that Aosta was after his job. Aosta was eager to promote the idea that there was a better alternative king ready and waiting. Victor Emmanuel, therefore, was reluctant to try to use force against the Fascists. He preferred the idea of 'taming' them by giving them a share of government.

Key profile

The Duke of Aosta (1869–1931)

Emanuele Filiberto, the second Duke of Aosta, was a cousin of King Victor Emmanuel III and an ally of Mussolini during his rise to power. Aosta commanded Italian armies in the First World War and had very nationalistic and militarist views. In the post-war crisis, he was sympathetic to the Fascist Party and provided a link between Mussolini and the ruling elites. He also hoped that Victor Emmanuel would abdicate 'in favour of a stronger man' – himself. Mussolini promoted Aosta to the rank of Marshal of Italy in 1936.

Fears of civil war

As King, Victor Emmanuel was Commander in Chief of the Royal Army. He was unsure whether the army would be strong enough to defeat the Fascists (all the evidence suggests that the army could easily have crushed Mussolini's Blackshirts, but the King was not certain of this at the time) and he was also unsure whether the army would be willing to act. The fascist movement was full of ex-soldiers. Several generals and senior officers were openly sympathetic to the Fascists; some, such as Emilio De Bono, were actually leaders in the movement.

The collapse of the liberal oligarchy

Stopping Mussolini meant giving power to somebody else, but the King was not willing to give full backing to Luigi Facta, someone he regarded as merely a temporary stopgap. He would have preferred Giolitti, but he was now 80 years old and had many political enemies. The King therefore accepted Antonio Salandra's plan to lead a new government that would share power with Mussolini and other fascist ministers. When Mussolini refused to accept the offer, Victor Emmanuel caved in and handed power to Mussolini rather than risk civil war. The King's decision in October 1922 had long-lasting effects. It made it almost impossible for the liberal oligarchy to fight its way back to power, because this would depend on the King intervening and there was little possibility of Victor Emmanuel opting for confrontation with Mussolini. In the years after 1922, Mussolini took over almost all aspects of the role of Head of State. The King did not turn against him for 20 years.

Activity

Thinking point

Use the evidence in this chapter and look ahead to later events such the Matteotti Affair in 1924, the introduction of the race laws in 1938, or the decision to go to war in 1940, when the King said and did nothing to oppose Mussolini. Evaluate the extent to which this was a 'psychological surrender' by King Victor Emmanuel, rather than a series of logical political decisions.

Other political movements

Mussolini's chief political enemies were the parties of the left and the Catholics. The PSI (*Partito Socialista Italiano* or Italian Socialist Party) had lost a lot of its political force during 1921 and 1922. The party was weakened in January 1921 when the Communists broke away to form a separate party. The PSI also suffered badly from fascist violence. According to figures produced by the PSI, fascist attacks killed 3,000 socialists between 1920 and October 1922. Fascist attacks had forced many elected socialist officials out of their posts. The general strike in August 1922 was a fiasco, partly because of fascist violence, but also because so few workers joined it. The rise of Catholic and fascist trade unions after 1919 also took members away from the socialist unions. The Socialists were divided and demoralised.

The Communists formed a separate party after splitting with the PSI early in 1921 – the PCI (*Partito Communista Italiano* or Italian Communist Party). The PCI gained considerable support in the main industrial centres such as Turin. They also succeeded in gaining control of local government in a number of smaller towns and cities. This made them a target for the fascist squads, who forcibly removed many elected officials from office.

Another factor weakening the PSI was the rise of the Catholic PPI. Before 1919, the Pope's ban on political activity by Catholics prevented the development of any Catholic party. Pope Benedict XIV lifted this ban and the PPI emerged under the leadership of a populist Sicilian priest, Don Luigi Sturzo. The PPI rapidly gained support from Catholics, both working class and middle class. This took support away from the PSI, and from the liberal and democratic parties.

The liberal parties had been split by the rise of Mussolini. Many were content to support the new fascist-led government because it promised to provide the stability the middle classes wanted. Some liberals stuck to

Exploring the detail

Although the PPI was a rival to the PNF, the rise of the Popolari actually helped Mussolini. The PPI gained enough support to make it difficult for other parties to form a government without its help. Don Sturzo hated Giolitti, for example, and Sturzo was partly responsible for keeping him out of power in 1922. In 1923, Mussolini cleverly undermined the PPI by improving relations with the papacy, going over Sturzo's head. The Pope withdrew support for the PPI and the party declined sharply.

Cross-reference

The decline and fall of the PPI is covered in Chapter 2 on pages 35–6.

their democratic principles and opposed Mussolini, but were too few to be effective.

To consolidate his power, Mussolini had to somehow get round the need to compromise with the other political parties. His emergency powers were only supposed to last 12 months. To gain permanent power, Mussolini needed to win an overall majority in the next elections. Until then, he had to manage the opposition parties by a mixture of threats and compromises.

The 1924 elections

The Acerbo Law

In theory, Italy was still a constitutional monarchy and a functioning democracy in 1923. To gain the legitimacy and the freedom of action he wanted, Mussolini had to gain an overall majority in the next elections; and to do this he had to change the existing electoral system – which he could only do with the agreement of other parties. One of Mussolini's most significant political achievements was to break free from the constraints of coalition government, and so gain real political power, through the Acerbo Law passed in July 1923.

Fig. 6 *'Vote for the National List', a poster displayed during the 1924 elections*

The arguments Mussolini used to get the Acerbo Law through were similar to the ones he had used a few months earlier to obtain the right to rule by decree: Italy needed the stability only a strong government could provide; the situation of one weak coalition after another collapsing within a few months had to be ended. The Acerbo Law (named after Giacomo Acerbo, the lawyer who framed it) offered a simple solution. The party gaining the most votes, provided it gained a minimum of 25 per cent, would receive two-thirds of the seats.

This plan was neatly designed to suit Mussolini's needs. The PNF was not capable of winning more than 50 per cent, the usual requirement to gain a majority, but it was capable of winning 25 per cent. With two-thirds of the seats, the PNF would be all but impossible to defeat. The dangers of Italy becoming a virtual one-party State if the Acerbo Law was passed should have been obvious, but it sailed through easily.

There was a considerable amount of intimidation by fascist Blackshirts during the voting in the Chamber, but the real reason the Law was passed by such a large vote in favour is that the deputies believed it was necessary. The fact that both Giolitti and Salandra voted in favour was reassuring. Many deputies were also taken in by Mussolini's promises to return to 'normality' as soon as the political crisis settled down.

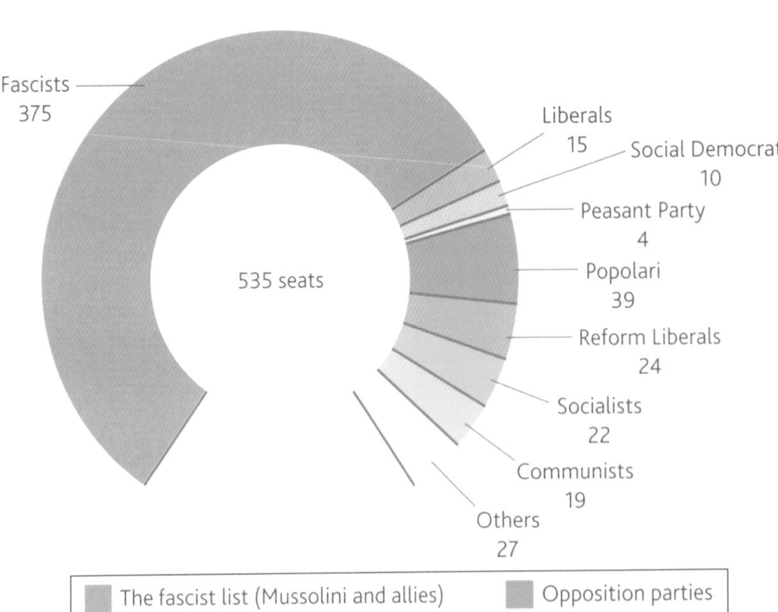

Fig. 7 *The 1924 election results*

The April 1924 election

Mussolini fought the election of April 1924 at the head of the *listone* (National List), allying the Fascists with conservative and liberal allies. Many politicians were tempted to join the fascist list, even though they disliked and distrusted Mussolini, because they knew they would be on the winning side. The Fascists duly gained 375 seats out of 535.

Mussolini's victory was not, however, as easy or as complete as it looked. The victories of fascist candidates had been accompanied by widespread intimidation and fraud. This was almost certainly unnecessary, as Mussolini had achieved widespread popularity by 1924 and the Fascists would have won anyway but the election campaign was marked by blatant irregularities. In spite of all this, the voting for the Socialists and Communists held up well and they gained more than 2 million votes.

The decisive election victory in April 1924 seemed to have made Mussolini completely secure. In reality, it plunged him into a crisis that almost toppled him from power. The violent and illegal actions carried out by Fascists in the election campaign led directly to the Matteotti Affair.

The Matteotti Affair and the repression of political opponents

Giacomo Matteotti was a young lawyer and leader of the Reformist Socialists in the Chamber of Deputies. He was a committed opponent of Fascism and had recently visited Britain and Austria trying to raise awareness of the true nature of Mussolini's regime. Matteotti also had acquired inside information on fascist financial scandals, especially a secret agreement between Mussolini and American oil companies.

Six weeks after the election, on 30 May, Matteotti launched a premeditated attack on the fascist violence, intimidation and ballot-rigging that had taken place. Matteotti's speech caused a storm in parliament and made Mussolini furious (Source 5).

> MATTEOTTI: ... if the government majority has obtained 4 million votes, we know that this result is the consequence of obscene violence.
>
> *(From their benches, Fascists brandish their fists at the speaker. The most violent try to throw themselves at Matteotti.)*
>
> MATTEOTTI: To support these government proposals there is now an armed militia, which is not at the service of the state but at the service of a party.
>
> *(Shouts on the right: Enough! Enough! Throw him out of the hall!)*
>
> MATTEOTTI: You want to hurl the country backwards, towards absolutism. We defend the free sovereignty of the Italian people, whose dignity we will defend by demanding that light be shed on the elections.
>
> *(The left rises to acclaim Matteotti. On the right there are cries of: Villain! Traitor! Provoker!)*
>
> MATTEOTTI (smiling to his friends): And now you can prepare my funeral oration.

5 *The session in the Chamber of Deputies, 30 May 1924. Quoted in C. Duggan,* ***Force of Destiny: Italy Since 1796****, 2007*

Mussolini did not just regard Matteotti as a nuisance, he saw him as a dangerous threat. On 1 June, Mussolini wrote an unsigned letter, published in *Il Popolo d'Italia*, denouncing Matteotti's 'monstrously

Activity

Thinking point

Assume you are local activists advising one of the candidates fighting the 1924 election on behalf of the Fascist Party. Working in two groups, devise a list of negative points that should be included to attack the other parties; and a list of positive points about the policies the Fascists will bring in if they are elected.

Activity

Revision exercise

Use the evidence in this chapter to make a list of reasons why you think the Fascist Party was able to rely on a large parliamentary majority after the general election of 1924.

Fig. 8 *Giacomo Matteotti (1885–1924), the Italian politician who was murdered in 1924*

Key chronology

The Matteotti Affair

1924 April	Fascist election victory
1924 May	Election violence exposed by Matteotti
1924 June	Abduction and murder of Matteotti
1925 January	Mussolini speech in parliament

provocative' speech and threatening to take revenge. Later, Mussolini calmed down and made a conciliatory speech in parliament, hoping to win over the Socialists. He won a vote of confidence by 361 votes to 107 and seemed to have re-established secure political control.

Three days later, however, Mussolini found himself deep in trouble. While walking from his home to the parliament building, Matteotti was seized by a gang of armed men, shoved into a car and driven away at high speed. The Fascists were immediately suspected but there was no sign of Matteotti until two months later, when his body was found dumped on the roadside on the outskirts of Rome.

The abduction and presumed murder of Matteotti caused a storm of protest, both inside and outside Italy. Mussolini was badly shaken by the universal denunciation of his regime. Nobody doubted that the abduction had been carried out by fascist thugs. There were eyewitness accounts to prove that the number plates of the car belonged to Amerigo Dumini, leader of the fascist 'punishment squad', the so-called ***Cheka***. It was clear that the abduction of Matteotti was a fascist crime. The key issue was whether it had been done on Mussolini's orders. It was known that Dumini reported to Cesare Rossi, in Mussolini's press office. Claims that the squad had acted on its own initiative were not very convincing.

Mussolini was extremely vulnerable in the summer of 1924. He had not yet consolidated his power. There were still opposition parties, independent newspapers and a king who had the constitutional authority to throw Mussolini out of office. His political allies in the fascist list refused to have anything to do with him, leaving him very isolated. If Mussolini's opponents organised a concerted political campaign against him, it would be very difficult for him to survive – but the opposition took no such action. Mussolini was saved by the **Aventine Secession**.

Key terms

Cheka: the secret police department of the fascist militia, the MVSN. The leader of the Cheka was Amerigo Dumini. The Cheka took its name from the secret police of the Bolshevik regime in Russia, set up by Lenin in 1921.

Aventine Secession: the name given to the boycott of parliament by the liberal and democratic opposition parties in 1924. This action was modelled on the practice in the Ancient Roman Republic of 'going to the Aventine Hill', hence the name Aventine Secession.

The Aventine Secession

The opposition parties made a serious miscalculation in June 1924. If they had exploited their position in parliament, they might have put Mussolini under such political pressure that the King would have been forced to intervene. Instead, the democratic parties (mainly the Liberals and Reformist Socialists) decided on a grand gesture, walking out of parliament to show their disgust.

The idea was to symbolise the moral purity of the opposition, leaving Mussolini to wallow in his own corruption. In reality, it left Mussolini free to make speeches in the Chamber with no opposition present, only tame fascist supporters. It also allowed the King to ignore the opposition. All Mussolini had to do was wait until the storm of protest died down and then win a vote in parliament allowing the government to continue its policies of 'pacification'.

This enabled Mussolini to get through the first stage of the Matteotti Affair in the summer of 1924, but he faced a serious problem in controlling the fascist militias. Mussolini badly needed the support of fascist leaders like Balbo, but he also needed the support of the armed forces, the King and the conservative elites. If Mussolini could not keep the fascist squadre d'azione in check, the old political establishment might turn against him. There was a danger of a split between the moderate and radical wings of the fascist movement. There was also a possibility that judges would begin a judicial inquiry into the murder of Matteotti. By December 1924, Mussolini was facing a crisis at least as bad as the one in June.

Mussolini had to act decisively to draw a line under the Matteotti Affair and prove that he was the man in charge. He did this by making a bold speech to parliament on 3 January. This could have gone badly wrong, but turned out to be a brilliant success. In the speech, Mussolini claimed he had nothing to do with the murder of Matteotti and that the killers would be tried and punished. However, Mussolini also went on the attack. He blamed the democratic parties for 'running away'. He said he took full responsibility for Fascism: 'I now accept, alone, full political, moral and historical responsibility for all that has happened.' This was a clever step. 'All that has happened' did not mean just the murder of Matteotti, it meant the whole fascist rise to power since 1922.

Above all, Mussolini made it clear he would get tough with the fascist radicals. This was enough to reassure the Liberals and Conservatives; Mussolini won the next big vote in parliament. He had survived the Matteotti Affair, just, but he was badly shaken by how close he had come to political disaster. It is important, therefore, to analyse the reasons why Mussolini was not toppled from power in 1924:

- The key decision was up to King Victor Emmanuel III, and he had already made up his mind in October 1922 that there was no credible alternative to Mussolini.
- Mussolini had just won the elections with a huge majority and this seemed to give his government legitimacy.
- The democratic parties badly misjudged the situation and took the wrong decisions.
- It was difficult to unite the opposition around a single leader – some people proposed Gabriele D'Annunzio but he was now unwilling to step forward (partly because Mussolini bombarded him with letters claiming he was innocent and begging D'Annunzio to hold back).
- Removing Mussolini would have required intervention by the armed forces and the generals were not keen to get involved in a civil war with the fascist militia.
- Mussolini was clever enough to avoid provoking further opposition. He waited the crisis out skilfully, made appropriate-sounding responses and sacked a number of fascist ministers. (The historian Doug Thompson claims that this was a turning point in Mussolini's rise to power, the moment when Fascism became the 'interrupted revolution'.)

Activity

Thinking point

Assess the validity of the view that: 'Mussolini survived the Matteotti Affair because of his own political skill'.

Propaganda and the cult of the leader

Dictators are human. Even Hitler and Stalin were human. The following pen-picture of Mussolini by the travelling American journalist, John Gunther, is useful because it was written in 1936, before Mussolini became a hate figure in the western democracies (Source 6).

> The things Mussolini hates most are Hitler, aristocrats, money, cats and old age. He detests old people, especially old women. He dislikes references to the fact that he is a grandfather; and when, on July 29, 1933, he reached the age of fifty, the Italian press was not allowed to mention it. The things Mussolini loves most are the city of Rome (he has assiduously fostered the 'cult of Rome'), his daughter Edda, peasants, books, aeroplanes and speed.

6 *J. Gunther, **Inside Europe**, 1938*

According to the propaganda myths, however, Il Duce was more than human. Mussolini had to be presented as the charismatic leader-figure for 40 million Italians. Mussolini had to be a cult.

> Central to the task of welding the nation into a homogenous whole was the cult of the Duce. Mussolini promoted himself with vainglorious abandon. His picture was everywhere and when he so forgot himself as to shake hands, the newspapers faked the photograph and showed him giving the Roman salute. Sculptures of the Leader also proliferated, among them equestrian statues whose eyes lit up at night, flashing green, white and red. Streets and squares were named after him and the Fascists even christened Mont Blanc, 'Monte Mussolini'. Slogans proliferated an: 'Mussolini is always right' and 'We shall go straight ahead' (famously displayed outside Naples on a hairpin bend). Cinema audiences had to stand when the Duce appeared on film.

7 *P. Brandon,* ***The Dark Valley****, 2000*

Il Duce was the star of the show. It was Mussolini's face (or sometimes shirtless upper body) that was projected in the posters and photographs. It was Mussolini's voice that was heard in speeches at rallies or over the radio. It was Mussolini's amazing personal abilities that were drummed into the minds of school children by the propaganda. Mussolini was a statesman. He was an intellectual. He was a man of action. He was a man of the people. Mussolini knew everything. Mussolini could do anything. Mussolini was always right.

Policies to consolidate power to 1927

It has been said that Mussolini followed a 'twin-track strategy' to consolidate power: on the one track using violence and intimidation, or the threat of it, to suppress political opponents, while, on the other track, appearing as a moderate in order to reassure the old elites and to make political deals with them. This is, in many ways, a valid interpretation but there were actually more than two tracks.

Fig. 9 *Mussolini addressing the Italian parliament*

Mussolini's position was strengthened by economic success. He was fortunate to come to power just as the underlying economic situation was beginning to improve. From 1922, there was a spurt of economic growth and a revival of international trade. Fascism had little to do with this economic recovery. Mussolini appointed Alberto De Stefani as Finance Minister and allowed him to follow traditional liberal economic policies based on free trade and support for industry. From 1925, Mussolini introduced more openly fascist policies, especially his 'economic battles', which were only partially successful in economic terms but did a lot to boost his popularity.

Mussolini also benefited from foreign policy successes. He had promised to rescue Italians from the shame and humiliation they thought they had suffered because previous governments had been too weak to stand up to the Great Powers. Between 1923 and 1925, Mussolini achieved a string of foreign policy successes, especially the acquisition of Fiume in January 1924.

These successes concerned relatively minor issues but helped to build up Mussolini's image as the man to restore national pride.

Mussolini also extended his control over the State through a series of legal and constitutional measures:

- The Palazzo Vidoni Pact of October 1925 provided a framework for industrial relations, bringing the trade unions under fascist control and strengthening the position of the employers.
- The *Leggi Fascistissime* (fascist laws) of December 1925 provided Mussolini with a new title as head of government, rather than prime minister. The Leggi Fascistissime banned opposition political parties and free trade unions and established tighter censorship of the press. The laws reorganised local government, replacing elected mayors with podestas – powerful local officials appointed directly by the State. In January 1926, the fascist laws were extended, giving Mussolini permanent powers to rule by decree.
- The Syndical Law (often known as the Rocco Law, after the Minister of Justice who devised it) was passed in April 1926. It made strikes illegal and laid the foundations for the Corporate State.
- The Press Law of 1926 suppressed the remaining independent newspapers and tightened up press censorship.
- The Charter of Labour in April 1927 extended the Rocco Law by forcing the fascist trade unions and the employers to enter into collective legally binding contracts.

Activity

Thinking point

For what reasons do you think Mussolini had his title changed from prime minister to head of government?

Mussolini increased his control over the fascist movement as well as the State. The Matteotti Affair had demonstrated the dangers of fascist radicalism running wild and the new national head of the PNF was Roberto Farinacci, the ras of Cremona, from the extreme radical wing of the fascist movement. In the first half of 1925, Farinacci supervised a wave of violence against 'anti-fascist elements' such as Catholic Action, bankers, industrialists and 'unreliable' civil servants.

Mussolini did not allow Farinacci's dominance over the PNF to last long. The Fascist Party Congress of 1925 turned out to be the last one. Farinacci was sacked in March 1926 and the PNF was gradually integrated into the State bureaucracy. The Party Statute of October 1926 ended the election of party officials and weakened the power of the ras. This allowed Mussolini to gradually get rid of pro-Farinacci radicals. By 1927, Mussolini had a much stronger grip on the PNF than before.

Exploring the detail

Attempts to assassinate Mussolini

1925 November:	Tito Zaniboni
1926 April:	Violet Gibson
1926 September:	Gino Lucetti
1926 October:	Anteo Zamboni

Violence and intimidation were still important elements of Fascism after 1926, but the repression of opponents became more systematic as Mussolini moved to establish a police state. This process was helped along by a sudden rush of attempts to assassinate Mussolini. Between November 1925 and October 1926, there were four such attempts (it has been estimated that the overall total during his rule was 13) and they were ideally timed to justify the introduction of new repressive police powers.

The first assassination attempt, by the socialist deputy Zaniboni, helped Mussolini pass the Law on the Powers of the head of government at the end of 1925. After the three attempts in 1926, a new police law introduced powers to imprison people without trial for 'special crimes'. In December 1926, the Law for the Defence of the State provided for the death penalty for attempts on the lives of members of the government or the royal family. The law also set up a new special tribunal for political trials.

In 1927, the secret police was formally established – the OVRA (Organisation for Vigilance and Repression against Anti-Fascism). Previously, repression had been carried out by the fascist militia, the MVSN. Now it was brought under the control of the Ministry of the Interior and became much more systematic. Political prisoners were sent to special camps on remote Mediterranean islands. The OVRA was quite small, especially in its early years, and the number of political prisoners was only about 4,000 at any one time; but the existence of the secret police and its network of informers was a powerful deterrent to anti-Fascists. Many chose to go into exile.

By 1927, Mussolini's consolidation of power was well advanced. He had transformed the political system of Italy into virtually a one-party State. He had suppressed, or otherwise neutralised, the main sources of potential opposition. He had proved his ability to dominate the fascist movement and he had survived the one really dangerous crisis of his regime over the murder of Matteotti. He had begun to establish the Corporate State. He had gained popularity through propaganda, economic recovery and foreign successes.

The process of consolidation was not fully complete, however. It was not until 1929 that Mussolini was finally able to neutralise the enormous influence of the Catholic Church by the Lateran Pacts with the papacy. It was not until the late 1930s that the fascist regime was really radicalised.

Activity

Revision exercise

Consider the evidence in this chapter about Mussolini's consolidation of power after his initial appointment as prime minister in 1922. Make two parallel lists:

a Successes that made Mussolini's political position more powerful and more secure.

b Factors that seriously limited Mussolini's freedom of action.

Summary questions

1. Explain why there was a March on Rome in 1922.
2. Explain why the democratic opposition failed to stop Fascism in the years 1922 to 1927.

2 Making Italians into Fascists

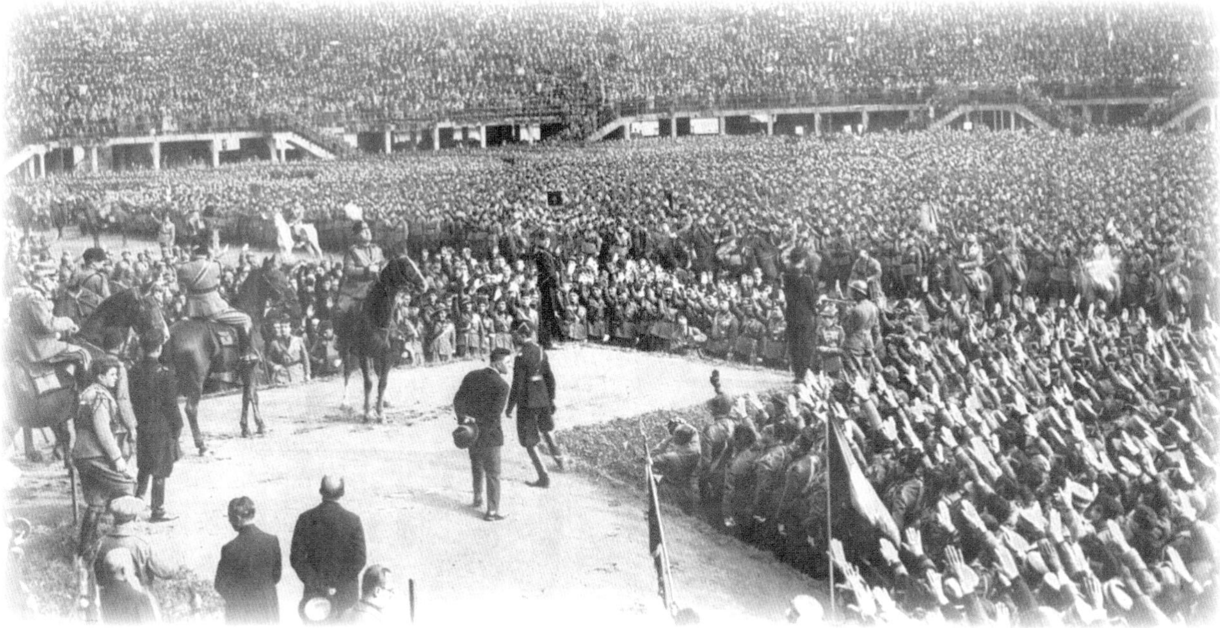

Fig. 1 *Mussolini at a fascist rally in the 1920s*

In this chapter you will learn about:

- the reasons for fascist political dominance under Mussolini
- the content of fascist propaganda
- the instruments of fascist propaganda
- the use of propaganda to support domestic and foreign policies
- the reasons why the Catholic Church came to terms with Mussolini in 1929.

Key terms

Totalitarian state: a state in which political power is totally controlled by one party and in which all individuals are totally merged into one coordinated mass society.

ARTICLE 36: Italy considers the teaching of Christian doctrine in accordance with Catholic tradition as both the basis and the crown of public education. It therefore agrees that the religious teaching now given in the public elementary schools shall be extended to the secondary schools.

ARTICLE 43: The Italian State recognises the organisations forming part of the Italian Catholic Action, in so far as they maintain their activity wholly apart from every political party and under the immediate control of the hierarchy of the Church, for the diffusion and practice of Catholic principles.

1 *Articles from* ***The Concordat Between The Papacy And Italian State****, February 1929. Quoted in J. Whittam,* ***Fascist Italy****, 1995*

Between 1922 and 1927, most political opposition was suppressed or marginalised as Mussolini made himself dictator of a one-party State. This rise, however, was based on what is often termed a 'block of consensus', rather than on the physical elimination of all opposition. Mussolini's rule was generally popular with wide sections of the Italian people, but this did not yet mean that there was universal enthusiasm for Fascism. Mussolini had taken power in Italy mostly by leaving things as they were before, not by transforming society.

After consolidating political power, therefore, Mussolini dreamed of 'turning Italians into Fascists' and making Italy a **totalitarian state**. To do this, it was necessary to change deep-rooted attitudes through the reorganisation of society and the extensive use of propaganda and indoctrination. It was also necessary to resolve the relationship between the fascist regime and the Catholic Church, which was in many ways a rival source of propaganda and indoctrination, competing with Fascism for hearts and minds.

Winning hearts and minds, 1924–29

Dictatorships rely on consent as well as coercion. The consolidation of the fascist regime was mostly achieved through political means, through repression and skilful tactics, but it was also essential for Mussolini to maintain high levels of public approval for his regime. This made propaganda a vital aspect of Mussolini's regime.

The content of propaganda

Key terms

Ideology: the ideas, values and beliefs of a political movement, as opposed to its specific practical policies.

Fascist **ideology** was complex and often contradictory. There were many competing interests within the fascist movement and within Italian society. The ideology that was transmitted through the content of the propaganda, therefore, was adapted to suit different audiences at different times, and fascist ideology went through significant changes during Mussolini's rise to power. The fascist message by October 1922 was very different from the ideology of fascist revolution put forward when Mussolini formed his Fasci di Combattimento in 1919.

1919: the ideology of social revolution – The ideology of Fascism in 1919 was based on extreme revolutionary ideas. Fascism was anti-capitalist, anti-monarchist and anti-Christian. Fascism called for a social revolution that would destroy the old elites. The ideology of 1919 was also very diverse, mixing nationalists with left-wing extremists, republicans with monarchists, working class with middle-class values and aspirations. Mussolini by no means had complete control over the movement and often had to give in to pressure from radical elements.

1922: the ideology of power – During the rise to power, many strands of ideology were discarded, or at least quietly hidden, as Mussolini attempted to reassure influential sections of society and to bring the wilder elements of the fascist movement under more disciplined control. Fascism no longer spoke in terms of Republicanism and overthrowing the monarchy, because the King would have an essential role if Mussolini wished to come to power by legal means. The anti-capitalist ideology was watered down in order to gain acceptance for Mussolini from big business. The anti-Christian ideology was played down as the Fascists began to stress how much it was on the same side as the Catholic Church in the fight against the 'Bolshevik threat' and 'godless socialism'.

It is, of course, very difficult to judge precisely how much the ideology really changed and how much it was temporarily covered up for tactical reasons. Mussolini himself later regretted some of his tactical decisions – in 1943 and 1944, in the days of the Salo Republic, he tried to return to some of the revolutionary ideals of early Fascism, admitting that he had been mistaken in the 1920s and 1930s by not being radical enough.

Cross-reference

Mussolini's leadership of the Salo Republic is covered in Chapter 10 on pages 131–4.

Another difficulty of interpretation is the vague and unstructured nature of fascist ideology, which can often seem confused and contradictory. Mussolini founded the ideals of Fascism in Italy but fascist movements emerged all over Europe between 1919 and 1945, notably Hitler and Nazism in Germany, the Falange in Franco's Spain and Oswald Mosley's British Union of Fascists. There was something that could be called the common ideals of international Fascism, even though these ideals were nothing like as organised and uniform as the common ideals of international Communism.

A closer look

Ideals of Fascism

The ideology of Fascism is easy to recognise but very difficult to define precisely. All fascist movements contained a diverse mixture of individuals and ideas. All fascist movements had their own special characteristics according to its national background and the personality of its leader. Fascism also tended to be a mixture of right-wing and left-wing ideas; above all, it was a mixture of negative hatreds and positive beliefs. The following diagram provides a summary of some of the main strands of Fascism.

Fig. 2 *'The First Book of Fascism', a poster depicting Mussolini as a strong leader*

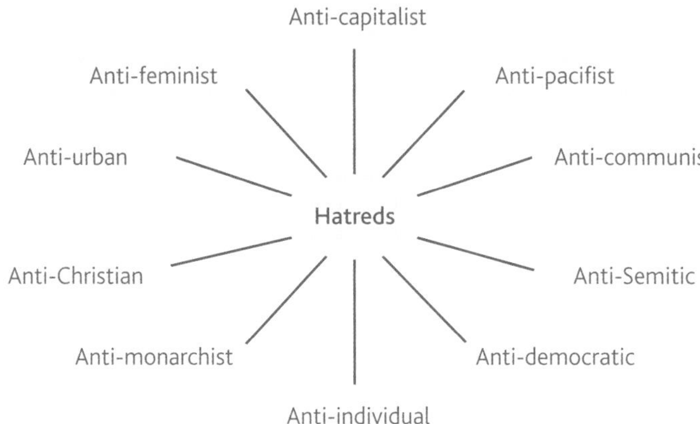

Fig. 3 *Fascist ideals*

Not all fascist movements shared all of these characteristics to the same degree. Hitler was obsessed above all by race, whereas Mussolini was obsessed by empire. Many individuals joined fascist movements because they were strongly motivated by one or two of these ideas but not others. The diagram above does not include all the ideals of Fascism. It does, however, provide a basic framework for defining fascist ideology – and it was from these broad ideas that Mussolini selected the key themes for fascist propaganda in Italy in the 1920s.

Propaganda in Fascist Italy in the 1920s revolved around the personality of Mussolini. Other leaders in the PNF were relegated to the sidelines, so much so that Fascism has been termed 'Mussolinianism'.

1. Remember that those who fell for the revolution and for the empire march at the head of your columns.
2. Your comrade is your brother.
3. Service to Italy can be given in all places and at all times. It can be given in work or in blood.
4. The enemy of Fascism is your enemy. Show him no mercy.
5. Discipline is the sunshine of armies. It illuminates the victory.
6. He who attacks with determination already has victory in his grasp.
7. Conscious and complete obedience is the virtue of the soldier.
8. There do not exist important or unimportant things. There is only duty.
9. The Fascist revolution depends on the bayonets of its soldiers.
10. Mussolini is always right.

2 *The **Fascist Decalogue**, introduced into secondary schools in 1938. Quoted in D. Evans, **Teach Yourself Mussolini's Italy**, 2005*

Cross-reference

The cult of the leader is discussed in Chapter 1 on page 23–4.

The *Fascist Decalogue* was not actually introduced into schools until 1938, but its ideological message is typical of fascist propaganda from the 1920s – the focus on youth, militarism, discipline and social order and on the idea of 'Mussolinianism'.

Ideology and the links to Ancient Rome

Fascist ideology looked both forwards and backwards. One key element in Fascism was the artistic, cultural and highly patriotic movement called 'Futurism', which had a strong influence on fascist ideology in the early stages of the movement. In the 1920s and early 1930s, several public buildings, especially railway stations and the planned new towns built during the Battle for Land, were built in accordance with futurist principles.

The influence of Futurism mostly faded away in the 1920s. Futurism was based on the excitement and modernity of the 'new city'. Mussolini, however, turned away from modernism and idealised the virtues of 'ruralism' and peasant values in preference to the 'wicked city'. Fascist propaganda was much more enthused by linking Fascist Italy to the past.

Did you know?

Fasces were the bundles of wooden rods with an axe that symbolised authority in Ancient Rome. The fasces provided the basis for the word 'Fascism'.

Fascism endlessly linked itself to the glories of Ancient Rome. Symbols such as the fasces provided Mussolini with the opportunity to make himself appear as the descendant of Roman emperors. The fascist organisation for very young boys and girls, the *Children of the She Wolf,* was named after the legend of Romulus and Remus, the founders of the city of Rome. Giving fascist officials the title of 'podesta' made Fascism seem both new and different but also old, in tune with the greatness of the past.

Fascist architecture, in the new towns created by the Battle for Land and in big public construction projects like the *autostrade,* was sometimes consciously designed to echo Ancient Rome. The city of Rome itself provided an ideal setting for the cult of *Romanita* ('Roman-ness') with its imposing ruins such as the Capitol and the Colosseum. State funding was poured into archaeological projects such as the tomb of the Roman Emperor Augustus and Rome's ancient sea port, Ostia. The regime's efforts to promote Romanita reached a peak in the late 1930s, but the links to Ancient Rome were already a central theme of propaganda from the early years of the regime.

> If you listen carefully, you may still hear the terrible tread of the Roman legions. Caesar has come to life again in the Duce. He rides at the head of the numberless cohorts, treading down all cowardice and impurities to re-establish the culture and the new might of Rome. Step into the ranks of his army.

3 *Teacher's manual for members of the Balilla. Quoted in C. Duggan,* ***The Force of Destiny: Italy Since 1796****, 2007*

Fig. 4 *Satirical cartoon showing Mussolini as the Roman leader Caesar*

One of the most important links to Ancient Rome was in foreign policy. Mussolini was obsessed with Italy's destiny to be a great empire. In the modern world, Italy was overshadowed by the power and prestige of Britain and Germany. In the days of the Roman Empire, however, Italian culture was highly advanced, dominating the culture of most of Europe at a time when Germany and Britain had been ruled by barbarian war bands. The concept of re-creating *Mare Nostrum* (the Mediterranean Sea as 'Our Sea') was one of Mussolini's main foreign policy aims.

Activity

Revision exercise

Make a list of **five** aspects of fascist propaganda using links to Ancient Rome. Explain why you think such propaganda might have been effective in winning support for Mussolini and his regime.

The importance of image

Like other totalitarian regimes, Fascist Italy based much of its propaganda on imagery and visual impact. Part of this was in the modern architecture and the allusions to Ancient Rome. Much of it was in the countless photographs of Il Duce – in uniform, in a racing car, piloting an aeroplane, sitting at his desk, stripped to the waist working in the fields. The most powerful images of Fascist Italy were live events staged as spectacle.

Mussolini perfected what A. J. P. Taylor called 'the Technique of the Balcony'. A Mussolini speech was not just something to be listened to, but an elaborate theatrical production. Below Mussolini was the cast of thousands, the cheering crowds. High on his balcony was Mussolini, alone and above, representing the will of the people but separate and superior. It was not necessary to hear the actual words (many of those in the crowd had little idea of what he was actually saying) – mass participation in a spectacular event made a deep impression anyway.

Exploring the detail

One aspect of the importance of image in Fascist Italy was the way in which the regime copied aspects of Catholic ritual. All Italians were familiar with the powerful visual images the Catholic Church had presented skilfully over past generations and fascist rituals were often shameless near-copies of Catholic traditions. This included the fascist images of the ideal woman and family, the god-like presentation of Mussolini and the ceremonies acted out in schools and youth groups.

The use of propaganda to support domestic and foreign policies

Mussolinianism became the basis of fascist policies in the early 1920s, both at home and abroad. There was a powerful propaganda element in the presentation of domestic policies and also in the policies themselves. This was not only a matter of using propaganda to win acceptance for Mussolini's policies; it was often the other way round. Some of Mussolini's policies, especially in foreign affairs, were designed at least as much to boost Mussolini's prestige as to pursue important foreign policy objectives.

Propaganda was a key component, for example, in Mussolini's 'economic battles', which were launched personally by Mussolini through big, set-piece speeches that maximised the impact of campaigns such as the

Battle for the Lira and the Battle for Births. These speeches hammered home the ideological messages of national pride, preparation for war and the greatness of Mussolini as leader. They were not only statements of economic policy, they were propaganda spectaculars used to reinforce 'Mussolinianism'.

In foreign policy, Mussolini was desperate to make an immediate impact on public opinion. He wanted to demonstrate the fact that he was the man to restore national pride after the sense of humiliation that hung over Italy after the First World War. This is why he intervened so forcefully in the Corfu incident in 1923, causing a major international fuss over a relatively trivial dispute. In 1925, Mussolini extracted the maximum propaganda value out of his role as a mediator alongside Britain when the Locarno Treaties were signed.

Mussolini gained respect abroad during the 1920s and exploited this to increase his popularity at home. His early foreign policy successes did not involve any serious risks or military commitments, thus providing a cheap and easy route to greater prestige in the eyes of Italians. Many different instruments of propaganda were used to 'brainwash' Italians into believing in Mussolini's achievements: radio and cinema, posters and school books, rallies and mass activities and, most of all, newspapers.

Cross-reference

Mussolini's 'economic battles' are covered in Chapter 3 on pages 42–6.

Italian foreign policies in the early 1920s are covered in Chapter 7 on pages 87–9.

Exploring the detail

Italy had no foreign policy issues at stake in the discussions at Locarno, which concerned Germany's eastern and western borders. However, it was a marvellous opportunity for Mussolini to play the part of international statesman, posing as the equal of the British Foreign Minister, Austen Chamberlain.

Cross-reference

Mussolini's exploitation of the meetings at Locarno for propaganda effect is covered in Chapter 7 on page 91.

Cross-reference

The development of 'minculpop' and fascist cultural propaganda in the 1930s is covered in Chapter 6 on pages 80–1.

The use of propaganda in the war years 1940–43 is covered in Chapter 9 on pages 121–2.

The instruments of propaganda

Radio and cinema

Mussolini was in many respects a brilliant propagandist, but his regime took a surprisingly long time to maximise the use of propaganda techniques. It was only in the 1930s that a ministry of propaganda was set up, named the Ministry of Popular Culture, generally known as 'minculpop'. Film propaganda was not fully exploited until the 1930s. There was no coordinated propaganda machine in Fascist Italy comparable to that controlled by Dr Josef Goebbels, Minister of Propaganda and Public Enlightenment, in Nazi Germany from 1933.

Mussolini's regime did exploit the new mass media, though it never matched the brilliant use of film propaganda by Nazi Germany or Soviet Russia. One reason for this was that technical developments, especially the arrival of talking pictures and the mass production of cheap radio sets, made things possible in the 1930s that could not have been done earlier. Another reason was that Mussolini's success in consolidating his regime in the 1920s was based on the 'block of consensus' in Italian society. It was only later that Fascism really aimed to make Italy a totalitarian state. 'Brainwashing' the people was less vital in the 1920s.

Radio was exploited to an extent, especially communal listening to broadcasts of Mussolini's speeches, but radio ownership was very limited outside the cities. Cinema became a major part of popular culture in Italy, but until the end of the 1920s the films people watched were silent films and most of them were American-made anyway. There was very limited use of film as propaganda until the 1930s.

Posters and school books

Posters were a key component of fascist propaganda. Posters conveyed a vivid message in a colourful and accessible form. They were especially important in the 1920s, before the arrival of cinema newsreels, but they continued to have a powerful impact in the 1930s and during the war years. Posters covered walls, advertising hoardings and school classrooms.

In the early 1920s, including the 1924 elections, there was a poster war between the Fascists and the opposition but from 1925 the fascist regime gained a virtual monopoly.

Posters were produced glorifying all aspects of Fascist Italy, especially the cult of Il Duce. Many of the posters reflected the influence of futurist art and the modernist 'fascist style' in architecture. Some very striking posters celebrated the two flights across the Atlantic by massed Italian flying-boats, led by Italo Balbo in 1930 and 1933. The second of these flights, to the Century of Progress exhibition in Chicago, caused an international sensation and gave a huge boost to Italian prestige.

Above all, fascist posters aimed to transform the image of youth. Countless posters portrayed youth as the future soldiers of Fascism. From 1921, there was a magazine dedicated to *Giovinezza* (youth); this became the lavish and expensively-produced magazine *Gioventù Fascista* (fascist youth) from 1931.

Poster propaganda was targeted at youth through schools as well as the youth organisations. Posters were used to illustrate classrooms and school books. There were dramatic poster illustrations on the front covers of *Il Capo Squadra Balilla,* a handbook for young Fascists, and *Quaderno,* a school exercise book. The Gentile Education Reform of 1923 put a fascist stamp on the school curriculum and the regime quickly ensured that schools used a new generation of textbooks full of propaganda material – though the regime's concessions to the Catholic Church meant that fascist propaganda in schools had to compete with Catholic religious instruction, especially in primary schools.

Fig. 5 *Italo Balbo, pictured on the front over of* Time *magazine after his flight to Chicago in 1933*

Did you know?

The propaganda impact of Balbo's famous flight to Chicago in 1933 was *too* successful for Mussolini – it made him furiously jealous of Balbo. Later, in 1933, Balbo was 'promoted' to be Governor of Libya as a way of lessening his influence within the fascist regime.

Rallies and mass activities

Image was also a vital part of mass rallies and sporting events. Mussolini had a propaganda flair for theatrical live performance. The militaristic marching formations, the carefully designed uniforms of the various youth organisations, the emphasis on sporting activities all carried the same messages of order, discipline, togetherness and action. The lone individual was small and insignificant, but the individual submerged in the mass was part of something massively powerful.

Some of the most visible and effective instruments of propaganda were the fascist organisations such as the ONB (*Opera Nazionale Balilla*), the OND (*Opera Nazionale Dopolavoro)* and the *Massaie Rurali* (Rural Housewives). People took part in the activities run by these organisations for many different motives. The focus on group participation enabled propaganda messages to be transmitted very effectively because the propaganda was not always blatant and it was associated with activities that were popular and enjoyable, even for those who were not fascist believers.

Newspapers

Newspapers provided the regime with its main instrument of propaganda in the 1920s. In his early career, Mussolini was above all a brilliant journalist. Many of the leading figures in the PNF also had experience as journalists. From the start, the regime exercised strict controls over the press. Money was poured in to support fascist newspapers and journals, such as *Il Popolo d'Italia* and *Critica Fascista.* There was censorship and harassment of non-fascist newspapers, some of which

Fig. 6 *Mussolini addressing a rally in the 1920s*

were virtually taken over by the regime. *Corriere della Sera*, formerly a liberal democratic paper, steadily became more and more a mouthpiece for the government.

There was also a lot of 'auto-censorship', the process by which editors and journalists tried to guess what the regime would and would not approve of and so censored themselves. The press was never completely coordinated, for example, *Osservatore Romano*, the Catholic Church newspaper, had a big readership and did not always follow the fascist line – but there was never any direct criticism or dissent. Mussolini was able to rely on the newspapers to report events and policies in exactly the way he wanted.

Activity

Thinking point

Write a letter to the editor of *Il Popolo d'Italia* in 1925 to express gratitude for Mussolini's role in 'saving Italy'.

There were also a number of publications controlled by the Fascist Party. It took some time for Mussolini to establish control over the PNF but, by the late 1920s, most of the radicals in the movement and most of the personalities big enough to challenge Mussolini had been sidelined. The PNF was increasingly run by nonentities and almost all propaganda put out by the PNF fitted in with 'Mussolinianism'.

> There was, from the beginning, the press office of the prime minister under Cesare Rossi, the close associate of the Duce. It had two sections, one dealing with Italian and the other with foreign newspapers and the state-controlled news agency *Agenzia Stefani*. Mussolini himself had risen to political prominence as a highly talented journalist and editor and he continued to take a close personal interest in the press, convinced that newspapers were the key to any propagandist success. Rossi and his successors imposed press censorship and this continued even after the last opposition newspapers had been closed down or taken over in 1926. Editors were forbidden to print news about crime, financial or sexual scandals, or indeed anything that suggested the regime had problems. Government subsidies were paid to editors and journalists but the newspapers did remain in private ownership. By the late 1920s, however, their staff were expected to become members of the Fascist union of journalists.
>
> 4 — J. Whittam, ***Fascist Italy***, 1995

The Catholic Church: rivalry and collaboration

Fig. 7 *Pope Pius XI*

The Church had many reasons to fear and hate Mussolini in 1922. The first was ideological. In his early career, Mussolini was a fierce atheist and anti-clerical who made frequent attacks on the 'evil influence' of the papacy. For Mussolini and many fascist radicals, the Church represented backward superstitions and was a barrier to modernity and progress. To the Church, Fascism represented 'godlessness' and a threat to the social order.

The second cause of conflict was political. Between 1919 and 1922, the new Catholic political party, the PPI, was an obstacle in the way of the rise of Fascism, competing for support from many of the same social groups. Before October 1922, Don Sturzo, the leader of the PPI, tried to join with other parties in order to keep Mussolini out of power. Even after this, the PPI was still a political danger to the new fascist regime. Another, related problem was the existence of Catholic trade unions, in competition with the fascist syndicates.

A third battleground was control over education and youth. Mussolini's dream of 'making Italians into Fascists' required extensive indoctrination of the young in order to establish fascist social values; this meant a head-on collision with the indoctrination of the young by the Church to establish Catholic social values. When the fascist regime moved to reform the education system and to set up new youth organisations, it came into conflict with the Church and with the Catholic **lay organisation**, Catholic Action.

Despite the potential for conflict, there were also reasons why the Church and the fascist regime might collaborate. Once Mussolini was securely in power, political realism pushed the Church to compromise with the government of the day. The same political realism pushed Mussolini towards gaining at least passive acceptance from the Church, just as he compromised with other traditional elites. For the Church, Mussolini seemed to be the man who could save Italy from the 'Bolshevik threat'. The Church hated and feared Fascism, but the Church hated and feared Communism a whole lot more.

Anti-Communism was a particularly powerful influence on the thinking of the new Pope, Pius XI. Before his election to the papacy in February 1922, Pius XI had witnessed the fighting in Warsaw when the Red Army invaded Poland during the civil war that followed the Bolshevik Revolution. Pius XI became almost fanatically anti-communist and this encouraged him to avoid open opposition to Mussolini.

Key profile

Pope Pius XI (1857–1939)

Pius XI (Cardinal Achille Ratti) was elected pope in February 1922, just before Mussolini's rise to power. Pius XI clashed with the fascist regime, often over issues connected to education and youth. He issued a papal encyclical denouncing totalitarianism in 1931. In 1938, he showed disapproval of Mussolini's race laws. The Pope was also ready to collaborate, however, especially in the historic Lateran Pacts of 1929. Pius XI negotiated similar treaties with foreign powers, such as Germany in 1933, and strongly supported Franco during the Spanish Civil War. He died in 1939.

On 2 October 1922, therefore, three weeks before the March on Rome, Pius XI issued a circular letter to the hierarchy of the Church in Italy. The circular ordered the Catholic clergy to remain politically neutral and not to give open support to the Catholic PPI. This was an important sign that the papacy was ready to make a deal with the Fascists once they came to power. In January 1923, Pius XI's Secretary of State, Cardinal Gasparri, had the first of a series of secret meetings with Mussolini. Through Gasparri, the papacy was offering to support the new regime, at least indirectly, by withdrawing support from the PPI. What the Church wanted from Mussolini in return was a continued attack on Socialism and guarantees of protection for the rights of the Catholic Church.

Mussolini was still in a relatively fragile position in 1923 and he was very willing to make concessions in order to secure support from the papacy. He committed extensive State funding to rescue the Bank of Rome, which managed the assets of the Church and was on the edge of bankruptcy. Concessions on the religious instruction in schools were also included in the education reforms introduced by the regime later in 1923.

Pius XI's decision to compromise with Mussolini was the beginning of the end for Luigi Sturzo and the PPI. In June 1923, the Pope ordered Sturzo to disband the Catholic Party. This was of great value to Mussolini

Key terms

Lay organisation: run by and on behalf of 'lay' people (that is, people who have not been ordained into the priesthood).

Exploring the detail

Azione Cattolica (Catholic Action) was the chief lay organisation for Catholics in Italy. Azione Cattolica comprised many different organisations, including youth groups, containing hundreds of thousands of members. It was well financed and well organised. There were frequent rivalries with fascist organisations and considerable friction between Mussolini's regime and the Catholic authorities. These clashes were reduced by the Concordat of 1929, but never completely eliminated.

Cross-reference

The 1923 Gentile Reform in education is covered in Chapter 5 on page 62.

Giovanni Gentile is profiled on page 42.

because the PPI still had 107 deputies in the Chamber and was capable of obstructing Mussolini's path to power. Sturzo reluctantly resigned (as a priest it was almost impossible for him to disobey the Pope), leaving the PPI badly weakened. There was little public protest from the Church against fascist violence in 1923, even when Catholics were the victims. Several bishops issued statements of admiration for Mussolini.

Exploring the detail

The Roman question

Since 1870, the Catholic Church had refused to recognise the legitimacy of the united Italy. The 'Roman question' was how to bring about a resolution of the legal and constitutional conflict between the papacy and the Italian State. One great problem, the permanent domination of government by anti-clerical liberal politicians, had been ended but many complicated issues were still not settled.

Solving the Roman question

By the end of 1923, collaboration between Mussolini's regime and the Church was well advanced, but there were still serious differences. Fascist radicals continued to inflict violence on Catholics as well as on Socialists. When Fascists talked about establishing a 'totalitarian' state, it inevitably aroused fear and opposition from the Church. The formation of the ONB in 1925 led to clashes between fascist youth organisations and those of Azione Cattolica. The PPI, although badly weakened, continued to exist, with strong support in country areas. The 'Roman question' had not been solved.

By 1926, Mussolini was in a stronger position and ready to seek a solution to the 'Roman question'. He forced the PPI to dissolve itself and made membership of it illegal. In August 1926, he opened formal negotiations with the papacy. There were several factors influencing the Church in favour of an agreement:

- It was clear by 1926 that Mussolini's regime would last and so the Church wanted to protect its position in society and not risk remaining outside the State.
- A formal agreement with Mussolini might bring an end to continuing violence from fascist extremists against Azione Cattolica.
- The Church was in agreement with Fascism on some ideological issues such as the need for social order and respect for authority.
- Fascist policies in relation to women and family, such as the Battle for Births and hostility to divorce, contraception and abortion, fitted in with Catholic beliefs.
- It was obvious that Mussolini wanted an agreement and so it was thought that he could be persuaded to make important concessions.

The negotiations were helped along by various goodwill gestures. After Mussolini survived an assassination attempt in 1926, the Pope was the first to deliver a message of congratulations and thanksgiving. In his Christmas message of December 1926, Pius XI declared that 'Mussolini is the man sent by Providence'. Even so, it took nearly three years of negotiations to conclude an agreement. In 1928, the talks were broken off for a time because of attempts to close down Catholic youth groups.

The Concordat of 1929

The Lateran Pacts were finally signed in February 1929, providing official recognition of the Italian nation-state by the papacy (at last accepting the loss of the Papal States seized by Italy in 1870) in return for official recognition by the State of the Vatican City as a separate independent State. The treaty also agreed massive financial compensation to the papacy for the loss of its territories when the Papal States were seized in 1870.

Exploring the detail

The Lateran Pacts

The Lateran Pacts took their name from the Pope's Lateran Palace within the Vatican City, the area round St Peter's in Rome that was the sovereign territory ruled by the papacy.

In addition to the treaty, a Concordat was signed recognising the dominant position of the Catholic Church in Italian society. Catholicism became the only officially recognised religion. Religious education was made compulsory in secondary schools. Teachers and textbooks had to be approved by the Church. The Church gained the right of censorship over books, newspapers and films. Civil marriage was no longer sufficient, there had to be a religious ceremony. Divorce was outlawed. Increased State financial support was given to priests and religious orders. Azione Cattolica was recognised as a legal organisation – the only non-fascist organisation in Italy to be given such status. It is easy to see why many Catholics rejoiced at the Lateran agreements.

Fig. 8 *The signing of the Lateran Pacts*

Mussolini had made significant concessions in order to secure the Lateran Pacts, but he also gained great rewards. The great majority of Italians were Catholics and now it was possible for them to support the regime with the favour of the Church. Any anti-fascist activity by Catholics was virtually eliminated. Mussolini had always known that Catholicism was too deeply rooted in Italian society for it to be crushed by direct attack. The Lateran Pacts meant his regime would be supported and approved by the vast network of priests.

Both internally and abroad, Mussolini gained massive prestige. He had achieved something no government in the 60 years of the united Italy had been able to do. It made him seem like a statesman and a man of peace. Special elections were held in 1929 to act as a referendum on the Lateran Pacts before they were ratified in parliament. The results showed a massive majority in favour. It was an important step towards being recognised as the legitimate ruler of Italy.

Activity

Talking point

Working in two groups, use the evidence in this chapter to support the rival arguments that:

a 'The papacy gained much more from the Lateran Pacts than Mussolini.'

b 'The Lateran Pacts gave Mussolini everything he had hoped for.'

The Lateran Pacts did not wipe away all the causes of conflict between Church and State. In 1931, Pius XI issued a papal encyclical denouncing the idea of a totalitarian state. Friction continued over fascist restrictions on Azione Cattolica. In 1937 and 1938, the Church made coded criticisms of Italy's links with Germany and the imposition of new race laws. There was no formal breach, however, and the Church continued to support the regime over almost all its policies, including the war in Ethiopia from 1935. Exactly who got the most from the bargain remains an open question.

Learning outcomes

Through reading this section, you have gained an understanding of the complex process by which Mussolini established his fascist regime in Italy. You have seen the inter-relationship between ideology and political calculation – and how Mussolini was able to gain the support, or at least acceptance, from many different elements in Italian society and politics. You have also examined the particular importance of fascist propaganda in promoting the cult of Mussolini and the idea that there was no alternative – so that by 1929, even the Catholic Church had decided to compromise with the fascist regime.

Practice questions

However much we deplore violence, it is obvious that, in order to make our ideas understood, we must beat stupid skulls with heavy blows. But we are violent only because it is necessary to be so. Our Fascist punitive expeditions, all those acts of violence that are reported in the newspapers, must always have the character of legitimate reprisal. Because we are the first to recognise how sad it is, after having fought the external enemy in the war, to have to fight the enemy within. The Socialists had formed a State within a State. This State is more tyrannical and illiberal than the old one. So the violence we are causing today is a necessary revolution to smash the Bolshevist State.

Speech by Mussolini to the Fascists of Bologna, April 1921. Quoted in M. Robson, ***Italy: The Rise of Fascism 1915–1945****, 2006*

This is the secret: motivated solely by ambition, Mussolini sought to keep one door open, be it to the Right or to the Left, so that he would always be able to emerge as leader, either at the head of a revolutionary movement or a right-wing reactionary movement. When he saw that the Socialist Party was torn by internal divisions, that it could not march towards power, Mussolini threw into the sea his Left ideas and dedicated himself to the forces of the Right. Leading a socialist revolution would be too difficult and dangerous for him – he realised how much easier it would be to arrive in power if he followed the ultra-nationalist line, renounced his past and betrayed his old companions.

Comments made in 1936 by Bruno Buozzi, Secretary of the metallurgical workers union (FIOM). Quoted in G. Seldes, ***Sawdust Caesar****, 1936*

Prime ministers Ivanoe Bonomi and Luigi Facta, Giolitti's successors, lacked authority. Facta, especially, was regarded merely as a stand-in for Giolitti during his two governments from February to October 1922. Former prime ministers, Orlando, Nitti, Salandra and Giolitti sought to return to power by striking a deal with Mussolini. When the actual crisis in government leading to the installation of a Fascist government began, it became difficult for political leaders to use force to prevent something which most had already accepted as inevitable.

A. De Grand, ***Italian Fascism****, 2000*

(a) Use Sources A and B and your own knowledge. Explain how far the views in Source B differ from those in Source A in relation to Mussolini's aims before he came to power in 1922. *(12 marks)*

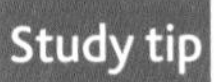

In these part a) questions, it is essential to make a direct comparison between the views in the two sources, not just to provide a literal paraphrase of the words of each source in turn. What is the 'message' of each source? In what ways (and why) are the comments about Mussolini's views by Buozzi and Mussolini himself different? What similarities are there? And, using your own knowledge, can you explain and comment on the degree of difference or similarity?

(b) Use Sources A, B and C and your own knowledge. How important was fear of Socialism in winning support for Fascism in 1922? *(24 marks)*

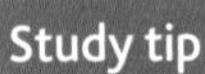

Questions like this require a coherent overall argument showing the ability to evaluate the relative importance of fear of Socialism alongside a range of other factors, such as violence and intimidation, the popularity of Mussolini, or his political skill in compromising with the elites. It is also important to have a good grasp of the chronology of events in 1922 – but used selectively, not as a descriptive account. It is also desirable to be concise. A lengthy answer full of detailed information may be less effective than a shorter answer that is more structured and controlled. Remember, too, that it is essential to use the sources to support your answer, not to plod through each source line-by-line.

2 The Corporate State

3 The Italian economy

In this chapter you will learn about:

- the economic aims of Mussolini's fascist regime
- the economic 'battles' in agriculture, industry and finance
- the ideology of 'autarchia' and its effects on the economy
- economic management and the Corporate State
- the situation of the Italian economy by 1940.

Fig. 1 *Making a new Italy: an artwork from* La Domenica del Corriere *(an Italian weekly newspaper) in 1935*

Exploring the detail

Natural resources

One serious problem for the Italian economy was the shortage of natural resources. Italy relied on imports for almost all major raw materials, especially coal, oil and iron ore. This made manufacturing in Italy very expensive, not least the armaments industries producing tanks, aircraft and warships. This shortage of natural resources made Italy vulnerable to economic sanctions by other European powers and was a key reason why Mussolini adopted the policy of autarky in the 1930s.

> Italy has become the Mecca for political scientists and economists looking for a new world order in a world trapped between capitalist depression and communist dictatorship.

1 *The exiled Italian academic, Gaetano Salvemimi. Quoted in R. Eatwell,* ***Fascism: A History****, 1995*

When he came to power, Mussolini faced two major problems with the economy. One was historic – 'dualism' and the gulf between the economic development of the agrarian South compared with the more industrialised North. The second was immediate – the pressing problem of the post-war economic crisis, with the dangers of runaway inflation

Cross-reference

The problems of the Italian economy before 1922 are covered in the Introduction on pages 2–3.

and of a complete breakdown in industrial relations. Between 1922 and 1940, Mussolini's regime had a major impact on the Italian economy, both for the better and for the worse, but fascist policies were often driven by priorities other than economics. There were political considerations, the desire for social transformation and, above all, the drive to make Italy a major military power.

The fascist regime and the economy

Mussolini was lucky in the timing of his accession to power. By late 1922, world trade was beginning to recover from the post-war crisis and Mussolini arrived at the right time to benefit from this. At first, Mussolini was very cautious in dealing with the economy. He did not rush to implement fascist ideology and satisfy the expectations of impatient Fascists who wanted an economic revolution. His priority was to win acceptance from conservative business interests. He appointed Alberto De Stefani as Finance Minister and allowed him to follow 'safe', pro-business policies. Taxes were lowered. The telephone industry was taken out of State control and given back to private ownership. Government money was used to help the privately-owned Ansaldo steel and shipping firm. There was a boom in industrial production.

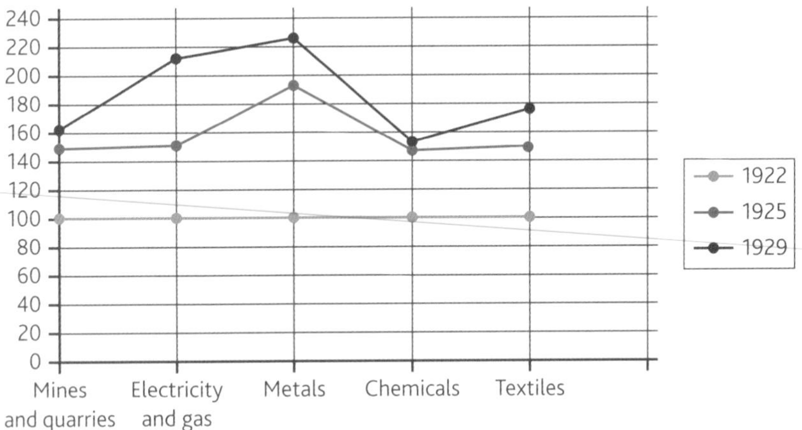

Fig. 2 *Industrial production, 1922–29*

Key profile

Alberto De Stefani (1879–1969)

De Stefani was an orthodox liberal economist, who was Mussolini's first Finance Minister from 1922 to 1925. He was a fascist sympathiser but he was already a respected politician before Mussolini came to power. His credibility with business and with the old liberal elite made him very useful to Mussolini in the early stages of the consolidation of power. De Stefani's policies were generally successful in balancing the budget and reassuring the Conservatives, but he was sacked in 1925. Mussolini moved towards more State intervention in the economy.

By 1925, there was a balanced budget and Mussolini could claim that economic stability had been achieved. Much of this success was due to De Stefani (even though there was a problem with rising inflation as a result of the industrial boom), but in 1925 Mussolini sacked De Stefani and replaced him with a pro-fascist businessman, Count Giuseppe Volpi.

At the same time, Mussolini gave Alfredo Rocco the task of preparing plans for the introduction of the Corporate State.

Key profile

Giuseppe Volpi (1877–1947)

Count Volpi was an influential businessman from Venice who provided an important link between Mussolini and big business. Volpi was governor of the province of Tripolitania in North Africa from 1921 until 1925 and was Mussolini's Finance Minister from 1925 to 1928, playing an important role in the development of the Corporate State. In 1928–29, he negotiated the financial aspects of the Concordat with the papacy. He became a member of the Fascist Grand Council and was president of the federation of employers, Confindustria, from 1934.

Fascist economic ideals

The economy was vitally important for Mussolini's regime. To maintain popular support for his regime, he needed people to have a sense of economic well-being and rising living standards. He needed to win support from big business to consolidate his regime. He needed to control the trade unions and put an end to the industrial unrest that had almost paralysed Italy between 1919 and 1922. He needed to please the radical Fascists. Many of these factors were more political and social than economic, but it was absolutely vital for Mussolini to get the economy under control and to prove that Fascism worked.

In addition to all these practical considerations, there was also fascist ideology. In theory, the fascist movement was based on revolutionary ideas – anti-Catholic, anti-bourgeois and anti-capitalist. Radical Fascists wanted immediate action to overthrow the old system. Many Fascists were enthusiastic about the ideas of syndicalism, which had emerged in France in the years before 1914. There was a sharp increase in the membership of fascist unions, calling themselves fascist syndicates, in 1922 and 1923.

Exploring the detail

The fascist syndicates

From January 1922, there had been growing support for fascist trade unions led by Edmondo Rossoni. The fascist syndicates wanted to use trade union power for political purposes. They demanded a corporatist system in which employers would be forced to cooperate with the workers (in other words that the employers would give in to union demands). Big business was very nervous of the influence of the syndicates; so was Mussolini.

Key profile

Edmondo Rossoni (1884–1965)

Rossoni was a radical Socialist and syndicalist before the First World War. He joined the Fascists in 1921 and led the fascist syndicates in the early 1920s. Later, he came Minister of Agriculture and served on the Fascist Grand Council. He voted against Mussolini on 25 July 1943; as a result, the Salo Republic sentenced him to death but he had already escaped to Canada.

In 1926, the Justice Minister, Alfredo Rocco, brought in the Syndical Law (often called the Rocco Law), which set up the structure of the Corporate State. Fascist leaders such as Giuseppe Bottai liked to call the Corporate State the 'third way' between Capitalism and Communism. The Corporate State fitted the fascist ideology of national unity and dynamic state action to solve the serious problems of industrial unrest in post-war Italy. Employers and workers would be brought together as part of a national plan. Exploitation of the workers by special interests would be prevented. Strikes would become unnecessary.

Cross-reference

The structures and development of the Corporate State are covered in more depth later in this chapter on pages 49–51.

Even in 1926, the ideology of the Corporate State was not fully developed; many ideas and propaganda slogans were added as time went on. Mussolini's thinking was strongly influenced by the philosopher, Giovanni Gentile. It was not until 1932, for example, that Mussolini produced a coherent overview in *The Doctrine of Fascism*, published in the fascist encyclopedia. This has led to the widespread belief that there was no coherent economic thinking in corporatism. It has also been claimed that the Corporate State was a sham policy, pretending to make workers equal partners with employers but actually used by Mussolini to bring the trade unions under control and to give big business everything it wanted.

Key profile

Giovanni Gentile (1875–1944)

Gentile was a respected philosopher and university professor who strongly influenced the ideas of Fascism. In 1923, Mussolini made him Minister of Public Education to reform school textbooks along fascist lines. The Gentile Reform shaped education policy in the 1920s. Gentile also influenced Mussolini's ideas about the ideology of Fascism and the Corporate State. Mussolini's book *The Doctrine of Fascism*, published in 1932, was mostly authored by Gentile. He was murdered by anti-fascist partisans in April 1944.

Activity

Thinking point

Make a list of **five** key reasons why Mussolini regarded economic policy as a high priority in the 1920s. Rank these reasons in order of importance.

Mussolini's economic 'battles'

In order to unify the nation and to put his ideology into practice, Mussolini launched a series of economic 'battles': the Battle for Grain, the Battle for the Lira, the Battle for Births and the Battle for Land. The aims of these battles were not only economic, they were all part of the drive to transform Italian society and they were also exercises in State propaganda, trying to maximise popular support for the regime.

According to the historian John Pollard, 'the great advantage of Mussolini's economic "battles" was that the Italian people could be mobilised in a non-class, non-political way for nationalistic economic ends'. The Italian historian Renzo De Felice believed that Mussolini succeeded in this aim: The economic battles were a decisive aspect of the national consensus around Mussolini between the end of the 1920s and the beginning of the 1930s.

> Mussolini's ambitions in 1925–26 were boundless. He wanted visible, dramatic successes and he wanted a leading role for himself. He had already ended strikes and made the trains run on time. Now he launched a series of spectacular 'campaigns', or 'battles' – the military terminology was revealing – on other key economic and social issues. The Fascist regime would save the lira, crush the Mafia, make the country self-sufficient in wheat, drain and resettle the Pontine marshes near Rome, rebuild Rome itself on imperial lines, and even boost the birth rate. These issues were carefully chosen. They were certainly dramatic gesture policies, demanding tough action and determined management but they were not *too* frightening or disruptive, and they were likely to prove popular.
>
> **2** M. Clark, **Mussolini**, 2005

Cross-reference

The Battle for Births is covered in Chapter 5 on pages 68–9 and the Battle against the Mafia is covered in Chapter 6 on pages 78–9.

Agriculture

From 1925 to 1935, there was a period of crisis for Italian agriculture. The landlords maintained economic power and many labourers were forced to become sharecroppers. There was a decline in the rural standard of living. The importance of agriculture steadily declined in relation to industry. This was not what Mussolini's regime wanted. During the first few years, the fascist movement promoted urbanisation and modernisation, but from the mid-1920s the regime placed huge emphasis on the importance of agriculture and the traditional values of rural society.

Much of Italian agriculture, especially in the South, was backward and inefficient. Mussolini's approach to solving the problems in agriculture was rather contradictory. On the one hand, the regime talked a lot about the need for modernisation. On the other hand, the regime also heavily promoted the policy of 'ruralisation', which idealised the old-style peasant values and encouraged a back-to-the-land movement, trying to stop the movement of people from the countryside into the cities – one propaganda slogan was: 'Empty the cities!' The most dramatic expression of the policy of ruralism was the Battle for Grain.

The Battle for Grain

Mussolini announced the Battle for Grain (*Battaglia del Grano*) in July 1925, promising to 'liberate Italy from the slavery of foreign bread'. There was a strong emphasis on the importance of self-sufficiency and making Italy less dependent on imports (and thus improving Italy's **balance of payments**). The propaganda also made grandiose claims about proving to the world that Italy was a major power, capable of dynamic expansion. An underlying assumption was that Italy's population would soon be growing rapidly and that much more food would need to be produced.

Ambitious targets were set for increases in the production of wheat and other cereals. To encourage this, the regime introduced high tariffs (import duties) on foreign imports. The price of Italian wheat rose higher than the price on world markets. Generous government grants were given to farmers for investment in machinery and fertilisers. The government also promised to bring under cultivation land that had previously been neglected because it was uneconomic to farm.

Wheat production did increase sharply (by more than 50 per cent) because of the Battle for Grain. Large-scale farms in the Po valley in the North did particularly well out of the Battle for Grain because they were able to maximise the use of mechanised farming techniques and fertilisers. In turn, this boosted the industrial firms producing agricultural machinery and the chemical industries producing the fertilisers.

In other ways, the effects were less beneficial to the economy. Other valuable export crops, such as olives, fruit and vegetables, were neglected. There was also a decline in animal farming because the costs of fodder were so high; after the first two years of the Battle for Grain, Italy's total livestock had fallen by more than 500,000. Meat and egg production fell, with the result that prices rose and living standards declined. The high import duties and the government subsidies enabled inefficient farms to survive; there was little or no agricultural modernisation in the South. Despite the big increases in grain production, Italy was still dependent on foreign imports – in 1933, for example, more than 500 million tonnes were imported.

Key terms

Balance of payments: the relationship between the total economic value of income, from exports, compared with the total economic costs of imports. A balance of payments surplus is the sign of a healthy economy; a balance of payments deficit can push governments into economic crisis.

Fig. 3 *Mussolini poses bare-chested*

Activity

Thinking point

Using Sources 3, 4 and 5 and the other evidence in this chapter, assemble a list of points for and against the argument that: 'Economically and politically, Mussolini's Battle for Grain achieved significant success.' Decide whether you agree or disagree with this statement, and why.

I am pleased to inform you that the harvest of wheat this year has risen to more than 75 million quintals. This year's production is the highest ever in Italy, greater even than the 70.9 million that was considered extraordinary in 1929. During the six years before the war, the average annual production stood at 49 million. These increases in the harvest are not due to an increase in the land under cultivation, which was 4.7 million hectares in 1914 and was 4.9 million in 1932. It is productivity that has increased. The rural population is now working in the rhythm set for it by the Fascist regime.

3 *A speech by Mussolini to the Permanent Wheat Committee, September 1932*

One key economic battle was the Battle for Grain. At that time, grain accounted for half of Italy's imports. In order to cut Italy's massive balance of payments deficit, Mussolini set in motion a campaign to increase production. Propaganda, including pictures of a bare-chested *Duce,* and a range of incentives persuaded farmers to switch to grain production. While cereals output did increase enormously, the campaign had its drawbacks. It encouraged farmers to abandon vital export crops such as vines, olives and citrus fruits and to cultivate land that was often not suitable for grain.

4 *J. Pollard, **The Fascist Experience in Italy**, 1998*

Success in the Battle for Grain was yet another illusory propaganda victory, won at the expense of the Italian economy in general and of consumers in particular.

5 *D. Mack Smith, **Mussolini**, 1981*

The Battle for Land

The Battle for Land, sometimes known as the Battle of the Marshes, was a massive land reclamation project launched in 1928. It was in some ways a continuation of the Battle for Grain, in that it was intended to make extensive new land available for wheat production, but there were other important motives. Like most of Mussolini's 'battles', it was designed to impress the outside world by showing how Fascism had galvanised Italy into coordinated action. Draining the marshlands would conquer malaria and improve the health of the nation. When the Great Depression hit Italy from 1930, the land reclamation project became an important way of providing employment and stimulating the economy.

The new towns built on the reclaimed land, such as Latina, Pontina, Littoria and Sabaudia, were intended to boost the economy and to provide jobs; but they were also meant to be showpieces of fascist architecture and town planning – suitably impressive homes for the expanding population. Not all of the 13 new towns were located in the area reclaimed from the Pontine marshes. One new town was built near Mussolini's birthplace, Predappio. Another new town, named Mussolinia, was built in Sicily.

The Battle for Land produced mixed results. It was largely successful in terms of propaganda. The Pontine marshes were near Rome and it was easy to dazzle the foreign visitors who toured the showpiece new towns. The massive public works involved in land reclamation also provided work for thousands of labourers. Many of the promises of the

Battle for Land were unfulfilled, however. The total amount of land reclaimed was much less than the ambitious targets set in 1928. Only 58 per cent of reclamation projects and about one in three irrigation schemes were completed.

Ruralisation

The Battle for Land was closely linked to the policy of ruralisation. From the late 1920s, the fascist regime placed more and more emphasis on the superiority of peasant ideals compared with the 'wicked cities' and attempted to stop the flow of migration from the countryside into urban areas. This policy had only limited success. The number of people who were resettled on the reclaimed land was very small in comparison to the original expectations. Small farmers, who were supposedly going to be the chief beneficiaries of the increased land under cultivation, gained very little; most of the benefits went to large landowners through government subsidies. The policy of ruralisation may possibly have slowed down the migration of people from the countryside into the cities, but it certainly failed to stop it altogether.

> This policy [of encouraging a return to the land and a high rural birth rate] flew in the face of Italian social trends. Italians were migrating to cities from relatively overpopulated rural areas. By encouraging a higher birth rate, the regime added to unemployment and did little to ease the problems of rural Italy.

6

A. De Grand, ***Italian Fascism****, 2000*

Fig. 4 *A poster for the 'Agenda Agricola', 1934*

Cross-reference

The effort to increase the rural population through the Battle for Births is covered in Chapter 5 on pages 68–9.

Activity

Group activity

Working in two groups, assemble evidence and arguments for and against the proposition that: 'Mussolini's Battle for Land succeeded more than it failed.'

Table 1 *Agriculture as a percentage of national income*

	Agriculture	Industry	Service sector
1911–20	45.9	28.7	25.4
1921–30	38.2	31.4	30.4
1931–40	29.8	32.8	37.4

Finance

The Battle for the Lira

One of the pressing economic problems of the post-war crisis that helped Mussolini come to power was inflation. Although there was an economic recovery from 1922 and government spending was brought under better control, price inflation remained a worry – it started going up again in 1925. As a result, the Italian currency, the lira, was falling in value in relation to other currencies in the international exchange markets. In 1922, the rate of exchange was £1 – 90 lire; by 1926 it was £1 – 138 lire and the value of the lira seemed likely to fall further. There were fears that Italy might suffer a complete collapse of the currency.

The Battle for the Lira, launched in 1926, was Mussolini's attempt to bring about an upward revaluation of the lira. Typically, Mussolini's motives were only partly economic. There was also a rather simplistic belief that a strong lira would show that Italy was a strong country. Mussolini also hoped to make Italy more economically independent in relation to foreign countries, especially the United States. As with so many of his policies, it was also supposed to play well as propaganda, demonstrating his ability to take bold and decisive actions.

In August 1926, Mussolini launched the Battle for the Lira in a big open-air speech at Pesaro (Source 7).

Activity

Thinking point

Read Source 7. To what extent was Mussolini's speech launching the Battle for the Lira motivated by political, rather than economic considerations?

I want to tell you that we will fight the economic battle to defend the lira with the utmost firmness. To the people in this square and to the whole of the world I declare that I will defend the lira to my last breath, to the last drop of my blood. I will never inflict upon the marvellous people of Italy, who for four years have worked like heroes and suffered like saints, the moral and economic disaster that would follow the collapse of the lira. The Fascist regime will resist the speculation of hostile financial forces. Our lira, the symbol of the nation must and will be defended.

7 *Speech by Mussolini, 18 August 1926. Quoted in J. Pollard,* ***Fascist Experience in Italy****, 1998*

Exploring the detail

Exchange rates fix the value (buying power) of a currency in relation to leading international currencies – in the 1920s, exchange rates were usually measured against the British £ sterling or the US dollar. A high exchange rate makes exports expensive and imports cheaper. Industrialists in Italy wanted a lower value of the lira to help exports; Mussolini wanted a higher exchange rate as a matter of national pride.

There was general agreement that the government should act to stop the fall in the value of the lira. The big issue was to decide at what level to revalue the lira. In 1927, Mussolini decided to peg the lira at *Quota Novanta*, (Quota 90) a rate of £1 – 90 lire. This valued the lira at a higher level than Italian business wanted or could cope with – big business and the Finance Minister, Count Volpi, wanted an exchange rate of £1 – 120 lire. At Mussolini's Quota Novanta, exports were hit because they cost more to foreign buyers. There were big cuts to prices and wages in Italy and the living standards of industrial workers worsened sharply. Many savings banks closed down. In 1928–29, there were many mergers, as struggling small businesses were taken over by bigger firms.

In the end, the Battle for the Lira achieved several of Mussolini's aims and benefited sectors of industry, such as steel, chemicals and armaments, because imports were cheaper. On the other hand, it caused intense economic difficulties that lasted long after the revaluation. When the world depression began after 1929, the Italian economy was only just getting over the adverse effects of the Battle for the Lira.

Industry and transport

There was substantial industrial growth in Italy during the fascist era. Many of the foundations for this had been laid down before the First World War, with the development of big industrial centres in the 'northern triangle' (between Milan, Turin and Genoa). General economic trends meant that industrialisation would have continued in Italy anyway, with or without the fascist regime, but Mussolini established close links with ***Confindustria***, the association of major industrial employers, and the policies of the regime did influence some of the key developments in the industrial economy.

Key terms

Confindustria: was the Italian Employers Federation founded in 1910. After 1922, Confindustria gave financial support to Mussolini in return for fascist actions against workers and trade unions. From 1925, Confindustria was an important part of the Corporate State.

Total industrial output in Italy was considerably smaller than in major European economies such as Britain and Germany, but there were several Italian industries of real size and significance:

- The Ansaldo steelmaking and shipbuilding firm, which received government financial support in 1923.
- The giant Montecatini chemical firm, which was originally based on copper mining but diversified into the production of vital chemical products such as phosphates, sulphuric acids, fertilisers, commercial dyes, aluminium and explosives. By 1939, Montecatini had a virtual monopoly of Italy's chemical industries.
- Fiat of Turin, which produced almost 80 per cent of cars for the Italian market. Fiat also diversified into a wide range of other areas, including agricultural machinery, mining, smelting and cement. Another key

player in the car industry was Alfa Romeo, based in Milan, producing luxury cars and racing cars.

- The Pirelli Rubber Company, which expanded rapidly due to the massive demand for tyres for the motor industry.
- The Italian division of the American-owned Edison Electric Company.
- The oil industry, with big new refineries constructed at Bari and Livorno.
- New industrial centres, such as the hinterland of Venice with the town of Mestre and the new sea port of Venezia Porto Marghera.

In the 1920s, the fascist regime assisted industry through generous tax arrangements and by muzzling the trade unions so that employers had secure control over their workers. In the early 1930s, when the Great Depression hit Italian industry, there was more State intervention. The IMI (*Istituto Mobiliare Italiano*) was set up in 1931 to save the banking system from complete collapse. In January 1933, the regime founded another agency, IRI (Institute for the Reconstruction of Industry), to provide financial and management support to industry.

Cross-reference

The impact of the Great Depression on the economy is covered later in this chapter on page 51.

Table 2 *Italian steel production, 1918–40 (million tonnes)*

	Italy	Germany
1918	0.3	15.0
1930	0.5	11.5
1940	1.2	19.0

Transport was one of the success stories of fascist economic policy. Italy became a world leader in the construction of autostrade. The first motorway, the *Autostrada of the Lakes*, linked Milan with Lake Como and Lake Maggiore. Strictly speaking, it was not a fascist achievement because construction began in 1921, although it was only finished in 1924. Later autostrade connected major cities such as Milan, Turin, Florence and Naples. Another 800 miles of existing roads were upgraded. The new roads were ideal prestige symbols. They were highly visible, well-designed examples of modern architecture, with stunning bridges and viaducts. They also fitted the fascist ideology of war.

Italy's railways also attracted admiration from abroad. Mussolini's propaganda boast was that he 'made the trains run on time'. Italy was one of the first countries in the world to opt for electrification of an extensive rail network, using new technology pioneered in Hungary. Some 5,000 km of track were electrified, providing fast, modern connections from the hub of Milan south to Rome and Naples and north to Austria and Switzerland.

Like the road building, the electrification of the railways did contribute much to the economic modernisation of Italy, but was also used for maximum propaganda effect. The same was true of shipping, with the construction of two huge ocean liners, *Rex* and *Count of Savoy*, and the car industry, where the regime gave massive support to Fiat and took State control of Alfa Romeo in 1932. Overall, transport policy had many successes, but this did not apply to all areas of the economy. Many parts of the country (especially, of course, the South) continued to suffer from inadequate transport links.

Fascist Italy also promoted aviation. Italo Balbo led two highly-publicised mass flights across the Atlantic, to Brazil in 1930 and to the United States in 1933 (the 1933 flight is covered in Chapter 2, page 33) and fascist propaganda made a lot of the fact that Mussolini was a qualified pilot.

Activity

Revision exercise

Use the evidence in this chapter to write a paragraph explaining the reasons why Mussolini's economic policies were often admired in foreign countries.

The fascist regime saw aviation almost entirely in terms of prestige projects and military aircraft, however, and it had little or no impact on the economy.

Trade and taxation

Italy's trade position was vulnerable to international fluctuations. The massive government debts incurred during the war made Italy very dependent on the United States. Italy lacked raw materials and was not self-sufficient in food – it was the dependence on imported wheat and the 'slavery to foreign bread' that prompted Mussolini into the Battle for Grain in 1925. Fascism was also very nationalistic. Mussolini was anxious to gain greater State control over trade. The high levels of government spending also put a lot of strain on taxation as the regime looked for ways to raise money without alienating business or public opinion.

Trade

Fascist trade policies were very inconsistent. In the first stages of the rise of the Fascist Party, its ideas were strongly anti-capitalist, threatening to completely tear apart Italy's whole economic system. Ideologically, Fascism was very hostile to the traditional liberal principle of free trade. As he came to power in 1922, however, Mussolini badly needed support from big business and the old elites. That is why he appointed Alberto De Stefani as Finance Minister and allowed him to pursue traditional free trade policies.

Between 1922 and 1925, Italian trade did well, with rising exports. This was partly because De Stefani's policies were successful, but was mostly due to the post-war boom in international trade and access to American loans. Unemployment was reduced and living standards improved. In 1925, however, Italy's trade position worsened because of the poor grain harvest in 1924 and the problems caused by rising inflation and the fall in the value of the lira. The regime turned away from free trade policies. The Battle for Grain, for example, imposed high **protective tariffs** on imported grain.

Key terms

Protective tariffs: duties imposed on imported goods to make them more expensive and thus 'protect' goods produced in the home country.

Trade was not an important priority for the fascist regime. The main aims of the regime were political. In any case, Italian trade was small in scale compared with the major European economies. Many of the most successful industries in Italy were focused on internal markets rather than exports. From 1926, Italy's trade position was badly affected by the side-effects of the Battle for the Lira, Mussolini's policy of strengthening the Italian currency, because the high valuation of the lira made Italian exports more expensive for foreigners to buy. The statistics on imports and exports in Table 3 show how relatively undeveloped Italian trade was by 1933, more than 10 years after the Fascists had taken over power.

Table 3 *Italy's trade balance in 1933: imports and exports*

Imports (millions of lire)		Exports (millions of lire)	
Raw cotton	767	Fruits and garden produce	1,091
Coal	685	Raw and synthetic silk	820
Wheat	504	Cotton fabrics	676
Machinery	365	Cheese and dairy products	241

Taxation policies

In the early 1920s, the fascist regime tried hard to keep taxes as low as possible in order to gain favour with business and to attract foreign investment. These business-friendly policies were carried through by the

Finance Minister, Alberto De Stefani, who re-organised the tax system in February 1925. The 10 per cent tax that had previously existed was repealed. Taxes on luxury goods and on foreign capital investment were abolished. Inheritance tax was ended as long as inheritance remained within the family.

The regime did not wish to be seen to impose high taxes on ordinary people, but it badly needed to raise money. The Decree Law of 1927, allowed the government to take money direct from workers' pay packets as 'deductions' in return for social benefits. Between 1927 and 1931, these deductions were heavily exploited. In theory, taxes remained low but workers' pay was squeezed hard, with a damaging effect on living standards.

Autarky

'Autarky' refers to policies to achieve economic self-sufficiency by reducing imports and maximising domestic production. It became a major priority in the mid-1930s as Mussolini developed his plans for military expansion and war, but autarchic ideas were already influencing fascist economic policies long before then. Italy lacked natural resources and was dependent upon foreign imports for vital raw materials. Mussolini's policy of *autarchia* (self-sufficiency) was partly an attempt to overcome this problem and to lessen the pressure on Italy's balance of payments. However, autarky mattered most to Mussolini as an expression of national pride and as a way of ensuring Italy's status as a world military power.

Autarky involved more and more State intervention in industry and increased support for industries that would be needed for military purposes. Foreign competition to the leading Italian industries was virtually eliminated because prices were fixed by the State. There were many joint ventures between the State and key industries like Montecatini, especially in finding ways of reducing imports of strategic resources.

One example of this was exploration for oil and gas in Albania, carried out by AGIP (Italian Petroleum), which had been established in 1926. Similar giant firms with links to the State controlled the production of coal and strategic metals such as copper and nickel. The effects of the policy of autarky worked in exactly the opposite direction to the regime's stated aim to bring about 'ruralisation'.

Activity

Group activity

Working in four groups, prepare a propaganda poster using appropriate slogans to dramatise the successes the regime claimed to have achieved in:

- the Battle for Grain
- the Battle for Land
- the Battle for the Lira
- policies for industry and transport.

Economic management: the establishment and structure of the Corporate State

Starting with the Rocco Law in 1926, the fascist regime introduced a series of measures leading towards what became known as the Corporate State. The establishment of the Corporate State was not carried out according to a clear-cut plan – the structures and even the ideology behind them, evolved only slowly and was still taking shape as late as 1934. Many observers, both at the time and later, claimed that the process was never completed and that the Corporate State did not really exist outside fascist propaganda. In the eyes of the fascist regime, of course, the Corporate State was a triumphant success, avoiding the errors of Capitalism and Communism and finding an ideal 'third way' to organise society and the economy.

There were two inter-related aims behind the Corporate State. The first aim was to solve the problems of class conflict and industrial unrest. The second aim was to increase the extent of State intervention in the economy. Both of these aims increased tensions within the fascist movement because key groups and individuals had rival ambitions and wanted to pursue different policies.

Between 1922 and 1925, the driving force behind corporatist ideas was Edmondo Rossoni, leader of the fascist syndicates. Under Rossoni's leadership, the fascist syndicates (unions) greatly increased their membership. The socialist unions were divided and losing support. In the Palazzo Vidoni Pact, the fascist syndicates gained a monopoly of the right to negotiate with employers. In April 1926, Mussolini's Justice Minister, Alfredo Rocco, introduced the Syndical Law (Rocco Law), banning strikes and providing for cooperation between workers' syndicates and employers. This was the real beginning of the Corporate State.

There were three very different views of how the Corporate State ought to work:

1 The view of the fascist unions, who had nearly 3 million members and expected to be able to dominate the employers.

2 The view of the big employers, who were very nervous of the power of the unions and wanted Mussolini to get them under control.

3 The view of fascist politicians who really believed in the ideology of corporativism and wanted to make the system of corporations work.

Rossoni expected his fascist syndicates to exercise real power in the new system, but Mussolini did not want to offend big business or to allow the syndicates to become too powerful. Outwardly, the Syndical Law was even-handed, but it was actually designed to weaken union rights, especially by removing the right to strike. The regime was not neutral but firmly on the side of Confindustria and the big employers.

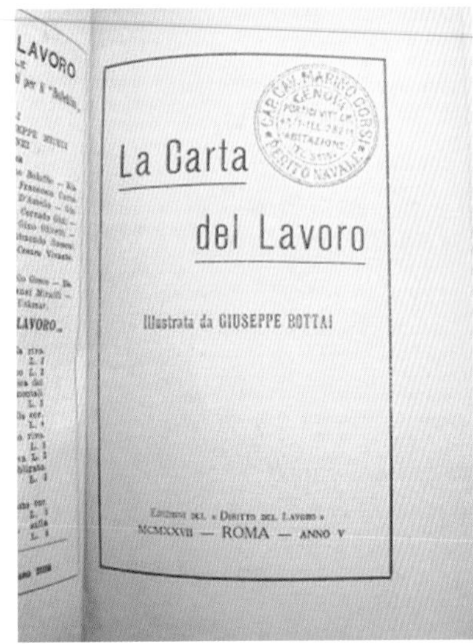
La Carta
del Lavoro
Illustrata da GIUSEPPE BOTTAI
MCMXXVII — ROMA — ANNO V

Fig. 5 *The Carta del Lavoro (Charter of Labour) document, published in 1927*

The Ministry of Corporations set up in July 1926 put industrial relations even more firmly under State control. In 1927, the Charter of Labour set out detailed rules for negotiating agreements between workers and employers. In 1928, the fascist syndicates were broken up into six smaller federations for different areas of the economy. Rossoni and the old leaders of the syndicates lost all their power. Whatever was going to happen in the Corporate State, it was not going to be dominated by the fascist unions.

In theory, it was still possible that the corporations might be made to work on the basis of cooperation. In 1929, Mussolini reorganised the government and promoted a group of capable young ministers, known as the 'Ministry of all the Talents'. The new Minister of Corporations was Giuseppe Bottai, an ambitious and ideologically committed Fascist. According to Alexander De Grand: 'the only serious attempt to realise a corporative policy in Italy occurred between 1929 and 1932 under Giuseppe Bottai.'

Cross-reference

Giuseppe Bottai is profiled on page 73.

Bottai supervised the reform of the National Council of Corporations (CNC) in April 1930. The CNC was like a pyramid: at the top it was run by Mussolini and government ministers; on the second level were civil servants and Fascist Party officials, at the bottom were representatives of the corporations from each sector of the economy. Bottai genuinely hoped that this system could be made to work efficiently and that it would bring about economic modernisation and social unity.

There were three main reasons why this did not happen.

- First, the system of power in Fascist Italy was very complicated and implementing coherent policies was always difficult. The ideology of the Corporate State was not fully worked out until 1932 and the structure of the corporations was only finalised in 1934.
- Second, the unions had been weakened so much and the employers had gained such a strong position that the CNC could not impose policies the employers did not like.

- Third, Mussolini was not willing to have a confrontation with the big industrialists, so Bottai could not rely on backing from Il Duce. In 1932, Bottai was moved from the Ministry of Corporations and the momentum behind the policy slackened off.

The economic impact upon Italy of the Great Depression

All advanced industrial economies were badly affected by the great world depression in the early 1930s. In some ways, Italy was less badly affected by the depression than some other countries, but there was still a serious slowdown of the economy:

- The value of Italian stocks and shares went down by more than 35 per cent (this was less dramatic than in countries like the United States, where stock market values had been much higher to start with).
- In 1931 and 1932, manufacturing production was 14 per cent down on 1929.
- The balance of payments worsened, with imports costing more than exports.
- Money sent back to Italy from the millions of Italians living abroad, which had always been one of the most important sources of capital in Italy, stopped flowing in. This worsened the banking crisis.
- Unemployment went up from about 300,000 to more than 1 million. To deal with this, the government increased the number of public works projects. Public spending went up to pay for them.

One major impact of the depression in Italy was a massive increase in State intervention in the economy. In 1931, the fascist regime acted to deal with the crisis facing Italy's banks, which were failing to provide businesses with the loans they needed. In December 1931, the IMI was set up to save the banking system. In January 1933, the regime founded the IRI to provide financial stability for Italy's major industries.

A closer look

The IRI and the economy, 1933–40

The IRI (Institute for the Reconstruction of Industry) was established in January 1933 as part of government action to rescue industries in danger of collapse because of the Great Depression. The IRI used State money to buy up shares that had become worthless and to lend money to industries so they could keep working. In addition to providing investment, the IRI also played a big role in management techniques and mobilising resources.

Originally, the IRI was supposed to be a temporary measure, saving industries in the short term and selling off the shares when the economy improved, but it was so successful it became a permanent part of the economic system. By 1940, the IRI controlled numerous industrial enterprises: nearly half the steelworks, almost all the shipping lines, 80 per cent of shipbuilding for the Italian navy, most of the electricity industry and the telephone system.

Although firms controlled by the IRI remained technically in the private sector, they were virtually State owned and State run. Fascist

Key chronology

The structures of the Corporate State

1925 October	Palazzo Vidoni Pact
1926 April	The Syndical Law (Rocco Law)
1926 July	Ministry of Corporations set up
1927 April	Charter of Labour
1928 November	Break-up of the fascist syndicates
1929 March	Giuseppe Bottai, Minister of Corporations
1930 March	Council of National Corporations set up
1931 December	IMI established
1933 January	IRI established
1934 February	Launch of 22 reformed corporations

Exploring the detail

The Great Depression was triggered by the Wall Street Crash – the sudden collapse of the American stock market in October 1929, which cut off the flow of American loans and damaged international trade. It is a mistake to assume that the Wall Street Crash immediately led to the Great Depression. There were serious problems in 1930 but it was in 1931 and 1932 that the economic crisis, especially mass unemployment, was at its worst.

Key terms

Cartelisation: the encouragement of the growth of big conglomerate economic enterprises (cartels) through mergers and takeovers, in order to remove competition and to monopolise key industries.

propaganda made it seem as if IRI was part of the Corporate State, but it actually had nothing to do with the corporations. The people who ran the IRI were able managers with direct industrial experience, not the inefficient party bureaucrats who mismanaged the corporations.

The IMI and especially the IRI were very successful in stabilising the economic situation in Italy in the 1930s. Their impact forms the main basis of claims that Italy coped with the depression better than other countries. The IRI, for example, took over many loss-making industries that the private sector would not invest in. On the other hand, the IRI was mostly concerned with rescuing existing industries through **cartelisation**, not with creating new ones. The industries that benefited most were the big cartels, based in the northern industrial triangle. There was much less help for smaller firms, or for the South.

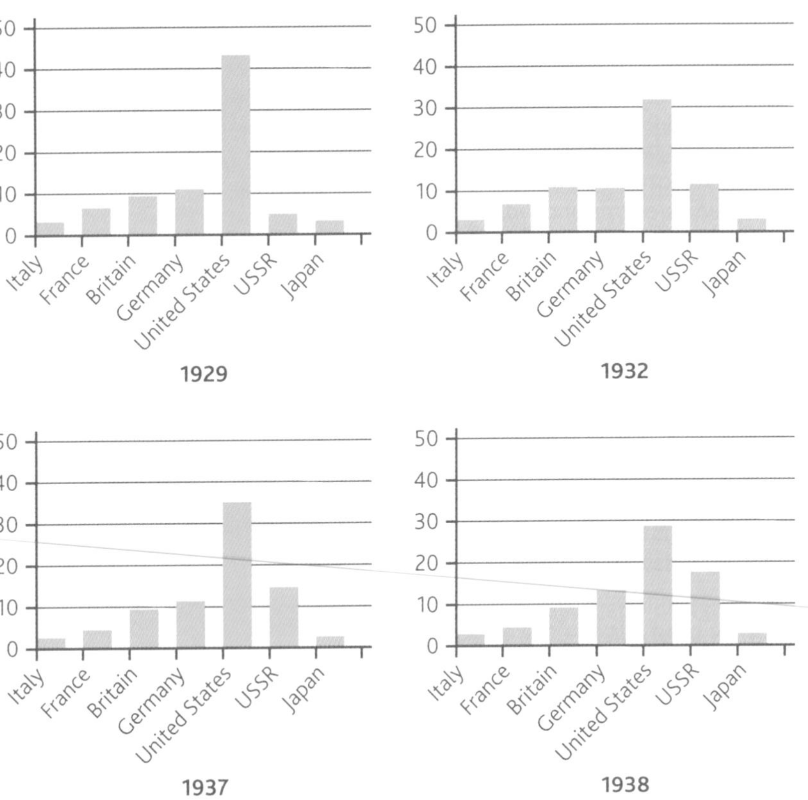

Fig. 6 *Percentage share of world industrial production, 1929–38*

Overall, it remains difficult to assess how seriously the Italian economy was affected by the depression and how well the fascist regime coped with the consequences. Comparisons with other countries indicate that there was lower unemployment in Italy and that there were less dramatic fluctuations in production. On the other hand, Italy was starting from a lower economic base.

The state of the Italian economy by 1940

It is difficult for historians to reach a decisive judgement about the achievements of the fascist economy by 1940 because of the gap between the propaganda myths and the actual economic realities. Mussolini successfully promoted the image of dynamic and effective action, through his economic 'battles' and the prestige public projects in areas like transport and land reclamation, but there were also mistaken policies and poor economic management. Industrial production in Italy lagged behind other advanced economies; so did the living standards of Italians. It remains a matter of debate how much economic progress there really was and how far this progress occurred because of Mussolini, or in spite of him.

According to the historian Martin Clark: 'In the late 1930s, Italian economic policy can be summed up in three words: Autarky, Rearmament and Empire, and the greatest of these was Empire.' Autarky was an aim of the regime from the mid-1920s but Mussolini's foreign policy made autarky much more urgent from 1935. Italy was almost constantly at war in the late 1930s: first the war

Activity

Statistical analysis

Look at the economic statistics in Figure 6. Find **three** reasons why it could be argued that:

- **a** Italy's economy coped well with the Great Depression compared with other countries.
- **b** Italy did badly compared with other countries.

against Ethiopia, then military intervention in the Spanish Civil War from 1936 to 1938, then the invasion of Albania in April 1939. The invasion of Ethiopia led to economic sanctions being imposed on Italy by the League of Nations and cut off imports of strategic raw materials.

The demands of rearmament and military expansion put the economy under terrific strain. Annual spending on the military was about 15 billion lire, more than 30 per cent of all public spending. Ethiopia soaked up oceans of money without producing any benefits to Italy. The intervention in Spain added huge costs between 1936 and 1938. Total government spending in 1935–36 was 30 billion lire, dangerously high. By 1939–40 it had doubled again, to nearly 60 billion lire. The scale of government spending made it impossible for Mussolini to keep the lira at the high valuation set by the Battle of the Lira since 1927. In October 1936, the regime was forced to devalue the lira by 40 per cent. This resulted in sharp price rises.

The concentration on war and the empire was not only expensive in itself, it also distorted the economy because many industries switched production to rearmament (where the profits were high) and away from goods for export, such as cotton and silk textiles. Olivetti, the internationally famous typewriter firm, started producing machine guns as well as typewriters. Producing aircraft, tanks and guns was profitable for industry and also helped to keep workers employed, but it had harmful effects on Italy's balance of payments.

These pressures made autarky even more desirable and priority was given to products that could be manufactured without reliance on imports. One example of this was the big effort to promote the production and consumption of *lanital* in the late 1930s.

Italy's economy might just have been able to cope with the strain of high military spending if hard choices had been made in other areas, but they were not. At the same time as the high military spending, welfare costs also shot up. In 1930, the total spending on welfare was about 1.5 billion lire. By 1940, the total welfare spending was four times higher, at 6.7 billion lire. This amounted to more than 20 per cent of government income. Taken together, military and welfare spending was more than half the national budget.

On top of this, there were enormous costs involved in keeping so many people in useless jobs in the bureaucracy. The fascist regime set up a huge range of organisations and administrative departments; packing these posts with party members and hangers-on was one of the ways to reward its supporters. However, it was a very expensive way of keeping people happy and it resulted in a lot of inefficiency in the system.

By 1940, the Italian economy was becoming very dependent upon Germany. About 25 per cent of Italian exports, especially agricultural produce, was going to Germany; large numbers of Italian labourers worked in Germany. In the other direction, Germany supplied Italy with coal, machinery and manufactured goods. Some Italian businessmen and leading Fascists feared Italy would become the inferior partner of a more powerful ally, merely supplying the German economy with its agricultural needs. From 1935 to 1940, the Italian economy had been put under massive strain by the demands of autarky and military spending; but the Italian economy was nowhere near ready to fight a major war in 1940.

Cross-reference

Italian foreign policy between 1935 and 1940 is covered in Chapter 8 on pages 95–108.

Exploring the detail

Lanital

Lanital was a synthetic fabric invented in 1935. Lanital was actually made from milk (the milk protein, casein). It had a soft texture and was often mixed with wool and fur to make inexpensive clothing, manufactured and marketed by the big textile firm SNIA Viscosa from 1936 to 1940. Lanital was heavily promoted by the fascist regime as a triumph of autarky and national pride.

Summary questions

1. Explain why the Corporate State was introduced by Mussolini's regime from 1926.
2. Assess the extent to which Mussolini's 'economic battles' achieved their objectives.

4 The living standards of the Italian people under the Corporate State

Fig. 1 *Fascist postcard contrasting the poverty of rural Italy before 1922 with the prosperity brought by Mussolini*

In this chapter you will learn about:

- the impact of fascist economic policies on living standards
- the extent to which the Italian people benefited from fascist policies on welfare and the OND
- the impact of the Corporate State by 1940.

There was more to the economy of Fascist Italy than the economic battles launched by Mussolini in the 1920s. It can also be argued that fascist leisure and welfare policies improved people's lives in important respects, such as preventing mass unemployment. During the fascist era, many foreign observers were convinced that Italy was coping with the Great Depression better than the Western democracies. On the other hand, there was often a wide gap between the extravagant propaganda promises and actual examples of poor economic management and wasteful bureaucracy. There is a genuine debate about the extent to which Mussolini's regime improved living standards and economic conditions in Italy; and how far ordinary Italians believed they were better off under Fascism.

Living standards

Like all dictatorships, Mussolini's regime was very anxious about maintaining popular support. Improving living standards (perhaps even more importantly, convincing ordinary Italians that living standards were getting better) was a key aim. There were both winners and losers in terms of improvements in living standards. Agricultural workers generally did relatively badly. Industrial workers, especially skilled workers, generally fared much better. White-collar workers, especially those who held posts in government or in fascist organisations, benefited from fascist policies both in terms of income and job security.

A closer look

The problems in assessing living standards

Assessment of the true standard of living in Fascist Italy is complicated because of a range of special factors:

- The propaganda claims and the unreliable official statistics produced by the regime make it difficult for historians to agree about the evidence for measuring living standards.
- The fascist regime prided itself on offering people extensive benefits through social and welfare policies. The term 'living standards' might include not only the levels of prices and wages, but also levels of 'well-being', which are much more subjective.
- International comparisons between Italy and other countries can be misleading because the Italian economy inherited by the Fascists in 1922 was more fragile and less developed than advanced economies such as Britain, France and the United States.
- There were almost never 'normal' economic conditions in Mussolini's Italy. After the short economic recovery of 1922–25, the Italian economy was always facing extreme pressures. From 1927, there were the pressures (including wage cuts) caused by the Battle of the Lira. From 1930 to 1935, the economy was affected by the impact of the Great Depression. From 1935, Italy was almost permanently at war.

Cross-reference

The impact of the Great Depression upon the Italian economy (and the role of IMI and IRI) is discussed in Chapter 3 on pages 51–2.

The impact of fascist social policies is covered in Chapter 6 on pages 76–80.

The living standards of most Italians improved considerably in the early 1920s as the economy recovered from the post-war crisis. **Real wages** increased, though more so for middle-class, white-collar jobs than for industrial or agricultural workers.

From 1926, living standards were adversely affected by two major developments:

- The first was the changed context of industrial relations, with the Palazzo Vidoni Pact of 1925, which weakened the bargaining power of the trade unions and the Syndical Law of 1926, which banned strikes. As a result, employers were able to keep wages low.
- The second was the impact of Mussolini's Battle for the Lira. In order to maintain the value of the lira at the high level of Quota Noventa, it was necessary for the regime to implement a number of deflationary policies. These measures did bring down the cost of living (by between 5 per cent and 10 per cent) but they also involved a series of painful wage cuts.

Key terms

Real wages: the value of wages after prices have been taken into account – a pay rise may actually be the same as a pay cut if prices rise by a greater amount. The best measurement of real wages is the calculation of how many hours work would be required in order to pay for necessities like food and rent.

Between 1927 and 1931, it is estimated that there were six separate wage cuts, reducing average wage levels by at least 25 per cent and, in some instances, by as much as 40 per cent. Wage rates in Italy were far lower than in most other countries. This was happening even before the onset of the Great Depression in the early 1930s. In most countries, there was an economic boom in the late 1920s, followed by a severe downturn and cuts in wages and living standards after 1929. When the Great Depression hit Italy, such belt-tightening had already been going on for some years.

From 1930, the effects of the Great Depression led to further State intervention to hold down prices and wages. A 12 per cent wage cut was imposed in November 1930. In addition to official cuts imposed by the regime, employers sometimes added unofficial cuts of their own. Unemployment tripled between 1928 and 1935, from 300,000 to just

Cross-reference

Welfare and leisure provision is covered later in this chapter on pages 57–9.

over 1 million according to the official statistics. Hours of work were reduced, which meant lower weekly incomes. In 1934, this policy resulted in the introduction of the 40-hour week. The decline in living standards prompted the regime to improve provision of welfare and leisure activities to soften the impact.

The decline in living standards did not affect all sections of society equally:

- The people whose living standards suffered most were agricultural workers. They were always vulnerable to seasonal unemployment and had very low wages even before they were cut. There was an increase in migration from the countryside to the cities, even though the fascist policy of 'ruralisation' was supposed to prevent this. Living standards were especially low in the slums around big cities like Rome, Milan and Turin, where these agricultural migrants ended up.
- Industrial workers generally did better than peasants, but they also suffered a drop in living standards. One measurement of this was diet. The amount and variety of food was reduced – one academic study in 1932 claimed that daily consumption was 200 calories less than the recommended minimum level for adults. At a time when unemployment was high and the unions were strictly controlled, there was little to stop employers from imposing harsh working conditions.
- Living standards among the middle classes and white-collar workers, were not hit quite as badly as those of the working classes. Their wage levels went down, but they were less likely to lose their jobs because the number of people employed by government agencies actually increased in the 1930s and because they were often party members who received a lot of 'perks' and fringe benefits.

Fig. 2 *Fascists and their eager supporters*

Despite the low living standards, there was no surge of anti-fascist feeling and there were few strikes or expressions of protest. It was only between 1940 and 1943, during the Second World War, that people began to turn against the regime. In the 1930s, the regime was able to maintain social stability. This was at least partly because of the impact of its policies in welfare and leisure.

A negative view of Fascist Italy would stress the decline in living standards and the extent to which fascist propaganda concealed how bad things really were. A positive view would stress the success of State intervention in the economy, maintaining economic stability, and would point to the success of the Corporate State in maintaining popular support by its policies on welfare, leisure and social cohesion.

The standards of living of the Italian people have improved from 1913 to the present. This improvement has been particularly marked during the twelve years of the Fascist regime; and it has not been interrupted by the world economic crisis. The economic and social achievements of Fascism are truly impressive. Italy is a more prosperous and happy nation.

1 *From an article in the journal 'Current History' by Prof. H. Marraro of Columbia University, New York, 1935. Quoted in G. Seldes, **Sawdust Caesar**, 1936*

The record of Fascism is one of repression, brutality and terrorism. Personal liberty has been destroyed, trade unionism has been crushed, and the status of the citizen has been reduced to that of a serf. Far from having been saved by Fascism, Italy has been brought to the edge of economic bankruptcy. Since 1922, wages have been reduced 40 to 50 per cent and are now the lowest in Western Europe. Even Mussolini admits that the living standards of Italian workers can be reduced no further.

2 *Speech by Walter Citrine, Secretary of the British Trades Union Congress, October 1934. Quoted in G. Seldes, **Sawdust Caesar**, 1936*

> **Activity**
>
> **Source analysis**
>
> Read Sources 1 and 2. Using your own knowledge and the evidence given, explain which source you find more useful and reliable, and why.

Welfare

The Corporate State deprived Italian workers of the right to strike and severely limited the bargaining power of the trade unions. In return for this, it was vital for the regime to convince workers that they were genuinely benefiting from its welfare policies. New organisations were created in order to provide these improvements in welfare. The role of these organisations was partly political, gaining consent for the regime, and partly social and economic, compensating for wage cuts and low living standards.

The main party welfare organisations were the EOAs (*Ente Opera Assistenziali*). They were originally set up to run summer health camps for children, but became involved in providing adult welfare during the Great Depression. From 1931, the EOAs organised a programme of winter relief. This was an especially important issue in Italy, where there was a tradition of seasonal work in agriculture and tourism, with many people unemployed in the winter months.

Money for the welfare schemes was raised from the corporations, by what were virtually forced loans imposed on workers and employers, or from banks and local businesses, and then doled out by the EOA. Winter welfare operated on a large scale. The PNF estimated that about 3 million people were receiving welfare assistance every day during the winter months in 1934–35.

There was nothing like a comprehensive welfare state, but the regime pressured employers into including benefits like accident and sickness insurance in pay settlements. The fascist syndicates made special local arrangements in times of severe hardship. In Turin, for example, workers agreed to give 1 per cent of their weekly pay to help the unemployed during the depression. In 1934, family allowances were introduced in many areas because weekly wages had gone down after the 40-hour working week was brought in. Other forms of welfare were Christmas bonuses and holiday pay.

Welfare did have an effect in defusing the dangers of unrest that might have arisen because of depressed living standards. It also helped to gain acceptance for the fascist regime. Local fascist officials and women volunteers played a big part in welfare work and this enabled the PNF to gain supporters in areas where the party had not been popular previously. Alongside the welfare provision, the regime also had considerable success with schemes to provide people with opportunities for leisure and recreation.

Leisure and the *Opera Nazionale Dopolavoro* (OND)

From the mid-1920s, the fascist regime made a huge effort to coordinate the leisure activities of the people. Numerous new organisations were created to provide facilities and to encourage participation. This policy was driven by two key aims:

- The first aim was social control – to brainwash Italians into becoming loyal fascists and to break the influence of the old independent trade unions.

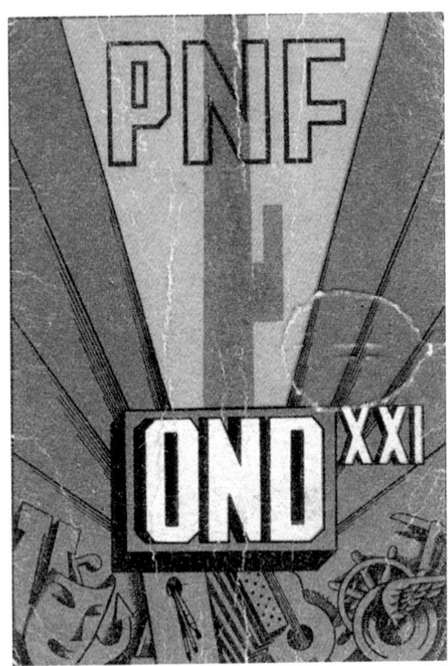

Fig. 3 *A poster for the OND, the Italian fascist leisure and recreational organisation*

- The second aim was to foster a sense of well-being – to compensate people for low pay and living standards, social welfare and opportunities for leisure and enjoyment. The most important way of providing this was the OND, the National After-work Group.

The OND was established on 1 May 1925. The day was deliberately chosen – 1 May was traditionally 'Labour Day', celebrated by Socialists and trade unionists across Europe. It was all part of the attempt by the regime to persuade people, especially workers, that their lives would be better as members of a fascist organisation than if they stuck to their old trade union loyalties. The OND was a State organisation responsible to the Ministry of National Economy. From 1927, it was taken over by the PNF and most of its local organisers were party members.

The OND rapidly became one of the most popular and successful of all the policies of the fascist regime. The activities run by the OND were financed by the State, but not lavishly. Equipment and facilities were often basic. Even so, the OND proved massively popular. Unlike many other aspects of Fascist Italy, there was no need for coercion. People joined in the activities of the OND because they wanted to. In its first year, it attracted about 300,000 members. By 1939, total membership was nearly 4 million.

A wide range of activities was provided by the OND. There were thousands of local theatres and drama societies, music societies, mobile cinemas and libraries. The OND virtually monopolised all the amateur football in Italy. In many towns and villages, social life revolved around the OND clubhouse, the OND sports ground and the OND radio.

One important reason for the success of the OND was that it did not over-emphasise ideology and propaganda, but concentrated on involvement and enjoyment. The result was that it was easier to manipulate opinion and consolidate support for the regime, precisely because the propaganda message was indirect and the main emphasis was on having a good time.

The OND was also important as a channel for social welfare benefits. OND members got cheap rail tickets, discounts in shops and subsidised holidays and excursions. In times of hardship, there might be emergency help with money or food. According to Philip Morgan: 'the OND's cumulative impact was probably to alleviate and divert some of the social distress and discontent arising during the Depression years.'

Cross-reference

Italy's war economy is covered in Chapter 9 on pages 119–121.

Evaluating the Corporate State

By the time the National Council of Corporations was finally set up in 1934, eight years had passed since the Syndical Law set the wheels of the Corporate State turning. The development of corporativism was slow and often confused. By 1934, there was a wide gap between the propaganda boasting about the 'third way' between Capitalism and Communism and what existed in practice. There are convincing reasons, therefore, to regard the Corporate State as almost a complete failure:

- It never had real power over the economy and was easily by passed by big business.
- It was not an economic policy at all, only a confidence trick to take away the power of the unions and allow the bosses and the State to exploit the workers. Wages and living standards were kept down deliberately.

- The Corporate State was based on sound policies, but these were never implemented properly because of the inefficiency of the system and the internal divisions within the fascist regime.

On the other hand, it can be argued that the Corporate State was at least partially successful, especially in terms of politics and propaganda:

- It was admired and imitated abroad. British and American trade union leaders, for example, genuinely believed Italy was coping better with the Great Depression than their own countries. Hitler in Germany and Oswald Mosley in Britain copied many of Mussolini's ideas on bringing people together in one united 'national community'.
- The original aim, to prevent strikes and industrial unrest, was achieved. Industrialists had virtually complete control over their workers. Italian workers were at least partially satisfied by the benefits provided by fascist social policies.
- Politically, Mussolini won the backing of big business and strengthened his regime.

The Corporate State provided the basis for increased State intervention in the economy. Government action was effective in limiting the problems caused when the world economic crisis affected Italy from 1930. The establishment of IMI in December 1931 saved several banks and businesses from going under. The establishment of IRI in January 1933 gave vital support to key industries. Strictly speaking, IMI and IRI were not part of the Corporate State, but they showed how the regime's interventionist approach could work; and they boosted the propaganda claims made on behalf of the Corporate State.

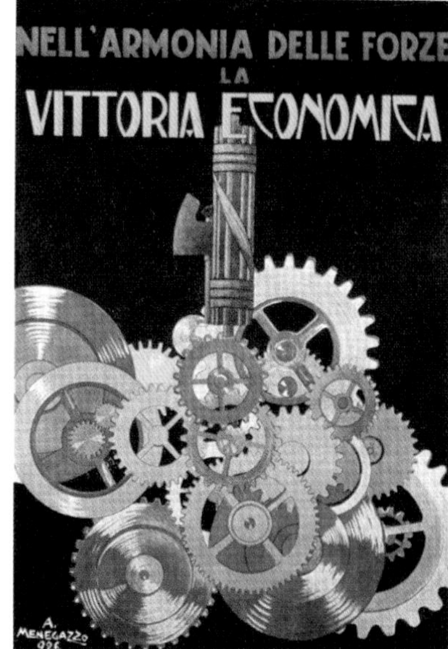

Fig. 4 *An Italian Fascist Party manifesto from 1926, with an industrial motif on the cover*

What do we mean by the 'Fascist corporative system'? What we mean is a form of decentralised control of the economy, delegated by the political authorities in the state to the various economic categories, properly organised. In the corporations, the power of employers and employees is balanced and reconciled. In this respect, the corporative regime in Italy has already achieved brilliant results, even before the institution of the corporation themselves.

3 *The magazine 'Critica Fascista', 1934. Quoted in J. Pollard,* ***The Fascist Experience in Italy****, 1998*

The new corporative state only amounts to a new and costly bureaucracy, from which those industrialists who can spend the necessary amount can get almost anything they want and put into practice the worst kind of monopolistic practices at the expense of the little fellow who is squeezed out in the process.

4 *Article in 'The Economist', 1935. Quoted in J. Laver and R. Wolfson,* ***Years of Change: Europe 1890–1945****, 1999*

Economically, Fascism was a failure. The Corporate State did nothing to improve economic conditions; in fact it never existed at all except on paper. Italy became almost self-sufficient in wheat production at the expense of the rest of her agriculture. The Fascist regime did more to hinder than to aid economic growth and modernisation. Even before the disastrous losses of the Second World War, growth in national income was held back by restrictive cartels, discouragement of urban growth, the spread of autarky, and the promotion of war industry.

5 *E. Tannenbaum,* ***Fascism in Italy****, 1973*

Activity

Thinking point

Read Sources 3–5. Consider the conflicting views of the Corporate State set out in the light of the other evidence in this chapter. Select the quotation that you find the most convincing. Give brief reasons to justify your selection.

Learning outcomes

This section should have provided you with a better understanding of the relationship between fascist ideology and the realities of the Italian economy during the 1920s and 1930s. You should be able to judge the effectiveness of Mussolini's economic battles and the extent to which the goal of autarky was achieved. The section has also explored how the creation of the 'Corporate State' affected the conditions of workers, unions and employers, and how forces such as the Great Depression and policies such as rearmament altered the economic life of the nation. Finally, you should understand how Mussolini's policies changed the living conditions for all sectors of society, including the nature of leisure time.

Practice questions

(a) Explain why Mussolini launched the Battle for Grain in 1925. *(12 marks)*

Study tip Answers to part a) questions need, above all, to be concise and direct. There is no time to waste on introductions or 'background' – what is required is a concise, focused explanation. First, you will need to think about a range of three or more reasons behind the decision to announce the Battle for Grain. Were Mussolini's aims purely economic, or were there other factors? Why did he launch the campaign in 1925, and not sooner or later? It is then a good idea to think about the relative importance of the reasons you have selected. Level 4 answers will not only assemble a list of relevant explanations, they will also provide comment and differentiation.

(b) 'Between 1925 and 1940, fascist economic policies completely failed to achieve their objectives.'
Explain why you agree or disagree with this view. *(24 marks)*

Study tip Effective answers to part b) questions need to provide a balanced argument, supported by selected specific evidence. It would not be a good idea to try to describe all the numerous and sometimes complicated economic policies of the regime. It would also be a mistake to assume that the only policies you need to consider are Mussolini's 'economic battles'. They were indeed important, especially in the 1920s, but the end date of this question is 1940 and key issues during the 1930s need to be addressed, such as the role of the IRI and the influence of war on the economy from 1935. Be careful, too, about the Battle for Births, which was not entirely an economic policy, so you might choose to focus more on other policies. The key to a successful answer is to decide exactly how much you agree or disagree with the quotation in the question – and why.

3 Fascist ideology and social change

5 Society and culture in Fascist Italy

In this chapter you will learn about:

- fascist policies in education
- the coordination of youth through fascist organisations
- the role of women in fascist society.

Fig. 1 *'Revista della Famiglie', Milan, June 1936. Although this publication purported to be a monthly magazine dedicated to women and family issues, it consisted mainly of speeches by Mussolini and other fascist-related articles*

Mussolini's dream was to 'turn Italians into Fascists'. To achieve this, it was necessary above all to win the hearts and minds of youth – indoctrinating the young generation through education in schools and universities and through a fascist takeover of youth organisations. Fascist policies towards education and youth aimed to transform Italian girls into little future mothers and Italian boys into little future warriors. The regime also gave high priority to shaping the lives of women. One of Mussolini's aims was to increase Italy's population from 40 million to 60 million. This required Italian women to regard motherhood as their 'patriotic duty'. Their role was to be at the heart of traditional family life, preferably in a rural environment, giving birth to as many children as possible. This led to the keystone of fascist policy towards women and the family, the Battle for Births. As time went on, particularly during the 1930s, there was increasing State intervention in society, altering patterns of female employment and involving women in the process of '**fascistisation**'.

Key terms

Fascistisation: (in Italian, *l'Inquadramento*, or 'totalitarian regimentation') aimed at the complete coordination of society according to the principles of fascist ideology.

Cross-reference

Giovanni Gentile is profiled on page 42.

Educational developments in schools and universities

Education policy was given a high profile from the start of the regime. In 1923, the Gentile Reform was introduced, which was a major re-structuring of the education system. Mussolini chose as his Minister of Education the respected philosopher Giovanni Gentile, who was regarded with suspicion by party activists, who did not think he was

Fig. 2 *Poster for* Il Balilla, *a newspaper for fascist youth, 1927*

fascist enough. The Gentile Reform followed a very elitist and academic approach, including strict (that is, difficult) national examinations. Gentile also defended academic freedom in the universities. This was popular with intellectuals and traditional Conservatives, but provoked fierce opposition from other groups:

- Fascist extremists, who wanted to purge liberals and democrats from the teaching profession, above all from the universities, and make radical reforms in education to indoctrinate the young.
- Middle-class supporters of the Fascists, who wanted the education system to benefit their 'ordinary' children, not just the brilliant and best.
- The Catholic Church, who wanted the fascist regime to introduce Catholic instruction into secondary schools and to break away completely from the anti-clerical approach to education that had been in place in the old Liberal Italy.

Mussolini did not want to upset these competing groups. He removed Gentile from the education ministry in 1924. Many of Gentile's reforms were shelved or watered down and, as with many other aspects of Fascist Italy, education policies were mostly cautious during the 1920s. It was only later, after 1929, that there was a major effort to reorganise education along fascist lines.

Schools

The fascist regime made relatively few changes in nursery and primary education. The main issue was what was going to happen in secondary schools. In the Italian system, there were three main types of upper school:

- The Gymnasium, or Liceo (Grammar school), with an academic curriculum for the most-able students.
- The Normal school, for a general education.
- The Technical school, for vocational subjects.

The Gentile Reform neglected Normal and Technical schools in order to concentrate on the elite Grammar schools. After 1924, this policy was changed and secondary schools went through a period of instability. The curriculum was radically remodelled on at least three separate occasions between 1926 and 1933. Catholic religious education became compulsory in primary schools in 1923. After the Lateran Pacts of 1929, it was extended to secondary schools. Religious teachers gained even more authority and influence in 1935, when it was made compulsory to pass an examination in religious instruction each year in order to move up to the next form.

Propaganda was sometimes very direct. Generally speaking, the younger the age of the pupils, the more pressure was put on by the regime. Rural primary schools were placed under the control of the fascist youth organisation ONB (the Balilla). From 1926, history textbooks deemed to be 'unsuitable' were purged from schools. From 1928, it was compulsory to use the government textbook, the *libro unico* – there was a textbook for each year group in primary and secondary schools. The propaganda content of these textbooks was often very blatant and militaristic. Most head teachers were Fascists, or prudently opted to become Fascists. It was much easier to gain promotion if you joined the party or attended indoctrination courses. In 1931, teacher associations were coordinated into a single fascist association.

There were also powerful indirect influences on education. Pressure was placed on teachers by their head teachers and by 'concerned parents'. There was fear of being denounced as 'politically unreliable'. The 'background noise' of fascist propaganda created a stressful atmosphere in which it seemed easier to go along with the majority and not to stand out. Many young people were enthused by their participation in youth activities outside school and this intensified peer pressure and wanting to feel you belonged.

A lot of fascist education policy was implemented piece by piece, with no overall master plan. It was only in 1939 that Giuseppe Bottai produced the School Charter, aimed at completing the fascistisation of schools. Bottai wanted to integrate all schools and children from all social classes into one system, following the principles of the Corporate State. Bottai also proposed making technical and vocational education as important as academic subjects. However, by 1939, war was already imminent and Bottai's School Charter never had time to take effect, even if the regime had been capable of putting it into practice.

Universities

The fascist regime mostly left the universities alone. This was partly because of the Gentile Reform in 1923, but mostly because it seemed more urgent to focus on the younger age groups on the basis of 'catch them young'. As with the school system, the Church was allowed to extend its influence and the Catholic University of Milan was founded. A fascist teacher training college was established for teachers of sport and physical education. From 1931, university professors were compelled to swear an oath of allegiance to the State; most did so, whatever their private thoughts may have been. There was no major purge of the universities, at least until 1938 when Jewish professors were victimised under the new race laws.

The regime took more interest in the students than the professors. The GUF (*Gioventu Universitaria Fascisti*), Fascist University Youth, founded in 1929, was taken over by the PNF secretary, Achille Starace, and reorganised as GIL (*Gioventu Italiana del Littorio*) in 1937. It gained a large membership and was seen as the natural next step for boys who had come through ONB. The GUF also organised inter-university competitions, including the Littoriali Games. The regime never took full control of Italy's universities, but it did not really need to. The vast majority of students either supported the regime or was at least willing to conform. There was no hotbed of anti-fascist protest.

Cross-reference

Giovanni Gentile and his influence on fascist ideology is covered in Chapter 3 on page 42.

The Lateran Pacts are covered in Chapter 2 on pages 36–7.

Fig. 3 *The cover of an edition of* Gioventù Fascista *(fascist youth)*

Cross-reference

Giuseppe Bottai is profiled in Chapter 6 on page 73.

Cross-reference

Achille Starace is profiled in Chapter 1 on page 11.

The Littoriali Games are explained later in this chapter on page 66.

Activity

Group activity

Working in three groups, make a list of comparisons between present-day educational experiences of **one** of the following compared with those in Fascist Italy:

- Primary schools.
- Secondary schools.
- Universities.

Fascist youth organisations

All totalitarian regimes placed great emphasis on coordinating youth into uniformed organisations where they would be active and easily controlled. It would be a mistake, however, to think that only dictatorships like Mussolini's thought this way – it happened all over the world in the first half of the 20th century. There was a vast membership of the boy scouts in the British Empire and around the world. There were dozens of other uniformed youth organisations, each with its own oath of patriotic loyalty and enthusiasm for outdoor activities such as team games, hiking and swimming. The youth organisations of Fascist Italy were not unique, just part of a trend.

Though they were not unique, fascist youth groups were a high-profile part of Mussolini's Italy. The regime attempted to provide an overall structure that would include young people of all ages. Along with the OND, the ONB, the fascist boy scouts, was the spearhead of the drive to achieve the successful coordination of a whole society. The marching song of the ONB, *Giovinezza!* (Youth!) was the signature tune of Fascist Italy, especially in the armed forces.

Fig. 4 *Boys dressed in military-style uniforms make a fascist salute*

Hail, O people of heroes, Hail O immortal Fatherland!
Your children are reborn, with faith in the ideal.
Within the Italian borders, Italians have been re-made,
Re-made by Mussolini, for the war of tomorrow,

For the joy of labour, for peace and the laurels,
For the shaming of all who their country deny.
CHORUS: Youth! Youth!
Springtime of loveliness,
In the bitterness of our life,
Your song rings out and away!
The poets and the craftsmen, gentry and the peasants,
With the pride of Italians, swear loyalty to Mussolini.
There is no poor district that does not send its story,
That does not unfurl its banners of Fascism that redeems all.
REPEAT CHORUS

1 *The fascist hymn of youth,* ***Giovinezza!***

The Balilla (ONB)

The Balilla took its name from an 18th-century legend about a heroic teenaged boy in Genoa who threw a rock at the occupying Austrian army. The legend appealed neatly to key fascist themes about youth, Nationalism, courage and militarism. The Balilla was the name of the fascist boy scouts, but the ONB included other organisations as well – the name 'Balilla' was often used to cover all of these. The ONB was founded as a party organisation in 1926 and was taken over by the education ministry in 1929.

The ONB contained different separate organisations, for girls as well as boys, in the various age groups:

- Ages 6–8, mixed – Children of the She Wolf (named after the legend of the wolf that suckled Romulus and Remus, the founders of Rome).
- Ages 8–14, boys – Balilla.
- Ages 8–12, girls – *Piccolo Italiane.*
- Age 14–18, boys – *Avanguardisti* (Vanguard).
- Ages 13–18, girls – *Giovani Italiane.*
- Ages 18–21, mixed – GUF.
- Ages 18–21, mixed – GIL.

Fig. 5 *Youth on the march; fascist girls parading in 1931*

When the ONB was first founded, there were still rival youth organisations, especially those run by Azione Cattolica. There was a lot of tension between the Fascists and the Catholics. In 1928, the regime managed to force the Catholic boy scouts to close down and in 1929 the Church agreed the Lateran Pacts with Mussolini. In the 1930s, there was an increase in levels of propaganda pressure and indoctrination in the ONB as part of the policy of l'inquadramento, or 'fascistisation'. Even then, however, Azione Cattolica youth groups continued to exist.

> By the 1930s a host of groups dealt with over 5 million young people from the age of six until well into the twenties. Their functions and impact varied considerably. The groups for the very young tended to be like Wolf Cubs or Scouts in other countries, though there was always a more military side. Activities included drill and carrying toy guns – at least for the boys (girls were sometimes allowed bows and arrows). Boys in all areas were much more likely to join, especially in the South, where no self-respecting young female marched around in uniform. As such, the organisation of youth was part of the drive towards conformism and militarism.

2 *R. Eatwell, **Fascism: A History**, 1995*

A closer look

Youth and the cult of Mussolini

Mussolini's image was an inescapable feature for any young person growing up in Italy. Every classroom had a large portrait of Il Duce on the wall. Every school day and every meeting of the youth organisations began with proclamations of loyalty and obedience to Mussolini. Mussolini's voice on the radio dominated homes and public spaces so much that even the youngest children were familiar with it. Mussolini's image, swimming, skiing, piloting aeroplanes was just as familiar through pictures in the newspapers and cinema newsreels. Many impressionable young people accepted this cult of the personality as a normal state of affairs. They saw Mussolini as a second God, even though they lived in a society that also had a pope and a king. Many of them became idealistic and committed youth leaders.

The indoctrination did not work as well with all Italian youth. As in most families in any society, many young people were more influenced by their parents than by the world outside. In homes where the parents had Catholic, liberal, socialist or communist traditions (and there were hundreds of thousands of such homes), there was deep reluctance to accept fascist values. There were rebellious teenagers whose attitude was 'count me out' – because they hated the regimentation, or because they just did not like team games. There were people who *did* like team games but couldn't be bothered with all the ideological stuff. The fact that the fascist regime put so much intense effort and brilliant presentation into promoting the cult of Il Duce did not necessarily make it effective.

Activity

Group activity

Divide the class into three groups. The groups draw lots to decide which age group they belong to:

- The 8-year-old She Wolves have to learn the words and music of *Giovinezza!*, so they can sing it to the class.
- The 12-year-old group has to design a large poster to celebrate Il Duce's birthday and to think up a suitable slogan.
- The 16-year-old group has to compose a special poem for the occasion.

Sport and the Littoriali Games

The Littoriali Games were part of the 'staging of Fascism' through public spectacle and group activity. They were organised by the FGL (*Fascio Giovanile del Littorio*), established in 1930, until 1937 when all youth groups were merged into GIL. The Littoriali della Sport, begun in 1932 in Bologna, involved sport and physical education, with national competition between university students in athletics, swimming and so on, rather like the Olympic Games. The Littoriali moved around to a different city each year. In 1938, for example, it was held in Rome, followed by Naples in 1939, Milan in 1940 and Genoa in 1941. In most cities, imposing new sports facilities were built specially for the Littoriali, often with imposing modernist architecture, such as the massive new swimming pool built in Turin for the 1933 Games.

The Littoriali Games of Culture and Art, begun in 1934, was 'something between a student conference and an academic talent show', in which university students competed for the title of 'lictor' in activities such as painting, poetry, music, cinema, theatre criticism, storytelling, economics and science. This was almost a straight copy of the Cultural Olympiad held in the Soviet Union in 1931. The key fascist organisers were Alessandro Pavolino, the Fascist Party boss in Florence, and Giuseppe Bottai. Like the Littoriali della Sport, the Littoriali della Cultura was aimed at producing a new fascist elite, bridging the generation gap between the old Fascists of Mussolini's rise to power and the new youth generation. It was all part of the attempt to 'turn Italians into loyal Fascists' and to train the future leaders of Fascism.

Cross-reference

Fascist policies in culture and the arts are covered in Chapter 6 on pages 80–2.

Alessandro Pavolino is profiled in Chapter 10 on page 131.

The position of women in fascist society

Mussolini also wanted to promote the fascist ideology of womanhood, of 'submissive women and strong mothers'. This ideology was heavily emphasised in the education of girls at school and in the role of girls in fascist youth organisations. Mussolini's ideal Fascist woman would live a peasant's life in the countryside, content to raise her large family according to traditional values. (Several historians have pointed out the fact that this old-fashioned ideal strongly resembled Mussolini's own wife Rachele, with her five children, but was completely different from his sophisticated, well-educated mistresses like Margherita Sarfatti.)

Did you know?

Mussolini not only had 'permanent' mistresses like Margherita Sarfatti and, later, Clara Petacci, there were dozens, possibly hundreds, of short-term women as well. Mussolini's private secretary claimed that Mussolini had a brisk sexual encounter with a woman in his office almost every working day.

Key profiles

Dona Rachele (1892–1979)

Unlike many of Mussolini's rich and well-educated mistresses, Rachele was a peasant girl of 18 when she started living with him in 1910; they were married five years later. She bore Mussolini five children and was used by fascist propaganda as an ideal role model as housewife and mother. Rachele had little interest in politics, though she intensely disliked her son-in-law, Galeazzo Ciano, and frequently urged Mussolini to dismiss him from government. (Rachele was grimly satisfied when Ciano was executed for treason in 1944.) The Italian government gave her a pension after the war.

Margherita Sarfatti (1880–1961)

Sarfatti was the most important of Mussolini's mistresses, once nicknamed the 'Queen of Italy'. She was a married woman, nine years older than Mussolini, when their relationship began in 1911. Sarfatti was the well-educated daughter of a rich Italian-Jewish lawyer; she was credited with influencing many of Mussolini's ideas about art and culture. She worked as a journalist on *Il Popolo d'Italia*. In 1926, she wrote *Dux*, her biography of Mussolini. In 1938, after the introduction of the new anti-Semitic race laws, Sarfatti emigrated to Argentina. She returned to Italy in 1947.

Cross-reference

The third most important woman in Mussolini's life, Clara Petacci, is profiled in Chapter 10 on page 133.

The impact of the fascist regime on the lives of women was very mixed, partly because its policies were not always consistent (and often had unexpected effects), and partly because the place of women in society varied enormously from one part of Italy to another (Source 3).

> Interwar Italy was a highly regionalised and uneven society, characterised by a very diverse economy, in which state intervention had hugely different effects according to geographical location and social class.

3

P. Wilson, ***Women in Fascist Society***, 1996

Family life

Fascist propaganda idealised traditional family life, as did the Catholic Church. After the reconciliation between Church and State in 1929, the aims and policies of Mussolini's regime towards the family was strongly reinforced by Catholic teachings on issues such as motherhood, birth control and abortion. In 1930, Pope Pius XI, fearful about the future of family life, issued a **papal encyclical**, *Casti Conubi*, to re-state the importance of parental authority and discipline in the home, especially the role of women as full-time mothers.

Key terms

Papal encyclical: a letter containing official pronouncements from the Pope, circulated round the worldwide Catholic Church.

Both the Fascists and the Church regarded the modern, emancipated, urban woman as a threat to their vision of the ideal family unit. Modern woman was to be found in the cities, the places of corruption, crime and social breakdown. The ideal family was almost always visualised against the 'unspoiled' background of villages and small towns. This was one of the main reasons why Mussolini put so much emphasis on his policy of ruralisation from the late 1930s.

The ideal propaganda image was not always reflected in real life. The fascist view of women and family was essentially a male-dominated one that many Italian women were unwilling to accept. Modern culture, such as cinema, fashion and advertising, was moving in a different direction. Fascist propaganda, for example, liked to denounce the slim, sophisticated modern woman and idealise the rounded, maternal, submissive wife and mother; but a lot of Italian women wanted to look like the fashion models and film stars they saw in magazines and at the cinema. They did not have the same enthusiasm for slogans like 'Woman in the Home' as most men did. Fascism also changed family life by mobilising men into many organisations and activities, such as the OND. This had the effect of taking men out of the home, away from their roles as husbands and fathers.

For Mussolini, the role of the family was above all to produce babies. His vision of the future was of a land-hungry Italian Empire, providing living space for a population of 60 million. The family was to be the basis of his Battle for Births.

Fig. 6 *Winning the Battle for Births: a prizewinning family*

The Battle for Births

It is often stated that Mussolini launched his Battle for Births (sometimes known as Battle for Babies) in 1927, when there was a massive propaganda campaign to promote a higher birth rate and to idealise the role of women as mothers. In fact, this policy was begun rather earlier. In 1925, the ONMI (National Organisation for Maternity and Infants) was set up to provide help for abandoned children and pre-natal advice for mothers. This was part of a drive to prevent birth control and abortions – in 1926 the law against abortion was strengthened. Also in 1926, a special 'bachelor tax' was imposed on unmarried men. Then, in his Ascension Day speech in May 1927, Mussolini made his grand announcement of the 'demographic battle' to boost the birth rate.

Although the Battle for Births is often included among Mussolini's 'economic battles', the main aims were not directly economic – he was more concerned with social policy and national greatness. Mussolini was obsessed with the idea that national glory and military power depended upon having a large population – he hoped the overall total population would rise to 60 million by 1950, half as much again as the 1927 figure of 42 million.

Table 1 *Population in Fascist Italy*

Year	Births per 1,000	Deaths per 1,000	Total population (millions)
1910	33.0	23.8	36.4
1922	32.3	19.0	38.6
1930	26.7	14.1	44.3
1940	23.5	13.6	46.9

There was more to the Battle for Births than setting targets and exhorting women to produce more babies. The propaganda machine kept up the pressure during the late 1920s and early 1930s. Mussolini made many speeches praising marriage and motherhood. The annual Day of the Mother and Child was introduced in 1933, when 93 mothers with 13 or more children were invited to an official reception in Rome, presided over by Mussolini in person. Prizes and silver medals were awarded to mothers with the largest broods. Militia men were ordered to give the Roman salute to pregnant women in the street.

Activity

Group activity

Working in four groups, design propaganda posters to support the Battle for Births. Have a class vote to judge the best visual design and the best slogan.

Did you know?

Mussolini acted in accordance with his own propaganda. In 1927, Mussolini was 40 years old and already had three children – Edda, 17, Vittorio, 11, and Bruno, 9. He and Dona Rachele joined the Battle for Births and produced two more children – Romano in 1927 and Anna Maria in 1929. (Another motive for this may have been that it pleased the Catholic Church in the run-up to the Lateran Pacts.)

In addition to the propaganda campaign, there were financial inducements. Generous marriage loans were made available; wives who produced four children did not need to repay the loan. There were tax incentives, too. Families with 10 or more children did not have to pay income tax. Fathers got preference for jobs and promotions in the civil service. More State funding went into maternity care. Pressure was applied on those who did not do their 'national duty'. Laws against divorce and abortion were tightened and more strictly enforced. Both the fascist regime and the Catholic Church regularly denounced contraceptives and birth control.

The **demographic** changes of all these policies and propaganda pressures fell a long way short of what was intended. One political success was that the Catholic Church approved strongly of what the fascist regime was attempting (and so it was useful in preparing the way for the 1929 Concordat), but the policy was mostly a failure. The population did increase, though slowly, but this was mostly due to a declining death rate, especially for children. The birth rate actually went down. There was no increase in marriage rates and the average age at which women got married went up. The regime brought in more measures in 1936, recognising the previous failures. These new measures did not really work either. General economic trends proved stronger than the fascist State in shaping people's lives.

Activity

Thinking point

Using the evidence in this chapter:

1. List **five** aspects of demographic change that could be used to support the argument that Mussolini's Battle for Births was a failure.
2. List **three** reasons why it might be considered that Mussolini was right to launch the Battle for Births.

Women in employment

Fascist ideology was, of course, hostile to female employment, especially in industry. The regime made persistent attempts to reduce female employment, but it was impossible to eliminate it altogether. The strict measures taken by the regime in the 1930s were not fully enforced everywhere, because there were powerful economic considerations pushing women into work. There were also wide differences between different sectors of the economy and various parts of the country.

Fascist policies were most effective in keeping women out of white-collar jobs or positions in the professions, especially law. Women educated at university could very rarely find work that matched their talents and qualifications. The main reason for this was that the social policies of the regime were heavily influenced by the masculine expectations and prejudices of the mass of fascist supporters who were lower middle-class men, many of them ex-soldiers. Although many teachers were women, teaching posts in prestige secondary schools were reserved for men. Women teachers were also excluded form teaching certain 'higher-level' subjects like history, classics and philosophy.

The regime had less impact on working-class women. When the Fascists came to power, approximately one woman in three was in paid employment, mostly working on the land – in 1921, women made up about 44 per cent of all workers in agriculture. About 35 per cent

Key chronology

Fascist policies towards women

1925 ONMI founded

1926 Bachelor tax introduced

1926 Abortion made a 'crime against the State'

1927 Launch of Battle for Births

1929 Lateran Pacts with the Catholic Church

1930 Pope Pius XI's papal encyclical against birth control

1932 Rocco criminal code

1933 'Day of the Mother and Child' is launched

1934 Quota of 10 per cent on women's employment

Key terms

Demographic: demography is the scientific study of changes affecting population patterns, such as birth and death rates, where people live, or the age profile of the population.

Exploring the detail

One of the few important factors leading towards population increase in the 1930s was the fact that it was no longer easy for Italians to emigrate to the United States; if the traditionally high rates of Italian emigration before and after the First World War had been kept up, the Battle for Births would have been seen as an even bigger failure.

of industrial workers were women. The proportion of women in the workforce dropped slightly during the fascist era, especially between 1931 and 1936. This was mostly due to the Great Depression which intensified discrimination against women because it was seen as necessary to reserve jobs for male breadwinners at a time when unemployment was rising. This was not only due to fascist ideology – there were similar trends to exclude women, especially married women, from employment in democratic countries, including Britain, in the 1930s.

The regime continued to tighten the restrictions on women in employment in the late 1930s. The regime imposed a quota system on all State businesses and economic enterprises in 1933, limiting the proportion of women in the workforce to a maximum of 10 per cent. In 1938, the 10 per cent rule was applied to private enterprises. Employers found this difficult to comply with and, in 1939, exceptions were made for specific 'female' jobs, such as typists, telephone operators and nurses.

Fascist policies did not always work out as intended. In many sectors of the economy, such as agriculture and the textile industry, the numbers of women depended more on local economic needs than on State policies. More women started going to university, partly because dead-end jobs were no longer available. Even so, the pressure from the regime had a powerful negative influence on women's employment (Source 4).

Fascist policies towards women seem less drastic than those of Nazi Germany, which in 1934 expelled women outright from state employment. Yet Italian female labour participation was lower at the start and occupied less qualified positions than in pre-Nazi Germany. The combination of customary biases and new discriminations, operating in an economy where jobs were hard to find anyway, made Fascist Italy a uniquely hostile environment for the employment of women.

4 *V. De Grazia,* ***How Fascism Ruled Women: Italy 1922–1945****, 1992*

Activity

Thinking point

Carry out some independent research on the similarities and differences between the lives of women in Fascist Italy and Nazi Germany.

Women's political organisations

Mussolini's regime had contradictory ideas about the mobilisation of women into fascist organisations. On the one hand, it was part of involving people in fascist society. It was seen as a good thing that women got involved in volunteer work for the ONMI, or the OND, or helping with welfare, or as mothers of children involved in youth activities. Fascist women's organisations were a way of promoting the right values. On the other hand, the fascist view of women required them to be passive and submissive, minding the home and the children – perhaps it was neither necessary nor desirable to mobilise them at all.

Despite the doubts, fascist groups were established and hundreds of thousands of women joined. Even though many women were frustrated that the organisation never became as important as they had hoped in the beginning, the PNF organisation for female party members, the *Fasci femminili*, had 700,000 members at its peak, The Massaie Rurali had a membership of 500,000 peasant women by 1935. Their activities were very local and small scale, growing extra food to support the campaign for autarky, attending local meetings or going on group excursions. These activities were not very political, however, the rural housewives were not being mobilised on a totalitarian model.

Cross-reference

The Massaie Rurali (Rural Housewives) is introduced in Chapter 2 on page 33.

Summary questions

1. Why did the fascist regime place such emphasis on winning the loyalty of Italian youth?
2. In what ways and why did fascist ideology change the lives of women and girls in Italy?

6 The extent of social change

In this chapter you will learn about:

- the extent to which the social policies of the fascist regime became more radicalised in the 1930s
- the impact of Fascism on media and the arts
- the impact of racial ideas and anti-Semitism
- the impact of Fascism on the elites and the class structure
- opposition to the regime and the extent to which Fascist Italy was 'totalitarian'.

Fig. 1 *'Blackshirts! Arrest that Cow! It has failed to produce any wine!' (1926) Cartoon by Kurt Arnold satirising fascist agriculture.*

> Mussolini had hoped to transform the Italian character and Italian society into a Fascist mould but he was disappointed. The race of athletic, aggressive, obedient Fascists never materialised. Fascism did not penetrate the psyche of most Italians, changing traditional habits and attitudes. There was outward conformity but little inner conviction. Although Fascist propaganda claimed that it was transforming Italy, the reality was very different.
>
> **1** *M. Robson, **Italy: The Rise of Fascism, 1915–1945**, 2006*

In theory at least, fascist ideology was totalitarian. Mussolini hoped for the 'fascistisation' of Italian society and culture, moulding the lives of people at work, in leisure activities and in the home. Fascist ideology, however, was never implemented consistently or comprehensively and it has often been claimed that the ideology was actually incoherent and contradictory, and thus impossible to put into practice, or that it was only propaganda window-dressing and the regime never really tried to implement it. Another view is that the ideology was real enough but the regime simply was not strong enough or efficient enough to carry it through – especially after the fascist revolution was 'interrupted' in 1925, and also that regional differences were too strong for any national policy to be effective. A third view is that fascist social policies changed over time, becoming much more radical in the 1930s and that Fascism did indeed bring about very significant social change in Italy by 1940, if not quite the complete transformation the propaganda machine boasted about. Thus, there is a continuing historical debate about the impact of fascist social policies and the extent to which Italy had, or had not, become a totalitarian society by 1940.

Radicalisation from 1936

Fascism was always a radical ideology but it was often constrained by circumstances and political realities. It has been argued that there was a process of 'cumulative **radicalisation**' that intensified as the regime became more established and as the younger generation became indoctrinated. According to this theory, fascist social policy developed as follows:

- To about 1925 – uncontrolled and violent actions by the radical elements in the fascist movement were eventually 'tamed' by Mussolini in order to secure his political position.
- 1925–29 – during which Mussolini completed his consolidation of power and was careful not to fall out with key power groups such as big business or the Catholic Church.
- 1929–35 – known as l'inquadramento, (the 'fascistisation' or regimentation of the people), an attempt by the regime to coordinate and control society through increased State intervention and 'going to the people'.
- 1935–40 – of 'radicalisation', linked to the aims of autarky, empire and war. This phase was marked by massive propaganda in favour of militarism and by the imposition of harsher policies, such as the new anti-Semitic race laws introduced in 1938.

This timetable, of course, implies that the regime *did* have a coherent ideology and that it *did* know what it was doing. However, by no means would all historians agree with either of these assumptions.

Key terms

Radicalisation: imposing more radical and extreme policies in accordance with ideological aims.

Exploring the detail

The idea that there was a distinct radicalisation of fascist policies in the late 1930s is an issue for debate. Did it really happen? If it did, was it a rational, directed policy, or something uncontrolled or even accidental? There had always been radical elements in the fascist movement but these had mostly been kept on a leash, especially from 1925. In the 1930s, fascist leaders like Bottai and Starace attempted to push through radicalisation, though they did not always succeed.

The impact of the Abyssinian War

The central factor in radicalisation from 1935 to 1936 was the impact of the Abyssinian War, which led to an intensification of militarist propaganda. The war also made Mussolini's regime extremely popular, at least in the short term (Source 2).

> The powerful propaganda machine was instrumental in creating, at least almost up to the outbreak of the Second World War, a sense of national solidarity such as had rarely occurred in the history of the united Italy. The decisive point in the consensus was undoubtedly the successful colonial war in Ethiopia. This new popularity serves as a stimulus towards the intensification of the indoctrination programme at all levels of society, as well as towards its increasingly militaristic nature and growing involvement with Hitler's Germany.

2 *D. Thompson,* ***State Control in Fascist Italy****, 1991*

On the other hand, the war also exposed some of the weaknesses and failings of Fascism. Behind all the victory celebrations and claims that Italians had proved themselves a superior race, Mussolini knew that there had been a lot of incompetence in the armed forces. He was disappointed with the lack of military spirit among the troops and the people. By 1936, Mussolini wanted to launch a 'second revolution', to give Fascism a new lease of life. One typical Mussolini comment at this time was: 'Italians need stick, stick and more stick. To make a people great you have to send them off to fight, even if it means kicking them up the backside. That is what I will do.'

The war in Ethiopia also intensified the drive for autarky. This meant further State intervention in the economy and even more aggressive propaganda, for example, when Italy faced economic sanctions.

Cross-reference

The Abyssinian War and the issue of sanctions are covered in Chapter 8 on pages 96–100.

There were other important factors pushing the fascist regime towards radicalisation. Leaders on the radical wing of the PNF, such as the Party Secretary Achille Starace, began to assert themselves more aggressively in the late 1930s, demanding that 'real' Fascists should take the lead and the regime should weed out those who were uncommitted or opportunists. Starace played a leading role in the racial campaign against the Jews in 1938. He was also responsible for the efforts to fascistise the language and terms of address in 1939. It was also in the late 1930s that Giuseppe Bottai started a campaign to complete the process of 'fascistisation' of the school system.

The *Fascist Decalogue* (Source 2 on page 30 of Chapter 2) was introduced into secondary schools in 1938. The Fascist Charter for Schools announced in 1939 was a belated recognition that the fascist regime had only tinkered with education up to that point and that fundamental reform was required.

Key profile

Giuseppe Bottai (1895–1959)

Bottai was an ex-soldier who took part in the March on Rome in 1922. He was editor of *Il Popolo d'Italia* and other fascist publications in the 1920s. Bottai played a leading role in fascist social reforms between 1929 and 1932; later he was Minister of Education and Mayor of Rome. In July 1943, he voted against Mussolini at the Fascist Grand Council. He was sentenced to death for this but had already escaped to join the French Foreign Legion, thus fighting alongside the enemies of Fascism. After the war, Bottai was given an amnesty and resumed his political career.

Another powerful factor pushing Italian Fascism into more radical policies was the influence of Nazi Germany. By 1937, Mussolini was moving towards closer links with Hitler. On his State visit to Munich, Mussolini was deeply impressed by the dynamism and discipline of the massed crowds and parading troops. On his return to Italy, he insisted that Italian soldiers adopt the goose step, the exaggerated marching style, used by German troops. The Italian equivalent was to be known as the *passo Romano* – Mussolini even claimed that 'the goose is a Roman animal' – but Italian soldiers did not look very impressive doing it. It is easy to poke fun at the passo Romano. However, there was a serious issue involved. Mussolini's desire to make Italians more like the Germans was leading him towards more extreme policies, including anti-Semitism.

LA DIFESA DELLA RAZZA

ANNO V - NUMERO 9
5 MARZO 1942-XX

ESCE IL 5 E IL 20 DI OGNI MESE
UN NUMERO SEPARATO LIRE 1
ABBONAMENTO ANNUO LIRE 20
ABBONAMENTO SEMESTRALE » 12
ESTERO IL DOPPIO

Direttore: TELESIO INTERLANDI

Comitato di redazione:
prof. dott. GUIDO LANDRA - prof. dott. LIDIO CIPRIANI
Segretario di redazione: GIORGIO ALMIRANTE

A PALAZZO VENEZIA

Il Duce ha ricevuto Telesio Interlandi, che gli ha riferito su "La Difesa della Razza" che egli dirige. Il Duce ha preso atto con soddisfazione dell'andamento della rivista e ne ha approvato l'indirizzo.

Riproduciamo qui - per i molti che lo hanno dimenticato - il manifesto del Razzismo italiano, che fu pubblicato il 15 luglio 1938 - XVI e che a tutt'oggi costituisce in materia l'unico orientamento di carattere ufficiale

RAZZISMO ITALIANO

Un gruppo di studiosi fascisti docenti nelle Università italiane sotto l'egida del Ministero della Cultura Popolare ha fissato nei seguenti termini quella che è la posizione del Fascismo nei confronti dei problemi della razza:

1 LE RAZZE UMANE ESISTONO. — La esistenza delle razze umane non è già una astrazione del nostro spirito, ma corrisponde a una realtà fenomenica, materiale, percepibile con i nostri sensi. Questa realtà è rappresentata da masse, quasi sempre imponenti, di milioni di uomini, simili per caratteri fisici e psicologici che furono ereditati e che continuano ad ereditarsi. Dire che esistono le razze umane non vuol dire a priori che esistono razze umane superiori o inferiori, ma soltanto che esistono razze umane differenti.

2 ESISTONO GRANDI RAZZE E PICCOLE RAZZE. — Non bisogna soltanto ammettere che esistano i gruppi sistematici maggiori, che comunemente sono chiamati razze e che sono individualizzati solo da alcuni caratteri, ma bisogna anche ammettere che esistano gruppi sistematici minori (come per es. i nordici, i mediterranei, i dinarici, ecc.) individualizzati da un maggior numero di caratteri comuni. Questi gruppi costituiscono dal punto di vista biologico le vere razze, la esistenza delle quali è una verità evidente.

3 IL CONCETTO DI RAZZA E' CONCETTO PURAMENTE BIOLOGICO. Esso è quindi basato su altre considerazioni che non i concetti di popolo e di nazione, fondati essenzialmente su considerazioni storiche, linguistiche, religiose. Però alla base delle differenze di popolo e di nazione stanno delle differenze di razza. Se gli Italiani sono differenti dai Francesi, dai Tedeschi, dai Turchi, dai Greci, ecc., non è solo perchè essi hanno una lingua diversa e una storia diversa, ma perchè la costituzione razziale di questi popoli è diversa. Sono state proporzioni diverse di razze differenti che da tempo molto antico costituiscono i diversi popoli, sia che una razza abbia il dominio assoluto sulle altre, sia che tutte risultino fuse armonicamente, sia, infine, che persistano ancora inassimilate una alle altre le diverse razze.

4 LA POPOLAZIONE DELL'ITALIA ATTUALE E' DI ORIGINE ARIANA E LA SUA CIVILTA' E' ARIANA. — Questa popolazione a civiltà ariana abita da diversi millenni la nostra penisola; ben poco è rimasto della civiltà delle genti preariane. L'origine degli Italiani attuali parte essenzialmente da elementi di quelle stesse razze che costituiscono e costituirono il tessuto perennemente vivo dell'Europa.

5 E' UNA LEGGENDA L'APPORTO DI MASSE INGENTI DI UOMINI IN TEMPI STORICI. — Dopo l'invasione dei Longobardi non ci sono stati in Italia altri notevoli movimenti di popoli capaci di influenzare la fisonomia razziale della nazione. Da ciò deriva che, mentre per altre nazioni europee la composizione razziale è variata notevolmente in tempi anche moderni, per l'Italia, nelle sue grandi linee, la composizione razziale di oggi è la stessa di quella che era mille anni fa: i quarantaquattro milioni d'Italiani di oggi rimontano quindi nell'assoluta maggioranza a famiglie che abitano l'Italia da un millennio.

ESISTE ORMAI UNA PURA "RAZZA ITALIANA". — Questo enunciato non è basato sulla confusione del concetto biologico di razza con il concetto storico-linguistico di popolo e di nazione, ma sulla purissima parentela di sangue che unisce gli Italiani di oggi alle generazioni che da millenni popolano l'Italia. Questa antica purezza di sangue è il più grande titolo di nobiltà della Nazione italiana. 6

E' TEMPO CHE GLI ITALIANI SI PROCLAMINO FRANCAMENTE RAZZISTI. — Tutta l'opera che finora ha fatto il Regime in Italia è in fondo del razzismo. Frequentissimo è stato sempre nei discorsi del Capo il richiamo ai concetti di razza. 7
La questione del razzismo in Italia deve essere trattata da un punto di vista puramente biologico, senza intenzioni filosofiche o religiose.
La concezione del razzismo in Italia deve essere essenzialmente italiana e l'indirizzo ariano-nordico. Questo non vuole dire però introdurre in Italia le teorie del razzismo tedesco come sono o affermare che gli Italiani e gli Scandinavi sono la stessa cosa. Ma vuole soltanto additare agli Italiani un modello fisico e sopratutto psicologico di razza umana che per i suoi caratteri puramente europei si stacca completamente da tutte le razze extra europee, questo vuol dire elevare l'Italiano ad un ideale di superiore coscienza di se stesso e di maggiore responsabilità.

E' NECESSARIO FARE UNA NETTA DISTINZIONE TRA I MEDITERRANEI D'EUROPA (OCCIDENTALI) DA UNA PARTE GLI ORIENTALI E GLI AFRICANI DALL'ALTRA. — Sono perciò da considerarsi pericolose le teorie che sostengono l'origine africana di alcuni popoli europei e comprendono in una comune razza mediterranea anche le popolazioni semitiche e camitiche stabilendo relazioni e simpatie ideologiche assolutamente inammissibili. 8

GLI EBREI NON APPARTENGONO ALLA RAZZA ITALIANA. — Dei semiti che nel corso dei secoli sono approdati sul sacro suolo della nostra Patria nulla in generale è rimasto. Anche l'occupazione araba della Sicilia nulla ha lasciato all'infuori del ricordo di qualche nome; e del resto il processo di assimilazione fu sempre rapidissimo in Italia. 9
Gli ebrei rappresentano l'unica popolazione che non si è mai assimilata in Italia perchè essa è costituita da elementi razziali non europei, diversi in modo assoluto dagli elementi che hanno dato origine agli Italiani.

I CARATTERI FISICI E PSICOLOGICI PURAMENTE EUROPEI DEGLI ITALIANI NON DEVONO ESSERE ALTERATI IN NESSUN MODO. — L'unione è ammissibile solo nell'ambito delle razze europee, nel quale caso non si deve parlare di vero e proprio ibridismo, dato che queste razze appartengono ad un corpo comune e differiscono solo per alcuni caratteri, mentre sono uguali per moltissimi altri. Il carattere puramente europeo degli Italiani viene alterato dall'incrocio con qualsiasi razza extra-europea e portatrice di una civiltà diversa dalla millenaria civiltà degli ariani. 10

Fig. 2 *'The Manifesto of Race', 1938. Italian anti-Semitic laws stripped the Jews of Italian citizenship and any positions in government or professions*

Race and society: more extreme policies and anti-Semitism

Between August and November 1938, a series of new race laws, similar to those already in existence in Nazi Germany, were issued in Italy. Jews were forbidden to intermarry with non-Jews. Jews were excluded from State schools, universities, the armed forces and the professions. Jews were purged from the PNF and from all cultural organisations. Jews were not allowed to own large estates or big businesses and there were other restrictions on the employment of Jews by Italian businesses.

There was a clear connection between the introduction of the race laws in 1938 and Mussolini's growing closeness to an alliance with Hitler, but the new laws had home-grown causes, too. Mussolini had always believed history was about the struggle between superior and inferior races and cultures. The war in Ethiopia, and before that the pacification of Libya, were accompanied by many instances of brutality and racism, often deliberately encouraged by Mussolini himself. Italian forces used poison gas against the Ethiopians in 1935 and 1936. After the conquest of Ethiopia was completed, Mussolini established a system of strict racial segregation.

Mussolini himself made a link between colonial conquest and racist attitudes. In a speech made in September 1938, he declared that: 'The racial problem has not broken out suddenly. It is related to our conquest of our Empire, for history teaches us that empires are won by arms but are held by prestige – and prestige demands a clear-cut racial consciousness. The Jewish problem is merely one aspect of this phenomenon' (J. Whittam, *Fascist Italy*, 1995).

Many leading Fascists had blatant anti-Semitic attitudes. A book by Pietro Orano in 1937, *Who Are The Hebrew People in Italy?*, was a vicious attack on Jews as alien to Italian culture. Men like Giovanni Preziosi and Roberto Farinacci were ardent racists who admired German policies against Jews and wanted Italy to go the same way. This was certainly not true of the whole PNF (about one-third of Jewish men in Italy were members of the party) or of Mussolini himself, whose long-time mistress, Margherita Sarfatti, was Jewish. Mussolini once described Hitler's *Mein Kampf* as a 'truly appalling book' and thought

Cross-reference

Italian actions in Ethiopia are covered in Chapter 8 on page 98.

Cross-reference

Margherita Sarfatti is profiled in Chapter 5 on page 67.

Hitler's attitude to the Jewish people was 'illogical and crazy'. There were, however, enough anti-Semitic elements in the fascist movement ready to orchestrate an aggressive anti-Jewish propaganda campaign once Mussolini signalled them into action.

Such a propaganda campaign was necessary because few Italians believed there was a 'Jewish problem' in their country. The fascist press had to work hard to plant anti-Semitic prejudices in the minds of people who mostly thought of Jews as a separate religion, not a separate race. The minculpop published numerous pseudo-scientific journals on racial topics. The Manifesto of Racial Scientists, in July 1938, stated that: 'The Jews do not belong to the Italian race. The Jews represent the only people who have never been assimilated in Italy and that is because they are composed of non-European racial elements, absolutely different from those which produced Italians' (J. Whittam, *Fascist Italy*, 1995). The fascist press campaign also attacked the Church and Pope Pius XI, after they expressed their opposition to the regime's anti-Semitism.

The anti-Jewish discrimination in Italy was not on the same scale as in Nazi Germany. There were no deportations to concentration camps until 1943, when Italy was under German occupation. Even so, from 1938, many Jews suffered economic hardship and increasing social isolation. Nearly 4,000 Italian Jews opted to convert to Christianity. More than 5,000 emigrated.

A closer look

Jews, Italians and Germans

Comparisons are often made between the persecution of the Jews in Mussolini's Italy and Hitler's Third Reich. There were about 47,000 Jews in Italy in the 1930s, compared with nearly half a million in Germany. Racist indoctrination in Nazi Germany went far deeper than in Italy. Finally, Mussolini's racial thinking was mixed with many other political considerations but for Hitler it was an obsession. The best explanations of the links and comparisons between Italian and German anti-Semitism are in a brief overview by Alexander De Grand, *Fascist Italy and Nazi Germany* and a full-length analysis by Jonathan Steinberg, in *All Or Nothing: The Axis and the Holocaust.*

There is a danger of taking these comparisons too far, putting all the guilt and responsibility for the suffering of Italian Jews on to Germany. In reality, there was considerable Italian responsibility, too, not only among fascist extremists. Anti-Judaism (discrimination against Jews on the grounds of religion) was quite prevalent in parts of the Catholic Church. Pope Pius XI did speak out against anti-Semitism in 1937, criticising Germany for its persecution of Jews and warning Italy not to go the same way, but the Church was actually far more bothered about defending Azione Cattolica against Mussolini's regime than defending Jews. Many Italians were happy to benefit economically from the businesses or jobs taken away from Jews under the new laws. Even fascist leaders who opposed the new laws, such as Giuseppe Bottai, did not make a stand against them. Bottai decided to stay in his job as Minister of Education and implement the new laws in Italy's schools.

Exploring the detail

Among the prominent individuals who emigrated to escape the race laws was Margherita Sarfatti – Mussolini helped her get out to Argentina in 1939. Another was Enrico Fermi, the brilliant physicist who later played a leading role in the *Manhattan Project*, the development of the atomic bomb in the United States. Fermi was not Jewish but he wanted to show solidarity with his Jewish scientific colleagues.

Cross-reference

The deportations of Italian Jews in 1943 are covered in Chapter 10 on pages 133–4.

The minculpop is introduced in Chapter 2 on page 32.

Activity

Thinking point

Compose a report, to be sent by a fascist official to his superiors, warning of the adverse consequences for the regime of introducing a campaign of anti-Jewish discrimination.

Cross-reference

The growing German influence on Fascist Italy in the late 1930s is covered in Chapter 8 on pages 128–30.

Mussolini later came to regard his anti-Semitic policies as a mistake, but he could never openly say so. Italy became more closely allied to Germany in the 1939 Pact of Steel, and also both militarily and economically dependent on Germany. There was no way out. The consequences were disastrous for Mussolini's regime. The race policies and the alliance with Hitler did not lead to a surge of patriotism and enthusiasm for radical Fascism; they proved widely unpopular, helping to undermine the consensus that had previously existed in favour of Mussolini's regime.

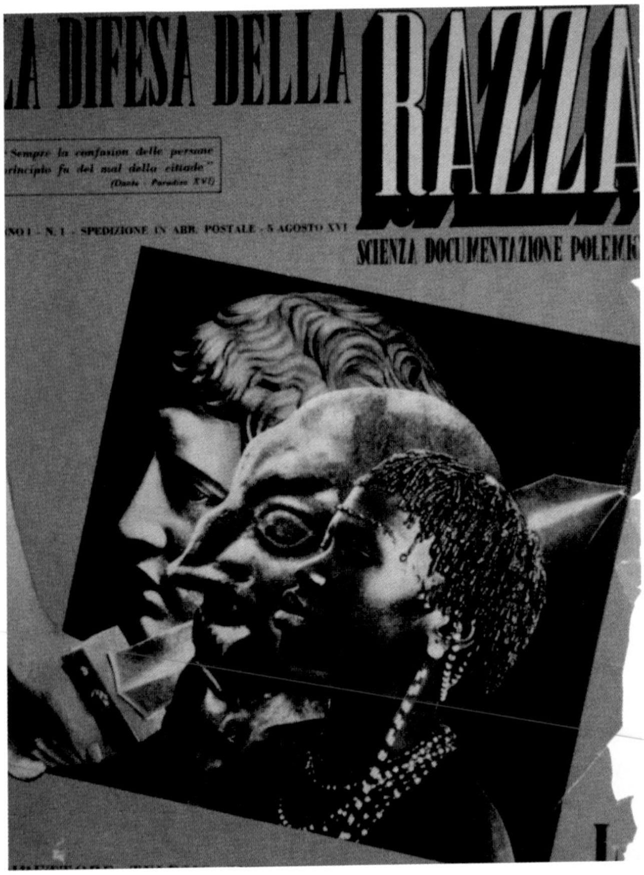

Fig. 3 *Cover of a magazine devoted to race stereotypes in Italy, c.1938*

The elites and the class structure

In the 1920s, Mussolini had backed away from any ideological crusade to smash the elites in Italy and to transform the class structure. The fascist regime usually preferred to avoid antagonising powerful interest groups and to leave things as they were rather than risk confrontations. The rush of radical initiatives at the end of the 1930s, such as the Starace reforms and the Fascist School Charter, were almost an admission by the regime that little had been achieved to break down the class structure and making Italy a more egalitarian society.

This does not mean that the elites had things all their own way under Fascism. They survived but, in many respects, they were severely weakened and could not easily challenge the regime.

- The monarchy and the aristocracy were almost completely overshadowed by Mussolini and had little remaining influence or prestige.
- The great landowners kept hold of their estates and were strong enough to obstruct many of the fascist regime's policies, especially in the South.
- The northern industrialists, were at first very afraid of the regime's promises of social revolution. They were very hostile to the Corporate State until they realised how much it neutralised the power of the unions, leaving them with an almost free hand. In the 1930s, however, business had to accept a lot more State intervention. They still had economic power but they could not easily challenge the regime.
- The academic elite remained more or less as they were. There was little attempt by the regime to force changes in the universities or the elite schools that provided most of their undergraduates.
- The artistic elite was mostly content to benefit from the support and patronage of fascist cultural organisations. Some famous individuals went into exile, such as the famous conductor Arturo Toscanini, but there was no general opposition to the regime.

Did you know?

Arturo Toscanini was an international superstar, the most famous conductor of classical music in the world. He emigrated to the United States in 1931 because he refused to accept the instruction to play the fascist anthem at the start of concerts. Toscanini was not Jewish, but his wife, the pianist Wanda Landowska, was a Jew.

The class system also remained more or less undisturbed. Little changed in the South, which remained trapped in poverty and isolated from the rest of the country. Organisations such as Massaie Rurali did more to reinforce class attitudes among peasants than to bring change. Two of Mussolini's main policies, the Battle for Births and the ruralisation campaign, would have kept the old peasant ways even more firmly in place if they had worked as intended but that was not the case. For the peasant classes, the biggest change was caused by migration to the industrialised cities.

The urban working classes also experienced relatively slow and limited change, at least until the end of the 1930s and the advent of war. The gap between skilled workers with reliable employment and the mass of unskilled labour was probably wider than the gap between skilled workers and the middle classes. The muzzling of the trade unions from 1925 held back any chance of fundamental social advances for the working classes. The regime talked a lot about egalitarianism but there was little actual change.

The middle classes, especially bureaucrats and white-collar workers, were strengthened by Fascism. Mussolini came to power with a lot of left-wing slogans about social revolution and the triumph of the have-nots, but the people who benefited from Fascism were those who had the jobs and the privileges of safe jobs as civil servants or in the party organisations. In all classes, Fascism tended to operate within the existing social order. Italian society remained male-dominated, marked by respect for authority and the continuation of social trends, not a break with the past.

The extent of opposition: was Fascism 'totalitarian'?

Totalitarianism in Italy was not very total. The fascist regime made many compromises with existing centres of power and authority. The Catholic Church was left more or less intact, with the Pope able to rival Mussolini as the arbiter of moral authority. The big industrialists continued to own their factories. The great southern landowners hung on to their estates. Even the Italian monarchy continued to exist, even though it was marginalised by the cult of Mussolini. If Italy had been a truly totalitarian system, like the Soviet Union under Stalin in the 1930s, there would not have been two separate heads of State.

Mussolini was not so much a totalitarian dictator as a cunning, manipulative politician who cleverly held the balance between competing power blocs. He depended upon consent as much as, or even more than, coercion. A true totalitarian regime would not have been as obsessive and anxious about police reports assessing the public mood. This does not mean that Fascist Italy was not a nasty repressive dictatorship that ruthlessly suppressed opposition and dissent. Mussolini's regime had its secret police and its prison camps for political prisoners. Parliamentary democracy was obliterated and Italy became a one-party State. The Fascists completely monopolised the press and controlled most of the media. The leader cult was promoted in true totalitarian style.

Mussolini's dictatorship also changed over time. Between 1922 and 1926, the fascist movement was very radical and violent, greatly feared by the existing elites such as big business and the Church. In the late 1920s, Mussolini gained greater control over the radical wing of the PNF and went out of his way to reassure the traditional elites that there would be no revolutionary extremism. In the 1930s, however, there was much more State intervention in society and the economy and considerable radicalisation in the policies of the regime.

Mussolini was extremely successful in suppressing political opposition. There was no anti-fascist opposition within Italy until the war was going badly wrong in 1943; even then, stirrings of anti-fascist activity had minimal impact. It was foreign armies that brought Mussolini down in the end, not internal opposition.

Key terms

Totalitarianism: the belief that all aspects of society must be coordinated by the State and that all individuals in society should become one single, united mass dedicated to the same ideological goals and loyal to the leader.

Did you know?

In 2009, the Italian prime minister, Silvio Berlusconi, made a supposedly light-hearted but politically loaded comment that political prisoners in Mussolini's Italy served their time in 'holiday camps'. Although typical of Berlusconi's provocative style, this comment was far from the truth. Fascist Italy was indeed a police State.

Exploring the detail

When Mussolini briefly returned to power as leader of the ISR (Salo Republic) from September 1943, surrounded by some of the most radical fascist leaders from the early days, his actions and words gave some indication of his inner desire to be a radical dictator – and of how he regretted not being more radical in the 1920s and 1930s. Mussolini said on several occasions in 1943–44 that he should have been much bolder in his social policies when he was at the peak of his power and prestige.

Cross-reference

To learn more about the Salo Republic, look ahead to Chapter 10, pages 131–3.

Mussolini was also extremely efficient at neutralising any potential rivals to himself or his regime. He moved quickly to sideline any fascist leader who seemed capable of challenging him. Leandro Arpinati found himself a political prisoner in 1930. Italo Balbo was shunted off to be Governor of Libya when he seemed to be gaining too much power and prestige. When Balbo was shot down and killed as his plane was landing at Tobruk in 1940, conspiracy theories were put about claiming Mussolini had ordered his death to eliminate a rival. This was not true – Balbo's death was indeed an accident – but it was not a completely unbelievable idea.

Another example of Mussolini's concern to limit rival power bases was his 'Battle against the Mafia'.

A closer look

The Battle against the Mafia

Mussolini made numerous attempts to overcome the backwardness of southern Italy. He thought many aspects of life in the South were out of tune with Fascism, resisting modernisation and sticking to out-dated traditions. After a personal visit to Sicily in 1924, Mussolini identified the high crime levels and the dominance of the Sicilian Mafia as a crisis that needed urgent action. (One cynical view is that the Fascists could not tolerate a rival gangster organisation to their own.) In 1925, Mussolini launched the Battle against the Mafia. A tough ex-policeman, Cesare Mori, was given the task of purging the fascist organisations in Sicily and rooting out the Mafia. Between 1925 and 1929, Mori expelled hundreds of Fascists from the party, especially in Palermo. Thousands of suspects were arrested across Sicily and there was a series of show trials. The regime claimed that the murder rate in Palermo dropped from 278 in 1924 to only 25 in 1928.

Mussolini did not completely eliminate the Mafia, partly because the courts could not be relied on to back up Mori's arrests. Many suspects were released. Mussolini also became anxious about the way public opinion in Sicily turned against his regime. In 1929, the 'Battle' was declared to be won and Mori's operations were hurriedly wound up. Even so, Mussolini had more success against the Mafia than Italian governments before and after him. One of the ironies of Mussolini's fall from power in 1943 is that the American secret service, the OSS, deliberately used American Mafia contacts, especially the Chicago gangster Lucky Luciano, to assist in the liberation of southern Italy and thus enabled a resurgence of the Mafia.

By the 1930s, there was very little direct political opposition to Mussolini. A small number of communist activists carried on operating secretly in factories and working-class districts, supported by comrades in exile. There were not many of them and they had little effect before the war started to go badly in 1942. A few liberals and democrats kept in contact with each other, but were not capable of effective political action until 1940, when the former prime minister, Ivanoe Bonomi, began organising anti-fascist opposition groups. Any form of direct political action was impossibly difficult because the system of repression was so well established.

Fascist Italy was an oppressive, nasty police State. The OVRA had been set up in 1927 as the Special Tribunal for Defence of the State. In the 1930s, it had about 5,000 secret police agents who controlled almost all aspects of domestic society in Italy. The OVRA was thus relatively small (the Gestapo in Nazi Germany had about 30,000 agents) and it was also sometimes inefficient and often corrupt. Its leader, Carmen Senise from Naples, was as corrupt as any of his men.

This did not prevent the repression from being highly effective. The OVRA could rely for its surveillance and intimidation upon many thousands of informers to denounce, usually anonymously, those guilty or suspected of anti-fascist behaviour – which meant anything the regime disapproved of, including homosexuality. By 1939, the OVRA had collected dossiers on 130,000 'suspects'. Serious offenders could be sentenced to imprisonment in the concentration camps on the Lipari Islands off Italy's south-west coast – about 9,000 were sent there during the regime. There was censorship and regular reports on the public mood from local police chiefs.

The OVRA also pursed enemies abroad – in 1937 two prominent anti-Fascists, the Roselli brothers, were murdered in France as a punishment for fighting on the side of the republican forces in the Spanish Civil War. In peacetime Italy, before 1940, there were very few executions – one estimate claims there were only nine (four of those were Slav nationalists, not Italians). These small numbers indicate that the regime did not need to worry much about the anti-fascist opposition. Conformity was the norm. At least up to 1938, there was a secure consensus that accepted and supported Mussolini's regime. The regime did worry, however, about indirect opposition, from those with Catholic or working-class loyalties.

The reconciliation between Church and State in 1929 did not mean that all friction between the regime and Catholics was ended. There was a brief period of tension and confrontation between the papacy and the regime over the Azione Cattolica in 1931. This was followed by several years of co-existence until 1938, when Catholic opposition to the race laws sparked another clash with the regime. At the time, Mussolini got in quite a state about the 'threat' from Azione Cattolica but, although the Church might be able to obstruct and annoy Mussolini, there was no prospect of the Church actually bringing the regime down.

The disputes over Azione Cattolica were one symptom of the breakdown of the national consensus the fascist regime had achieved up to 1937–38. Another symptom was dissatisfaction among the industrial workers. The mood of the workers was endlessly reported on by police reports and analysed by anxious party officials. Again, however, this was latent opposition rather than a direct threat to the regime.

> Discontentment is manifested in a number of different ways but most common is that of speaking badly about the regime and of the autarchic measures it is taking. You can hear these things being discussed among the workers as soon as they are together with old friends they can trust, or among the women in the city's markets, or when they are waiting for their children coming out of school. This insidious discontentment is very serious and seems to be spreading as each day goes by.

3 *Police report from Turin, October 1938. Quoted in D. Thompson,* ***State Control in Fascist Italy****, 1991*

Cross-reference

The foundation of the OVRA in 1927 is covered in Chapter 1 on page 26.

Cross-reference

The Lateran Pacts are covered in Chapter 2 on pages 36–7.

The Azione Cattolica is introduced in Chapter 2 on page 35.

Activity

Source analysis

Read carefully the police report from Turin in Source 3.

1. Make a list of **five** reasons why this source is useful and reliable evidence about attitudes to the fascist regime in 1938.
2. Make a list of **three** reasons why it might only be of limited value.

Propaganda and culture: the impact of fascist policy towards the media and the arts on the people of Italy

Key terms

Culture: all forms of the arts and entertainment (art, architecture, cinema, radio, literature, theatre and music), both 'high' culture for the elites and 'popular' culture for the masses. Like all other dictatorships, Mussolini's regime exploited and manipulated culture for propaganda purposes.

Like many other aspects of Fascism, there was increasing radicalisation of **culture** and the media in the 1930s. The word 'culture' meant many things in Fascist Italy. In theory, the regime was coordinating the cultural life of the nation into a single whole, carrying through a 'cultural revolution' based on shared national values. In reality, cultural organisations often followed their own agendas. There were also many competing interests and rivalries between the 'private empires' of leaders such as Roberto Farinacci and Giuseppe Bottai.

There was never one single approach to culture and fascist cultural policies often had different aims:

- To control the press and the media and the use of culture as propaganda.
- To control 'high culture' in art, architecture, literature and classical music.
- Coordination of the cultural lives of ordinary people through sport, festivals and mass entertainment.
- Coordination of the 'national memory' through such things as history textbooks and commemoration of suitable legends and heroic episodes in the past.

The process of radicalisation in the 1930s resulted in greater coordination of fascist propaganda. In 1937, the minculpop was set up under the leadership of Alessandro Pavolino. Minculpop got control

Fig. 4 *Mussolini addresses a crowd from a balcony, c.1935*

of radio and cinema as well as the newspapers. From 1937, the Ministry of National Education, run by Giuseppe Bottai, acted almost as a rival to minculpop. Although press and radio were important, the most influential aspect of the mass media was cinema. The 1930s was the first great age of talking pictures and films were the most exciting and glamorous form of mass entertainment. The regime tried to build up Italy's own film industry by establishing a modern well-financed production centre, *Cinecitta* (Film City).

There was official censorship of cinema, but only a few State-sponsored propaganda films were produced. The most popular films were light entertainment, especially escapist 'feel good' comedies. Cinecitta was successful in keeping the home film industry going but Italian films were outnumbered by foreign imports. In the late 1930s, 87 per cent of cinema attendances were for foreign-made films, mostly from Hollywood. As a result, culture in Italy became Americanised – the main effect of mass cinema-going was that many Italians were far more impressed by the Hollywood image of life in the United States than with the realities of life in Fascist Italy.

Cross-reference

The content and instruments of fascist propaganda, and the influence of Ancient Rome on fascist ideology, are covered in Chapter 2 on pages 28–31.

Mussolini had a personal interest in the links between art and power. The fascist regime promoted many cultural projects to demonstrate the power and modernity of Fascism. On the other hand, the regime liked to stress the importance of traditions from the past – the fascist approach to culture was naturally influenced by the classical styles of Ancient Rome. In other areas of Italian history, too, there were iconic themes and heroic individuals that the regime co-opted into the forerunners of Fascism. These themes made a big impression on beliefs and attitudes.

The regime promoted a series of big art festivals and exhibitions. The Venice *Biennale*, (held every two years) became a major international event, showcasing Italian art and culture. In 1932, a huge exhibition, the *Mostra della Rivoluzione Fascista* (Display of the Fascist Revolution) was mounted to show off the achievements of Italy in the 10 years since Mussolini came to power. The fascist regime was especially attracted to modernist architecture. This was shown in the construction of the new towns in the Battle for Land and also in the stylish design of the roadways and stunning bridges of the new autostrada. Italians were often impressed by fascist cultural achievements, partly because they got attention and admiration from abroad.

Exploring the detail

Mussolini's mistress, Margherita Sarfatti, was an acknowledged expert on art and architecture and did a lot to influence him in favour of modernist trends in art and culture.

The regime was successful in coordinating art and culture at the level of ordinary people. Fascist organisations such as the PNF and the OND ran countless exhibitions and competitions at a local level. This approach was successful in arousing enthusiasm and acceptance for 'fascist art'. It was also particularly effective in bringing cultural activities under the control of the regime. From 1928, this control was exercised by the National Confederation of Fascist Professional and Artistic Syndicates, a kind of 'corporate state of the arts'.

The regime also had a big cultural and propaganda impact through sport, which was an ideal way of promoting the fascist virtues of youth, fitness, discipline and struggle. A special training college for female PE teachers was set up at Orvieto. Mass participation in sporting activities was successfully encouraged by the education system, the ONB, the OND and the Littoriali Games (Source 4).

Activity

Source analysis

Analyse the attitudes towards sport and the fascist regime revealed in Source 4. To what extent do you feel these attitudes would be typical of young people:

a in Fascist Italy

b among your own classmates?

Our early years were a wonderful period. The days were too short for us, as we had to run from one sports facility to another. In the Fascist era, we youngsters became members of the Fascist Party from birth. A lot of adults had membership cards as well but my parents, who were not enrolled in any Fascist organisations, had no troubles because of this. In the course of my sporting life, I once met Mussolini, as a winner in the Littoriali. It happened in Rome, when the *Duce* gave the best athletes of both sexes a prize – a gold 'M' pin.

4 *G. Gori,* ***Italian Fascism and Female Body: Sport, Submissive Women and Strong Mothers****, 2004*

Sporting success was pursued as a symbol of national pride. The motor manufacturer Alfa Romeo was taken over by the State in 1932. Its lavishly-funded racing car teams became regular winners on the international Grand Prix circuit. Alberto Nuvolari was the most famous Alfa Romeo driver.

Did you know?

England refused to take part in the World Cup until 1950, but there was a prestige 'friendly' between England and Italy in 1934. By the standards of the time, this was a very rough and physical encounter, known ever afterwards as the 'Battle of Highbury'.

The Italian soccer team became the best in the world, partly because of State support, partly because a generation of brilliant players came together at the same time. Italy hosted the second-ever World Cup in 1934 (the first in Europe) and made a propaganda triumph out of the home team's victory in the final – 2–1 over Czechoslovakia. In 1936, Italy won the gold medal at the Olympic Games in Berlin. In 1938, an Italian team, thought by many observers to be the best ever, stormed through the 1938 World Cup, this time beating Hungary in the final, 4–2.

Fig. 5 *Olympic Champions: the Italian Football team, Berlin 1936*

Many, probably most, Italians were won over by the regime's emphasis on the greatness of Italy's past. The links between Mussolini's Italy and Ancient Rome, the great Italian city-states of medieval times and the heroes of national independence became deeply rooted in the educational experience and the cultural activities of the people.

Activity

Revision exercise

Consider the evidence in this chapter about the impact of fascist ideology and propaganda upon society and culture in Italy. Assemble **five** reasons for and against the proposition that: 'Between 1922 and 1940, there was a fascist revolution in Italy.'

Learning outcomes

In this section, you have examined fascist social policies and the ideologies concerning women and youth that lay behind them. You have also looked at some of the ways in which social policies were inter-related with the economic policies analysed in Section 2. You have gained an understanding of the methods and priorities of the fascist regime and the extent to which they succeeded (or not) in 'transforming Italians into Fascists'. Finally, you have considered the question of the radicalisation of the regime in the later 1930s, under the influence of war and the desire for imperial expansion.

Practice questions

(a) Explain why fascist propaganda in the 1920s emphasised the importance of traditional family life. *(12 marks)*

Study tip Answers to part a) questions need to be as direct and concise as possible. You need to think through a range of selected reasons and then explain them – not just as a list, but commenting on which factors were more influential than others. The best answers here will probably be aware of the ways in which economic and social policies were inter-related – such as ruralisation and the fascist ideal of women and motherhood. The Battle for Births will obviously be relevant here, but the question requires other evidence as well.

(b) 'Fascist attempts to transform Italian society in the years 1925 to 1939 completely failed to achieve their aims.'
Explain why you agree or disagree with this view. *(24 marks)*

Study tip Questions like this require a coherent overall argument showing the ability to respond to a provocative interpretation/argument with precisely selected evidence. Historiography could be useful – but only if it is applied to assessment and evaluation, not a prepared descriptive account of what historians have written. The most important interpretation should be your own!

4 Italian foreign policy, 1923–39

7 Mussolini the statesman, 1923–35

In this chapter you will learn about:

- the motives behind fascist foreign policies
- Italy's early successes in foreign policy in the 1920s
- Mussolini's policies in the early 1930s, including Austria, 1934, and the Stresa Front
- Mussolini's image as a world statesman to 1935.

Fig. 1 *Mussolini presenting himself as a great military commander, c.1935*

If a politician has to be assessed by whether his speeches are in any way profound or prophetic, or even just sensible, then Benito Mussolini was no better than third-rate. If instead the test is how far he changed his country and the rest of the world, the rating would be far more in his favour, although, if the test also includes whether he left the world a better place, the inventor of Fascism would in nearly everyone's estimation score no marks at all. Mussolini himself would have preferred to be judged by whether he succeeded in frightening Europe and making his country of greater account in the world, on which reckoning even his enemies would probably have to admit that he was a very considerable personality indeed.

1 *D. Mack Smith, **Mussolini's Roman Empire**, 1977*

One of the key themes of Italian Fascism was the promise to rescue the nation from the sense of national humiliation following the peace settlement after the First World War. Mussolini promised to restore national pride and make Italy an empire to be reckoned with on the international stage. Mussolini also talked the language of violence and war, promising to build up Italy's armed forces and to turn the Italian people 'from sheep into wolves'. Outwardly, at least, Mussolini achieved considerable foreign policy successes. Italy gained influence over smaller neighbours, including Austria and Albania; Mussolini gained prestige as a statesman on the world stage; the formation of the Stresa Front in 1935 seemed to mark British and French recognition of Italy's status as a European power. At the same time, however, Mussolini was seeking to expand Italian influence in the Mediterranean and Africa, if necessary by wars of aggression. Between 1923 and 1935, therefore, fascist foreign policies often seemed inconsistent and contradictory.

Key chronology

Italian foreign policy, 1923–35

1923 March	Corfu incident
1924 January	Italian acquisition of Fiume
1925 July	Italian-British mediation at Locarno
1930 May	Friendship Treaty with Austria
1933 June	Pact of Rome (Four Power Pact)
1934 June	Mussolini's first meeting with Hitler
1934 July	Italian action after death of Dollfuss
1935 April	Stresa Front
1935 October	Italian invasion of Abyssinia

A world power? Fascist foreign policy, 1923–35

At the time he came to power, Mussolini's attitude towards foreign affairs was not yet grandiose or aggressive. He actually announced that he did not want an ideological foreign policy and that he was more concerned with protecting Italy's interests than being adventurous. (In his early career, Mussolini had been a Socialist and a pacifist.) Mussolini was already thinking of extending Italian influence across the Adriatic to Dalmatia and Albania, but he did not make much fuss about the Treaty of Versailles and the 'Mutilated Victory'. That became a main theme of fascist foreign policy only gradually.

It took time for Mussolini to build up his authority. At first, he had to operate within the constraints of the traditional diplomacy of the foreign affairs department and its old-style Foreign Minister, Salvatore Contarini. In 1926, Mussolini took over the post himself, with Dino Grandi as his second-in-command.

Fig. 2 *Mussolini and the British Chancellor of the Exchequer, later prime minister, Neville Chamberlain, shake hands on the front cover of an Italian magazine*

Influences behind Mussolini's foreign policy

There were several key influences pushing Mussolini's Italy towards an ambitious, expansionist foreign policy:

- Mussolini's quest for personal glory on the world stage. Gaining prestige victories, even small-scale ones, was an important aspect of Mussolini's consolidation of power.
- The recent experience of the First World War and the 'Mutilated Victory'. Ever since unification, Italians had been motivated by a sense of frustrated Nationalism, the feeling that Italy *ought* to be a Great Power but had somehow been cheated out of the international recognition the nation deserved.
- Fascist ideology, with its emphasis on the concepts of national greatness, military strength and the glorification of war. In Italy, as in some other European countries, the experience of the First World War had fostered a cult of strength and violence, idealising the image of the storm trooper.
- The sense of history – a desire to recreate the glories of Ancient Rome and the domination of the Mediterranean world by Roman and Venetian Empires. Liberal Italy had missed out badly on the great age of European imperialism before 1914 and Mussolini was pledged to put this right.

Frustrated Nationalism: the legacy of the past

The *Risorgimento,* the movement for national independence in the 19th century, aroused patriotic fervour and great expectations for Italy's future as a great European power. These high expectations were not fulfilled. Italian unification coincided with Bismarck's unification of Germany, but the rapid rise of Imperial Germany to Great Power status was in sharp contrast to the halting progress of Italian expansion.

Italian ambitions to acquire a colonial empire produced negligible results and a good deal of frustration. In 1911, Italy did seize territory in North Africa from the Ottoman Empire following the invasion of Libya, but there were many failures. The most embarrassing failure was at the Battle of Adowa in 1896, when native armies decisively defeated Italian forces invading Abyssinia. The defeat at Adowa was especially humiliating at a time when other European powers were rapidly extending their empires in Africa and elsewhere, showing complete military superiority.

The hope of gaining territory from Austria-Hungary, the German Empire and Ottoman Turkey was a key motive for Italian intervention in the First World War in 1915, but these hopes were only partly fulfilled. Italian armies did not win the glorious victories that were expected. The most important battle of Italy's war, the Battle of Caporetto on the Alpine front, ended in a shattering defeat, with many Italian troops and their commanders accused of running away.

Exploring the detail

The Battle of Caporetto (now Kobarid in Slovenia) was an epic battle between Italian and Austrian forces, fought high in the Dolomite mountains over a period of many months in 1917. There is a brilliant account of the battle, and its impact on Italy, in *The White War* by Mark Thompson (2008) and a great fictional account in *For Whom The Bell Tolls,* by Ernest Hemingway.

After the war, Italy was dissatisfied with the peace settlement. The port of Fiume, disputed with Yugoslavia, was made a free city and not awarded to Italy. German colonies in Africa were not given to Italy but came under British rule or were made mandates of the League of Nations. Italian representatives at the post-war peace negotiations were angered by the actions of the 'Big Three' (Britain, France and the United States) who frequently met separately and froze Italy out of important discussions. Participation in the war had been intended to enhance Italy's prestige but, in reality, it had the opposite effect. One of the themes of fascist foreign policy was to right the wrongs of the 'Mutilated Victory'.

Cross-reference

The 'Mutilated Victory' is covered in the Introduction on page 4.

Mare Nostrum: Italy's Mediterranean empire

The concept of Mare Nostrum (Our Sea), of the Mediterranean Sea as an Italian sphere of influence, was very appealing to many Italians. It harked back to the glories of Ancient Rome and of the maritime empire of Venice. It fitted with the idea of Italian cultural superiority. It enabled Mussolini to project Fascism as something new and exciting that would wipe away the sense of national humiliation following the post-war peace settlement.

Mussolini hoped that control over the Adriatic would be expanded to include key strategic islands such as Malta and Crete. Further east, Mussolini aimed to replace British influence in Egypt and in East Africa with an Italian colonial empire. The Italian colonial possessions in Libya would be exploited to the full.

Exploring the detail

The Mediterranean and Mussolini

It is sometimes said that Mussolini wanted to make the Mediterranean an 'Italian Lake' but this is not really true. For Mussolini, a lake would be more like a prison than an empire because lakes do not have exits. He hated the fact that Italy was blocked at one end of the Mediterranean by British Gibraltar and, at the other end, by British control of the Suez Canal. Mussolini's dream of Mare Nostrum meant making Italy a great sea power capable of breaking out into the oceans.

The idea of Mare Nostrum included Italian dominance of North Africa. Libya (the Italian name for the combined territories of Tripolitania and Cyrenaica) had been an Italian possession since it was seized from the Ottoman Empire in 1911–12. Although huge in area, Libya had little economic value (nobody knew then about the huge oil reserves buried under the sand) but many nationalists like Luigi Federzoni promoted grandiose ideas about Italy's 'civilising mission' there. These pre-war nationalist ideas influenced the Fascists in the 1920s.

Fig. 3 *The Italian Mare Nostrum*

> The bastardised local population, composed of the most disgusting mixture of races, must be repelled and destroyed and replaced by good Italian blood.

2 *Maffeo Pantaleoni, a nationalist Italian journalist, writing in 1911. Quoted in R. J. B. Bosworth,* ***Mussolini's Italy: Life under the Dictatorship****, 2002*

Key profile

Luigi Federzoni (1878–1967)

Federzoni was a fanatical Italian nationalist who strongly supported Italy's participation in the First World War 'to make the nation feel unified at last'. After the war, he joined the Fascist Party and influenced Mussolini's thinking about Nationalism and foreign affairs. From 1924 to 1926, Federzoni was Minister of the Interior. In July 1943, he was one of the 17 men at the Fascist Grand Council who voted for the motion against Mussolini.

Key developments in fascist foreign policy

In 1922–23, most of Mussolini's grandiose aims were distant dreams; there was no prospect of achieving them straight away. He had to satisfy himself with small successes.

Corfu

Italian intervention in Corfu in the summer of 1923 was a propaganda success for Mussolini at an important time, though it was a relatively minor international incident and its significance was much more about image than any tangible foreign policy success.

The crisis originated in a dispute over the border between Greece and Albania. The Great Powers organised a Conference of Ambassadors to oversee the negotiations; Italian army officers formed part of the inspection team. The leader of this Italian delegation, General Enrico Tellini, and several of his men were killed inside Greek territory. There was no clear proof who was responsible for the murders but Mussolini seized the opportunity to uphold Italian national honour. He sent a harsh seven-point ultimatum to the Greek government, demanding a grovelling apology and massive financial compensation.

Greece issued the apology but claimed the compensation demanded was too much. Mussolini immediately bombarded the Greek island of Corfu, killing a number of civilians; Italian troops occupied Corfu. This may have been a sudden, opportunistic decision, but there was speculation at the time that Mussolini had pre-planned the occupation of Corfu and was simply looking for a convenient excuse.

Mussolini's actions amounted to a blatant act of war. Greece made furious protests and was supported by Britain. Greece went to the League of Nations (recently established at Geneva) but Mussolini refused to accept adjudication from the League and insisted that the Conference of Ambassadors should resolve the issue. In the end, the Corfu crisis fizzled out. Britain held back from punitive action because France wanted good relations with Italy. Greece lacked the military strength for a shooting war. Mussolini agreed to pull Italian forces out of Corfu and the whole affair blew over without any major confrontation.

Corfu did, however, have some important consequences. Mussolini had achieved exactly the kind of cheap boost to his prestige he was looking for as he consolidated his power – Corfu helped to win over public opinion in the lead-up to the 1924 elections. Mussolini was able to restore good relations with Britain but Italy's actions weakened the League of Nations at an important early stage in its development. On a smaller scale, Mussolini's actions over Corfu in 1923 were a dress rehearsal for his approach to the Abyssinian crisis 12 years later.

> Mussolini had wanted the Italian forces to stay in Corfu but he was obliged to submit to world opinion and withdraw them. This rankled with him but among Italians this first example of violence on an international scale won him a useful reputation for courage and patriotism. Such was the chorus of applause that Mussolini never realised what damage he had done, nor how dangerous for Italy as well as other countries this one-sided idea of national prestige might be. On the contrary, he took positive pleasure in having made people afraid of Italian power.

3 *D. Mack Smith,* ***Mussolini's Roman Empire****, 1977*

Fiume

Mussolini gained another significant foreign policy success in 1924, when he secured Italian possession of the sea port of Fiume (Rijeka) on the Dalmatian coast. Fiume was a disputed territory after the collapse of Austria-Hungary, claimed by both Italy and Yugoslavia. The post-war peace settlement established a compromise solution, by which Fiume became a free city. For 15 months in 1919–20, Fiume had been occupied by an unofficial force of 2,000 Italian volunteers led by

Gabriele D'Annunzio. After months of heavy pressure from the Great Powers, the Italian government of Vittorio Orlando reluctantly expelled D'Annunzio's forces from the city in December 1920. Inevitably, this was unpopular with most Italians and severely weakened the government. In acquiring Fiume, therefore, Mussolini was playing to a very receptive national audience.

Mussolini believed that Italy had the opportunity to establish political dominance in the Western Balkans, especially over Albania. In his speeches to enthusiastic fascist audiences, Mussolini often made boastful claims that the Adriatic Sea was 'by rights Italian'. On the other hand, he was still fairly cautious and realistic in his early years of power, and did not want to alarm foreign powers or the Italian Conservatives.

Mussolini showed more diplomatic skill over Fiume than he had over Corfu. He persuaded the government of Yugoslavia to accept Italian annexation of Fiume by the Treaty of Rome in January 1924. The situation in Fiume had remained very chaotic since 1921 and the Rome agreement promised to establish order there. Mussolini also toned down the more extreme claims he had been making against Yugoslavia. Economically, the acquisition of Fiume was useless (because the port was cut off from its hinterland) but what Mussolini cared about was prestige. Success over Fiume significantly strengthened his popularity, without him having to take any risks.

Mussolini's ambitions in the Balkans

By the late 1920s, Mussolini had grown much more confident and assertive in foreign policy. He was now ready to pursue his extensive ambitions in the Balkans. These ambitions were likely to lead to conflict with Yugoslavia, Greece and Albania:

- After acquiring Fiume, Mussolini hoped to extend his influence in Yugoslavia. He began giving secret aid to separatist groups within Yugoslavia, hoping one day that the break-up of the country would allow Italy to take control of Croatia and the whole Adriatic coast (something which he eventually achieved, if only temporarily, in the Second World War).
- Mussolini's ambitions were bound to cause tension with Greece, especially over the Mediterranean islands. The Treaty of Lausanne in 1923 confirmed Italian possession of the Dodecanese Islands. Italy aimed to make these Greek-speaking islands thoroughly 'italianised'. Mussolini also dreamed of using the Dodecanese as a springboard for seizing other important islands from Greece, especially Kos and Crete. Italian influence over Albania (which had a disputed border with Greece) also caused tension.
- Italy had already gained economic influence in Albania before the First World War; Mussolini set out to turn this influence into Italian dominance. Albania was increasingly dependent on military and economic assistance and Italy also exerted strong cultural influence, especially over the Catholic regions of Albania – there was strong pressure to make Italian a compulsory language in Catholic Albanian schools. By 1935, Albania was virtually an Italian protectorate.

Libya

The idea of Living Space for the expanding population was a key theme of fascist ideology. There was a lot of excited speculation about the millions of emigrants who would be settled in Italy's colonial empire and about

Fig. 4 *General Badoglio, photographed c.1921*

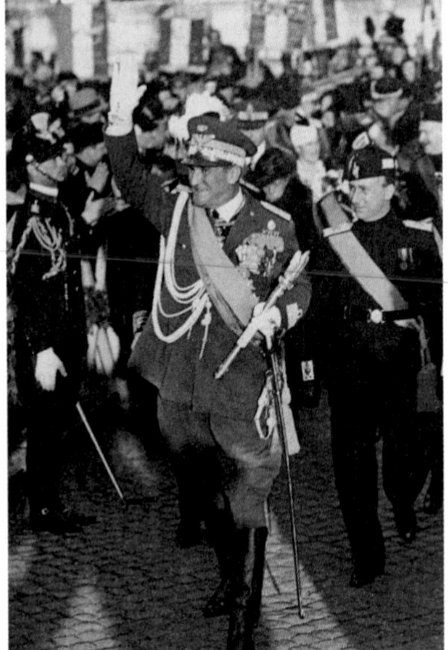

Fig. 5 *General Rodolfo Graziani*

the need to expand Italian colonial territories to make room for them. In reality, the number of Italians settled in North Africa was small. Instead of the 'millions' predicted by fascist propaganda, the real figure was about 50,000. Predictions about the wealth that would flow into Italy as a result of developing the colonial empire were also wildly unrealistic. The costs of running the colonies were always greater than any economic returns. These realities did not have any effect on Mussolini's policies and propaganda. Throughout the 1920s, his regime gave a high priority to the North African Empire.

Bringing Libya under fascist imperial rule was not only a matter of immigration from Italy and of developing agriculture and the economy; it was also necessary to use the armed forces to carry out the 'pacification' of the native population. This was carried out between 1928 and 1933. De Bono was in overall command but the actual military operations were carried out by two rising stars in the Italian army, Pietro Badoglio and Rodolfo Graziani, both of whom later played prominent roles in all of Mussolini's wars. They both gained big reputations in Libya, in spite of the fact that De Bono, Badoglio and Graziani did not get on with each other and were obsessed by personal and petty rivalries.

Key profiles

Pietro Badoglio (1871–1956)

Marshal Badoglio held high rank in the Italian army in the 1920s, despite being widely blamed for the terrible defeat at Caporetto in 1917. He was Governor of Libya from 1929 to 1933. In December 1935, he led Italian forces to victory in Abyssinia and was promoted to the rank of Marshal. Badoglio was opposed to the Pact of Steel. He resigned from his command in December 1940. When Mussolini was removed from power in 1943, the King appointed Badoglio temporary prime minister but he was later replaced by Bonomi.

Rodolfo Graziani (1882–1955)

General Graziani made his reputation in the 'pacification' of Libya from 1926 to 1934. He commanded Italian forces on the southern front in the Abyssinian War. From 1937, he was Governor-General of Abyssinia. He later became chief of the general staff but resigned in 1941 after failures in the campaign in Egypt. Graziani was the only senior general to stay loyal to Mussolini after July 1943 and was rewarded with the post of Defence Minister in the Salo Republic. In 1945, he was given a long prison sentence for collaboration with the Nazis but was released after a few months.

The 'pacification' was done by very brutal methods that nowadays would be described as 'ethnic cleansing'. More than 100,000 of the native population were expelled from their land and penned up in concentration camps in harsh conditions. Death rates were high. Badoglio openly encouraged his men to be 'firm' and 'ferocious'. In putting down a native rebellion in 1930–31, the Italian forces used poison gas to bomb the rebels. By 1933, the 're-conquest' of Libya was over and the concentration camps were closed. Mussolini was ready to move on to his next target, Abyssinia.

Locarno, 1925

Another prestige success for Mussolini was his role as mediator, signing the Locarno Treaties in 1925. The borders between France and Germany had been imposed on Germany by **diktat** in 1919. By the mid-1920s, relations between the two countries were much improved and diplomatic negotiations took place at Locarno, a lake resort in the Italian-speaking part of Switzerland, aiming to reach a voluntary agreement, recognising the borders between Germany, France and Belgium as permanent. Mussolini and the British Foreign Secretary, Austen Chamberlain, were present to act as mediators.

Key terms

Diktat: the idea of the Treaty of Versailles as a 'dictated peace', imposed upon the Germans without any negotiations.

Mussolini, of course, claimed that his role at Locarno was vital for international peace. He was happy for his supporters to make the suggestion that the Duce should be awarded a Nobel Peace Prize. In reality, his role was little more than symbolic. The real architects of Locarno were the Foreign Ministers of France and Germany, Aristide Briand and Gustav Stresemann. Reality, however, was not the issue for Mussolini in 1925; it was all about prestige and strutting impressively about on the international stage.

By 1925, Mussolini's prestige had grown considerably. His foreign successes, though not very substantial, increased his popularity within Italy and gained him respect from other European countries, especially France and Britain. Austen Chamberlain, for example, was quite impressed by Mussolini at Locarno and met him on several later occasions. This was all useful to Mussolini in gaining an image of importance and respectability.

In June 1933, Mussolini scored another apparent triumph by bringing Britain, France, Germany and Italy together in the Four Power Pact (sometimes called the Pact of Rome). Mussolini wanted the Pact to demonstrate his importance. He also wanted to by-pass the League of Nations in favour of direct agreements between the main European powers. The Four Power Pact never had any practical results. Hitler had only reluctantly signed the Pact and there was still an obvious danger that he would try to break free from the restrictions placed on Germany by Versailles. This raised fears for the continuation of the Locarno agreements, which was a vital issue for France. It also raised fears for the continued independence of Austria, which was a vital issue for Mussolini.

Activity

Thinking point

Write a brief article by a British journalist reporting from Italy, expressing admiration for Mussolini's foreign achievements by the end of 1925.

Mussolini and Austria

In 1929, Italy began providing arms and money to right-wing political groupings in Hungary and in Austria. In 1927, he made a treaty with Hungary, aligning both countries with opposition to the 'unfair' post-war peace settlement. This policy continued through the early 1930s. In 1930, Mussolini signed the Friendship Treaty with Austria. Mussolini was already very sensitive to the need to protect Italy's northern borders, on the Brenner Pass with Austria. When the Catholic conservative politician, Engelbert Dollfuss, came to power in 1932, Mussolini hoped that a right-wing government in Austria would come under his influence.

Mussolini established close links with Dollfuss, who made numerous social visits to the Italian Riviera, where Dollfuss, Mussolini and their wives met in friendly and informal circumstances. Italy also poured substantial financial assistance into Austria – the salaries of Austrian government officials and civil servants almost entirely depended on aid from Italy.

Key profile

Engelbert Dollfuss (1892–1934)

Dollfuss was a Catholic conservative politician who became Chancellor of Austria in 1932 at a time of political and economic crisis. In March 1933, Dollfuss suspended parliament and made himself dictator. He was threatened by the rise of the Austrian Nazis, backed by Hitler. In August 1933, Dollfuss banned the Austrian Nazi Party and established close links with Mussolini to defend Austrian independence. In February 1934, government forces defeated the Socialists in a brief civil war in Austria. On 25 July 1934, the Nazis launched a coup d'état. Dollfuss was murdered but the coup failed.

From January 1933, the situation in Austria was complicated by Hitler's rise to power in Germany. The Austrian Nazi Party became much stronger and received a lot of support from Germany. Dollfuss, therefore, faced dangerous opposition from two sides – from the Socialists on the left and from the Nazis on the right. During 1933, Mussolini and Dollfuss moved closer together. Italy increased its aid to the struggling Austrian economy. Mussolini pushed Dollfuss to increase his political authority over the Austrian parliament and to 'act decisively' against the socialist opposition.

In September 1933, Dollfuss suspended parliament and made himself virtually dictator. This provoked violent opposition from the left. In February 1934, there was a brief but vicious civil war in Vienna as government forces battled against left-wing militias who had taken over working-class areas of the city. Mussolini also supported Dollfuss against the rising threat from the Austrian Nazis, who had grown stronger since Hitler came to power in Germany at the start of 1933. At that time, Mussolini was confident that Italy could prevent any German attempt to carry through ***Anschluss*** with Austria.

Key terms

Anschluss: union between Germany and Austria, which had been specifically forbidden by the Treaty of Versailles in 1919. Hitler, himself of Austrian origin, eagerly supported the idea of Anschluss, along with many nationalists both in Germany and Austria.

The situation in Austria became very urgent for Mussolini in July 1934, when Austrian Nazis assassinated Dollfuss in Vienna during a failed attempt at a coup d'état. The coup failed mostly because it was uncoordinated and badly planned, but also because Mussolini seized the opportunity to make a show of Italian commitment to protect Austria by military force if necessary. Italy stationed an army of four divisions on the Austrian border at the Brenner Pass.

> Mussolini was revolted by the death of Dollfuss. "Hitler is the murderer of Dollfuss", he said, "a loathsome sexual degenerate, a dangerous madman" He strode up and down in his villa and then decided to send two divisions up to the Brenner. But for three hours the Nazis' failure had been obvious; so Mussolini was playing a sure thing, knowing he could not lose. The news of the troops' departure was given maximum publicity. Hitler, who had committed a major error, was compelled to withdraw, seemingly yielding to Italian military pressure.

4 *M. Gallo, **Mussolini's Italy**, 1973*

The show of strength on the Brenner boosted Mussolini's prestige but gave a misleading impression of his power and influence in relation to Germany. In the summer of 1934, Hitler was still in the process of consolidating his position within Germany. Mussolini knew there was no practical possibility of German military intervention in Austria. In June 1934, at his first face-to-face meeting with Hitler, in Venice, Hitler had reassured Mussolini that he did not intend to force Anschluss with Austria. In 1934, Mussolini could still act like the 'senior partner' in Fascism, assuming a position of leadership. Over the next four years, however, Hitler became massively stronger, both politically and militarily. Mussolini's position as protector of Austria became less and less secure.

Activity

Research exercise

Find out more about the meeting between Mussolini and Hitler in Venice in 1934, and the attitudes of the two leaders towards each other at that time.

The Stresa Front

The rising threat from Nazi Germany from 1934 onwards changed Mussolini's attitude to Hitler. It also raised deep concerns for Britain and France. In March 1935, Hitler announced his decision to ignore the Treaty of Versailles, which limited Germany's armed forces to 100,000 men, and to build up an army of 400,000 men. Hitler also announced plans to develop a German air force (also forbidden by Versailles) and to introduce conscription. Britain, France and Italy immediately started to seek joint action to guard against the German threat. Their response led to the Stresa Front in April 1935.

Mussolini had always had contradictory attitudes towards Britain and France, especially Britain. On the one hand, Mussolini regarded Britain as a colonial rival, blocking his foreign policy ambitions. On the other hand, Britain was potentially a useful ally in countering the rise of Germany. From 1932, Italy's ambassador to Britain was Dino Grandi, who was generally in favour of keeping good relations with Britain.

Fig. 6 *Italo Balbo, a Blackshirt and Marshal of the Italian Air Force*

Cross-reference

Pierre Laval is profiled in Chapter 8 on page 100.

Mussolini met the French Foreign Minister, Pierre Laval, and the British prime minister, Ramsay MacDonald, at Stresa, in the beautiful setting of the shores of Lake Maggiore. It was another occasion for Mussolini to show off on the international stage; he made a flamboyant arrival at Stresa, dashing across the lake by speedboat. On 14 April, the Final Declaration of the Stresa Conference set out the joint agreement by the three powers to underline their support for the Locarno Treaties of 1925 and to maintain the independence of Austria. Germany was never mentioned by name, but it was plain that the whole purpose of the conference was directed against Germany.

In theory, the Stresa Front ought to have brought Italy and the Western democracies closer together, but this did not happen. There were several reasons for this:

- The agreements made at Stresa were vaguely expressed and avoided specific commitments. None of the powers involved was willing to consider invading Germany, which meant that there was no effective way of stopping Hitler from carrying through his military expansion. Stresa was all protest and no action.
- The three powers all had slightly different aims. They all shared concerns about the rise of Hitler but were not agreed about how to deal with it. Italy and France talked in terms of taking a hard line towards Germany; Britain preferred to leave open the possibility of negotiating agreements with the Germans.
- Well before the Stresa meeting, Mussolini was already actively planning to launch a war against Abyssinia. This would be against the Covenant of the League of Nations and was bound to cause serious difficulties between Italy and Britain. Mussolini was careful to conceal many of his true intentions at Stresa and this was bound to weaken the agreement afterwards.

The Stresa Front started to fall apart within a matter of weeks. In June 1935, without consulting France or Italy, Britain negotiated the Anglo-German Naval Agreement. This reassured Britain by restricting the German Navy to 35 per cent of the size of the Royal Navy; but it broke the terms of the Versailles Treaty, which prohibited Germany from having a large battle fleet. Both Mussolini and the French government blamed the Anglo-German Agreement for undermining what had been achieved at Stresa but, for Mussolini, this was more of an excuse than a reason. By June 1935, Mussolini was already committed to the invasion of Abyssinia (something he had kept quiet about at Stresa) and this was bound to cause a breach with Britain anyway. The summer of 1935, therefore, was a turning point for Italian foreign policy.

Fig. 7 *Signing the Franco-Italian Pact, Rome 1935*

Activity

Talking point

Working in two groups, make a list of the reasons why the Stresa Front did not lead to an effective alliance between Italy and the Western democracies, placing the blame on:

a Mussolini

b Britain and France.

Summary questions

1 Explain why Mussolini's Italy regarded the acquisition of a colonial empire as important.

2 Assess the extent to which Mussolini deserved his reputation as an international statesman by 1935.

8 Fascist aggression, 1935–40

In this chapter you will learn about:

- the reasons for the invasion of Abyssinia and the consequences for Italy
- the impact of Mussolini's decision to intervene in the Spanish Civil War
- the reasons why Italy was drawn into an alliance with Hitler's Germany
- the reasons why Italy remained neutral when war began in Europe in September 1939.

Fig. 1 *'Italy has its own empire!' A poster of Mussolini and the AOI (Africa Orientale Italiana – Italian East Africa) 1936*

There is nothing original in the idea that modern Italy should found an Empire as great and as powerful as Ancient Rome. But until the Great War Italy had not been fortunate in colonial expansion. By 1927, economically, Italy was in a poor way. The lira had been fixed too high; foreign trade was declining; the closing of America to emigrants kept the rising population pressing more heavily on the available land. The home situation called for a military adventure that would absorb the whole nation. It must glorify Fascism abroad and also help to remove that suspicion of military incompetence which lurked at the back of every Italian brain – vague unhappy memories of Adowa and Caporetto.

1 *G. T. Garratt,* ***Mussolini's Roman Empire****, 1938*

Key chronology

Italy and fascist aggression, 1935–39

1935 October	Italian invasion of Abyssinia
1936 May	Final victory in Abyssinia
1936 December	Italian 'volunteers' sent to fight in Spain
1937 July	Mussolini's State visit to Munich
1938 March	Mussolini's acceptance of Anschluss with Austria
1938 September	Mussolini's mediation at Munich Conference
1939 April	Italian invasion of Albania
1939 May	Pact of Steel

Exploring the detail

The Wal Wal incident

In December 1934, there was a brief military confrontation at Wal Wal oasis in which 150 Abyssinians and 50 Italians were killed. The Italians had established a fort at Wal Wal in 1930, several miles inside the Abyssinian border, and their presence there was disputed – Haile Selassie appealed for international arbitration. The firefight at Wal Wal inflamed tensions between Italy and Abyssinia and brought the two countries closer to war – which may well have been what Mussolini wanted anyway.

Cross-reference

The Stresa Front is covered in Chapter 7 on pages 93–4.

At the beginning of 1935, France and Britain viewed Mussolini as a European statesman and a potential ally. By May 1939, however, Mussolini was allied to Hitler and Italy was one of the Axis powers alongside Nazi Germany and Imperial Japan. In the eyes of Britain and France, Mussolini had turned into a fascist dictator. This process was not sudden; between 1936 and 1939 there were still opportunities for Italy to rebuild relations with Britain and France. Step by step, however, Mussolini moved closer to Nazi Germany: the invasion of Abyssinia (the name used for Ethiopia in the 1930s), intervention in Spain, acceptance of the Nazi annexations of Austria and parts of Czechoslovakia in 1938, and finally the Pact of Steel in May 1939. When the European war began in September 1939, Mussolini held back, fearful of involving Italy in a real war. It might still have been just possible for Mussolini to avoid Hitler's clutches and for Italy to rebuild relations with Britain and France. Mussolini did not make this choice. In the end, the consequences of siding with Germany proved disastrous for Mussolini and Italy.

The invasion of Abyssinia

At the Stresa Conference in April 1935, France and Britain had been eager to achieve an agreement with Mussolini. They did give warnings to Mussolini about Abyssinia, but privately and in rather coded terms. Mussolini assumed, wrongly, that there would not be strong international opposition to an invasion.

Fig. 2 *A Parisian cartoon shows Mussolini threatening Abyssinia, shouting down the phone at Emperor Haile Selassie*

Mussolini had been thinking about invading Abyssinia for a very long time before the actual invasion. Italian forces in Eritrea, to the north of Abyssinia, had been building up since 1932. The Wal Wal incident of December 1934 showed how Italy was angling for an excuse to invade. The appointment of Emilio De Bono as Commander in Chief of all Italian forces in East Africa in March 1935 showed Mussolini's intentions. Italy continued with massive military preparations through the summer months. The Emperor of Abyssinia, Haile Selassie, was well aware of the Italian threat and was already seeking support from the League of Nations.

Key profile

Emperor Haile Selassie (1892–1975)

Haile Selassie was Emperor of Abyssinia from 1930 to 1974. He became famous for his appearance at the League of Nations in 1936, appealing for international action to defend his country against Italian aggression and to uphold the principle of collective security. Haile Selassie was in exile in England from 1935, during the period of Italian rule under the AOI. In 1941, he returned to Addis Ababa after the Italian occupiers were expelled by British forces.

The invasion began on 3 October. The main invasion force, led by Emilio De Bono, attacked from Eritrea in the North while General Graziani commanded smaller Italian forces on the southern front. The day before, Mussolini made a big set-piece speech in Rome. At the same time, in public meetings in towns and villages all over Italy, people listened to announcements by local officials and to the live radio broadcasts from Rome. A massive effort was made to whip up patriotic enthusiasm for the war.

à midi 5
à 19 heures 5
tous les jours
écoutez

ÉDITION DE 5 HEURES

LE JOURNAL

PARIS, 100, RUE DE RICHELIEU — SAMEDI 8 AVRIL 1939

au poste de l'Ile-de-France le 1/4 d'heure du "Journal"

ENVAHIE PAR L'ITALIE
L'ALBANIE SE DÉFEND...

Malgré une résistance acharnée des troupes du roi Zog les agresseurs avec de formidables moyens militaires ont réussi à prendre pied sur plusieurs points de la côte

Les Albanais reconnaissent qu'en fin de journée Durazzo, Valona, Santi Quaranteet Shengjin étaient aux mains de l'ennemi

LE GOUVERNEMENT DE TIRANA PROCLAME SA DÉCISION DE POURSUIVRE LA LUTTE

La reine Géraldine s'est réfugiée en Grèce

FIER MESSAGE AU DUCE du chef nationaliste albanais

"QUAND VOS FORCES AURONT ANNIHILÉ TOUS NOS HOMMES, NOS FEMMES COMBATTRONT"

UN TOUT RÉCENT PORTRAIT DU ROI ZOG

Fig. 3 *The French newspaper* Le Journal *announces the Italian invasion of Albania*

> From a window in one of the thick walls of the old palace, I looked down on the scene in the Piazza Venezia. It was a vast mosaic of pink faces under the soft evening light, gazing eagerly upward at the closed window of Mussolini's room. The square itself can hold 200 000 people but in the surrounding streets at least as many more were packed in solid masses. Every window and roof was crowded to capacity. Slowly, while the nation waited in suspense, a honey-coloured moon rose in the green evening sky. It hung over the broken outline of the Coliseum, which in 2000 years has looked down on so many mighty spectacles. Then at 7.30 a sudden roar like a huge volcanic eruption broke from the crowd. Mussolini, in the grey uniform and round black cap of the Fascist militia, had stepped out onto the floodlit balcony.

2 *Ward Price of the* ***Daily Mail*** *describing Mussolini's announcement of war against Abyssinia, 3 October 1935. Quoted in N. Farrell* ***Mussolini: A New Life****, 2003*

> Blackshirts of the revolution! Men and women of all Italy! Listen! A solemn hour is about to strike in the history of the fatherland. Twenty million men are at this moment occupying the piazzas in every corner of Italy. Twenty million men; but one single heart and one single will. It is not just an army that is moving towards victory but an entire people of 44 million souls. Attempts have been made by foreign powers to commit the blackest injustice against this people – that of depriving us of our little place in the sun. We have been patient for thirteen years. With Abyssinia we have been patient for forty years. Enough!

3 *Mussolini's speech to the Italian people, 2 October 1935. Quoted in C. Duggan,* ***The Force of Destiny: Italy Since 1796****, 2007*

Mussolini's plans depended on winning a quick victory. A symbolically important victory was gained with the capture of Adowa (scene of the humiliating defeat in 1896) on 6 October, but the advance of the Italian armies was frustratingly slow and Mussolini lost patience. In December, he sacked De Bono and replaced him with Pietro Badoglio. There was a counter-attack by the Abyssinian armies and the Italian advance stalled. Mussolini was now facing two serious problems: one was military – how to win the war; the other was diplomatic – how to cope with the threat of international action to force him to back down.

Activity

Source analysis

Examine the descriptions of the announcement of war in Sources 2 and 3.

1. What do they reveal about fascist aims and propaganda methods?
2. How effective were these methods in winning mass support?

Fig. 4 *A satirical cartoon in* Fortune *shows Abyssinia betrayed by the international community. At the bottom, on the left, is President Wilson and, on the right, Mussolini*

During 1936, Mussolini was able to win his war but only by the use of massive military force. In addition to the forces already stationed in East Africa, Italy mobilised more than 600,000 troops, equipped with modern weapons and with air support. Mussolini urged his generals to use brutal methods, including poison gas. Between February and April 1936, the Italians won a series of battles on both the northern and southern fronts. Badoglio launched his final assault, the so-called 'March of the Iron Will', determined to get to the Ethiopian capital, Addis Ababa, before Graziani did. Haile Selassie went into exile and the war ended on 5 May. On 9 May, Victor Emmanuel III was proclaimed Emperor of Ethiopia.

The consequences of the invasion of Abyssinia

In May 1936, Mussolini was able to bask in the glow of victory. Victor Emmanuel III was proclaimed Emperor of the Italian territories in East Africa, now re-named Africa Orientale Italiana (AOI) or Italian East Africa. There was mass national rejoicing and Mussolini's popularity rose higher than ever. In reality, the victory had been less than spectacular. It took far longer than originally planned, it was only achieved at massive cost to the national budget and the fighting was not yet finished. General Graziani, who took overall command in June, had to spend several months 'pacifying' the country and dealing with rebellions and guerrilla warfare. It was February 1937 before he established complete control.

People in Italy, however, took Mussolini's victory at face value. He gained approval from wide sections of society. There were mass demonstrations in favour of Mussolini and against 'foreign elements' who opposed his actions. From the beginning of the war, leaders of the Catholic Church expressed their approval. The Bishop of Cremona announced: 'The blessing of God be on our soldiers, who on African soil will conquer new and fertile lands for the spirit of Italy and will bring Roman and Christian culture to them. May Italy stand once again as a Christian model for the whole world.' There were many similar outpourings in the celebrations of victory.

Italy's victory on the battlefield did not bring an end to the diplomatic crisis caused by the war. Mussolini had hoped that the European powers would quickly accept the conquest of Italian East Africa and give diplomatic recognition to the AOI. He expected a brief outburst of disapproval, after which Britain and France would allow diplomatic relations to get back to where they were before the war. This did not happen. The international crisis Mussolini had provoked by invading Ethiopia rumbled on for two years. It did lasting damage to Italy's relations with Britain and France and helped to push Mussolini towards an alliance with Germany.

There were several reasons for this:

- Mussolini had simply misjudged the response of Britain and France. The warning signs had been there in 1935, but he ignored them.

Key chronology

The war in Abyssinia

1934 December	Wal Wal incident
1935 October	Start of invasion
1935 December	De Bono replaced by Badoglio
1936 January	Victory in the South at Genale Doria
1936 February	Victory in the North at Enderta
1936 April	'March of the Iron Will'
1936 May	Flight of Haile Selassie into exile
	Capture of Addis Ababa

Cross-reference

The impact of the war in Abyssinia on the Italian economy is covered in Chapter 3 on page 53.

The impact on attitudes within Italy towards the fascist regime is covered in Chapter 6 on pages 72–3.

- It had taken too long for the conquest of Ethiopia to be completed. A quick decisive victory might have enabled Mussolini to avoid a major international reaction but the war lasted eight months. This allowed time for opposition to the war to grow and for the League of Nations to become involved.
- Emperor Haile Selassie mounted a very effective campaign to exploit international condemnation of Italian aggression. Haile Selassie's emotional address to the League of Nations at Geneva, in July 1936, after he had been forced into exile, had a huge impact on public opinion around the world.
- The attitudes and actions of France and especially of Britain were influenced by public opinion against Mussolini's aggression. At government level, there was a strong desire to get around the problem of Abyssinia and to rebuild the Stresa Front, but the public mood made this very difficult.

British and French policy towards Mussolini was very uncertain and ambiguous, both during and after the war. On the one hand, there was a desire to support the League of Nations and to block fascist aggression. There was no question of doing this militarily, but there was pressure to punish Italy by introducing **economic sanctions**. After much diplomatic haggling, sanctions were imposed. There were numerous public statements condemning Italy and demanding respect for Ethiopian independence.

On the other hand, British and French policymakers did not want to drive Mussolini into the arms of Hitler. They still genuinely hoped to keep alive the Stresa Front. They were not completely against Mussolini gaining an empire in Africa, as long as he did not cause too much trouble in doing so. This weakened their response. Oil, for example, was excluded from the economic sanctions, and oil was the one item that might have forced Mussolini to take serious notice of the sanctions. The confused British and French position resulted in the Hoare–Laval Pact in December 1935. This Pact aimed at a compromise agreement, giving large parts of Ethiopia to Italy but preserving the independence of a smaller Ethiopia.

Fig. 5 *An Italian propaganda postcard shows Haile Selassie toppled by an Italian tank*

Key terms

Economic sanctions: a form of diplomatic blackmail. By cutting off imports of vital goods and raw materials, sanctions are intended to force a change in policy and behaviour by the country being targeted by sanctions. The idea of sanctions was popular in the 1930s as a way of taking action but avoiding war.

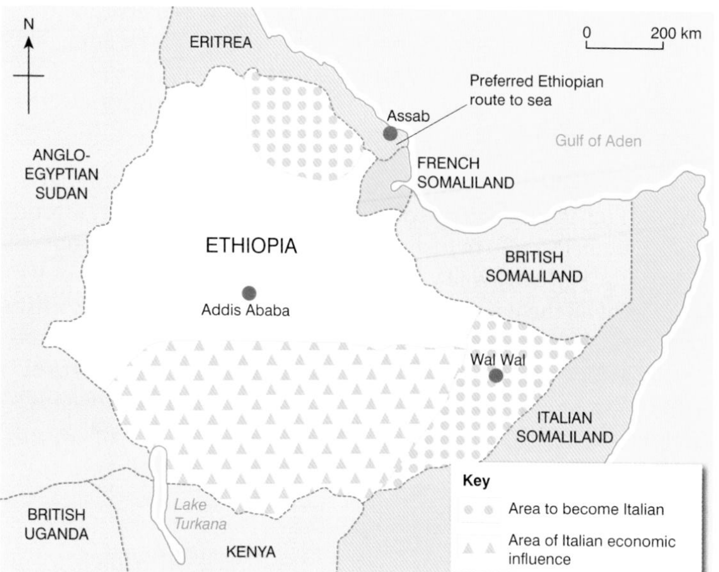

Fig. 6 *The Hoare–Laval Pact*

Exploring the detail

The Hoare–Laval Pact

In December 1935, the British Foreign Secretary, Samuel Hoare, met Pierre Laval, the French prime minister, for private talks in Paris. They agreed a pact aimed at tempting Mussolini to call off his war in Ethiopia in return for a favourable territorial settlement. There was a massive public reaction against their plan, especially in Britain. Hoare resigned and took all the blame but he had actually acted on behalf of the government as a whole.

There were two fatal weaknesses in the Hoare–Laval Pact: first, Mussolini would never have accepted it because he was already fixed on winning a military victory; second, there was a storm of public and political protest against the Pact's 'appeasement' of Mussolini. The Hoare–Laval Pact was sunk without trace. Hoare resigned and was replaced as Foreign Secretary by Anthony Eden. Laval also lost power when a new Popular Front government was formed in 1936.

Key profiles

Sir Samuel Hoare (1880–1959)

Hoare was Britain's Foreign Minister in 1935 but was forced to resign by the furious public condemnation of the Hoare–Laval Pact. (Hoare already knew Mussolini well. As an army intelligence officer during the First World War, Hoare paid £6,000 to the then unknown journalist, Benito Mussolini, to finance his propaganda campaign to keep Italy fighting in the war after the shock of defeat at Caporetto.) From 1940 to 1944, Hoare was British Ambassador in Spain and played an important role in persuading the Franco regime to remain neutral in the Second World War.

Pierre Laval (1883–1945)

Laval was a French politician who started his career as a Socialist but later adopted right-wing views. He was prime minister four times in all, first in 1931. In 1935, as Foreign Minister, he agreed the Hoare–Laval Pact, attempting to find a compromise solution to the crisis caused by the Italian invasion of Abyssinia. In 1940, he became prime minister in the pro-Nazi government of Vichy France headed by Marshal Pétain. Because of this collaboration, Laval was executed for treason in October 1945.

British and French policy continued to be half-hearted and contradictory, even after the war ended. They refused to grant recognition to the AOI until 1938. Some efforts were made to improve relations with Italy and to breathe life into the corpse of the Stresa Front but they did not get very far, partly because of Anthony Eden, who had a very hostile attitude to Mussolini and made it clear he did not think he would ever be a reliable ally. Mussolini occasionally gave indications that he would like better relations with Britain and France, but he could see the way things were going as early as June 1936 (Source 4).

> The present situation forces me to seek elsewhere the security I have lost on the French side and on the British side, with the aim of restoring the shattered balance to my advantage. Who should I turn to if not Hitler? I know perfectly well what will happen if I make an alliance with Hitler. First of all there will be the *Anschluss* with Austria. Then it will be Czechoslovakia, Poland, the German colonies, etc. To sum up, it means war, inevitably. That is why I have hesitated and why I still hesitate to take that path. But if the attitude of the French government towards me and the Fascist regime and Italy does not change, then I will accept Hitler's offers.

4 *Comments by Mussolini to a French Socialist, June 1936. Quoted in N. Farrell,* ***Mussolini: A New Life****, 2004*

Activity

Source analysis

Examine Mussolini's comments in Source 4 in the light of the evidence in the rest of this section.

1. What do you think his motives were in speaking to the French Socialist?
2. How reliable is Source 4 as a guide to Mussolini's real intentions in 1936?

From the summer of 1936, therefore, Mussolini's relationship with Britain and France was already damaged. Things were then made much worse by the consequences of Italian intervention in the Spanish Civil War.

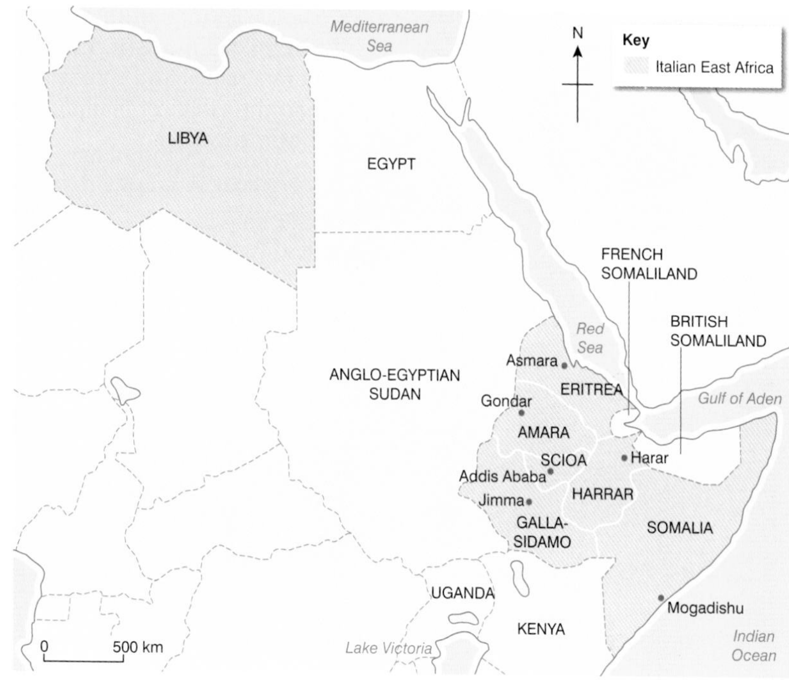

Fig. 7 *The AOI (Italian East African Empire) after the Abyssinian War*

Italian involvement in the Spanish Civil War

Mussolini's decision to support the nationalist rebellion against the legal government of the Spanish Republic was partly based on ideology. He was supporting a fellow Fascist against the dangers of Communism. There were also considerations of prestige – Mussolini was anxious, as always, to be seen as a decisive man of action and he wanted to prove the martial spirit of the new Italy. He was also keen to match anything that Hitler's Germany did to help Franco and did not want to be left behind.

A closer look

The Spanish Civil War

The Spanish Civil War was actually three inter-related wars:

- The first war was the nationalist revolt against the Spanish Republic, an internal struggle between the forces of the right (Francoists, Fascists, Catholic Conservatives and monarchists) against those of the left (Liberals, Socialists, trade unionists, Communists and republicans).
- The second war was between the centre and the regions – the struggle by the Francoists to prevent the Basques and the Catalans from achieving self-rule.
- The third war was the international trial of strength between fascist regimes and the Western democracies.

The civil war began in July 1936, with a revolt of right-wing army officers, led by Francisco Franco, against the Spanish republican government. The revolt soon widened into a bitter civil war with many atrocities on both sides. By March 1939, the nationalists had achieved a decisive victory. Franco continued to dominate Spain until 1975.

One key reason why Franco was able to win power in the end was that his rebellion received large-scale military support from Nazi Germany and Fascist Italy, whereas the legal republican government did not receive equivalent help from the Western democracies. Both Britain and France followed a policy of non-intervention, backed by economic sanctions. The republican forces did get military backing from Stalin and the USSR, and from the idealistic volunteer fighters in the International Brigades but this was ultimately ineffective – and the assistance from Stalin made the republican cause associated with Communism. Franco's victory weakened the Western democracies and strengthened the fascist regimes. The war also had the effect of bringing Hitler's Germany and Mussolini's Italy closer together.

Key profile

Francisco Franco Bahamonde (1892–1975)

General Franco made his reputation fighting Spain's colonial wars in Morocco. In July 1936, he led a coup d'état against the Spanish Republic and led the nationalist forces to victory in the Civil War by 1939, partly because of the help he received from Hitler's Germany and Mussolini's Italy. In 1940, Franco resisted Hitler's requests to join in the Second World War and kept Spain neutral – though he did allow the Spanish Blue Division to fight on the Eastern Front. Franco was widely hated in the West, but his authoritarian regime remained in power until his death in 1975.

Italian military assistance to the nationalists in Spain was on a large scale. Twelve Italian bombers were sent in July 1936. In December, the first force of 10,000 Italian 'volunteers' arrived in Cadiz. By February 1937, there were more than 50,000 Italian troops fighting in Spain. At the height of Italian involvement in 1937, the total reached 80,000, backed by 150 tanks. Air power provided by Fascist Italy and Nazi Germany was vital in tipping the balance of the Civil War away from the republicans and towards the nationalists. A total of 660 Italian aircraft were deployed in Spain. The Italian bombing raid on Barcelona in March 1938 was both militarily and psychologically very damaging to the republican cause.

Fig. 8 *Italian aircraft bombing Spain, 1936*

Intervention in Spain gained some of the prestige and political advantages Mussolini had hoped for, but it put severe strain on Italy's military and industrial strength. Mussolini had gambled on the involvement in Spain being short lived, but it lasted until the end of 1938. The total of Italian dead was nearly 4,000, most of them killed in the humiliating defeat by a smaller republican army at Guadalajara in November 1937. One of the problems of Italian intervention was that most of the troops involved were not trained regular army units but Blackshirt militiamen, who were not prepared for the intensity of the fighting in Spain. General Franco had not really wanted a large Italian fighting force anyway – what he wanted most was money and weapons.

The intervention in Spain had very important consequences for Italy afterwards, but it is not clear how far Mussolini realised this at the time (Source 5).

> As his rise to power in the 1920s had shown, Mussolini knew how to play people off against each other, how to threaten and bluff, how to make propaganda and how to exploit temporary advantages; but he knew little of other countries and he ignored the underlying strategic realities. For him, foreign policy was an exhilarating game, played for high stakes. It was also a marvellous way of rousing and transforming the Italian masses. As Mussolini told Ciano in 1937: 'When Spain is finished, I will think of something else. The character of the Italian people must be moulded by fighting.'
>
> **5** *M. Clark,* ***Modern Italy 1871–1982****, 1984*

Activity

Revision exercise

Using Source 5 and the evidence in this chapter, construct two parallel lists as a 'balance sheet' of Mussolini's gains and losses as a result of the military intervention in the Spanish Civil War.

In fact, Italy paid a high price diplomatically. In the Western democracies, there was strong support for defending democracy in Spain. 40,000 volunteers joined the International Brigade to fight in Spain. Franco became a hate figure for the left, especially in Britain, where public opinion turned sharply against Italy and Germany. It might still have been possible in 1936 and 1937 for Italy to rebuild relations with Britain and France, but links between Mussolini, Hitler and Franco in the Spanish Civil War made this much less likely. Intervention in Spain pushed Mussolini towards greater subservience to Nazi Germany.

Mussolini's relationship with Nazi Germany

The relationship between Fascist Italy and Nazi Germany was shaped to a great extent by the key personalities of Benito Mussolini and Adolf Hitler. Their personal relationship was marked by many contradictions. Mussolini admired and feared the strength of Nazi Germany, but he often had a negative attitude to Hitler. Mussolini's private comments about Hitler were often scathing: 'a gramophone record that knows only seven tunes'; 'a sexual degenerate' and so on. On the other side, Hitler looked down on Italy and had no respect for Italian military or economic strength, but he was always well disposed towards Mussolini personally, and remained loyal to him right up until the end of the war.

Hitler's ability to handle Mussolini, sometimes by flattery and sometimes by decisiveness and force of personality, was an important factor in shaping Mussolini's foreign policies. The relationship lasted for more than 10 years and involved 15 crucial face-to-face meetings.

When Hitler came to power in January 1933, he was already an admirer of Mussolini. Mussolini saw his rise to power as advantageous to Fascism and did not then see Germany as a threat. When the two dictators met for the first time, in Venice in June 1934, Mussolini still regarded himself as the senior partner (because he had been in power 10 years longer) and was not particularly impressed by what he saw and heard of Hitler.

In July 1934, Hitler supported the Austrian Nazis in a failed attempt to seize power in Austria that led to the assassination of Dollfuss. Mussolini ostentatiously sent troops to 'protect' Austria. Hitler was furious. Between 1934 and 1938, the issue of Austria was a constant source of friction between Mussolini and Germany. Mussolini became increasingly worried about the rapid growth of Germany's economic and military power. Several leading Fascists in Italy were hostile to Germany, including Italo Balbo. In 1935, Mussolini entered what was a virtually anti-Hitler alliance with Britain and France in the Stresa Front.

Other factors, however, combined to draw Mussolini and Hitler closer together. The war in Ethiopia caused a breach between Italy and the British and French. Intervention in Spain pushed Mussolini into the fascist camp. During 1936 and 1937, Italy became more dependent on the German economy. Relations between Italy and Britain continued to be difficult, partly because of the bad personal relationship between Mussolini and the British Foreign Secretary, Anthony Eden.

Key profile

Anthony Eden (1897–1977)

Eden became Britain's Foreign Minister in October 1936, after the resignation of Sir Samuel Hoare. Eden disliked Mussolini (who did not like him, either) and negotiations between the two were often difficult. Eden resigned in February 1938, partly because he was opposed to his prime minister, Neville Chamberlain, over how to deal with Mussolini. Eden came back as Foreign Minister of Churchill's wartime government from 1940 to 1945. He was later prime minister from 1955 to 1957, when he was forced to resign after the failed intervention at Suez.

Did you know?

Mussolini prided himself on his ability in foreign languages. At the Munich Conference in September 1938, he was the only leader present who did not need an interpreter. His German was not quite as good as he thought it was. His strong accent meant that the audience did not understand much of his big speech to the rally in Munich in 1937. More importantly, Mussolini did not always grasp everything Hitler said to him in private discussions, especially when Hitler launched into long monologues, but he was too proud to ask for a translation.

Mussolini became more and more impressed with the dynamism of Nazi Germany. In September 1937, Mussolini made a high-profile State visit to Munich. The highlight was his speech to a mass open-air rally, speaking in German, in the middle of a fierce thunderstorm. The propaganda presentation of the event made a great impression on Mussolini.

Exploring the detail

The Comintern (Third Communist International) was the worldwide association of communist parties, formed in 1919 under the leadership of the new Bolshevik regime in Russia. Germany and Japan signed their Anti-Comintern Pact in November 1936; Italy joined in November 1937.

In November 1937, Mussolini signed the Anti-Comintern Pact, thus joining Germany and Japan, who had signed their pact in 1936, in what became known as the Axis. Britain attempted to improve relations with Italy and Anglo-Italian talks were held in Rome in March 1938. Britain at last agreed to recognise Italian possession of Abyssinia – but the agreement was followed two days later by Hitler's annexation of Austria.

Inwardly, Mussolini was furious. Mussolini was a realist, however. He had already recognised the fact that it was no longer possible to prevent Germany from annexing Austria. Outwardly, therefore, Mussolini put a brave face on it and told Hitler that Italy would not interfere, even though he knew the Anschluss was a clear defeat for what had been a key policy since 1930. Hitler was delighted and expressed his gratitude to Mussolini in effusive terms.

Cross-reference

Mussolini's policy towards Austria is covered in Chapter 7 on pages 91–3.

Another consequence of the Anschluss was that the Austrian economy was integrated with the Third Reich and this increased Italian economic dependence on Germany. The prospects of an Italian-German alliance grew stronger. In September 1938, Hitler began pressuring Czechoslovakia over the Sudetenland and there was growing international tension. The British prime minister, Neville Chamberlain, made several visits to meet Hitler, attempting to prevent war by compromise over Hitler's demands.

Mussolini had no direct interest in Czechoslovakia, but he seized the opportunity to act the part of an international statesman and mediator. He proposed a Four Power Conference, to be held in Munich, to discuss the Italian 'peace plan'. In reality, Mussolini did not have any peace plan – it was drawn up by the Germans and rubber-stamped by Mussolini. Nor was Mussolini acting as a neutral mediator – he was simply giving Hitler a useful cover for imposing his demands. However, Mussolini succeeded in posing as a peacemaker and there was a huge surge in his popularity when he returned to Italy after Munich.

Mussolini was not yet fully committed to an alliance with Hitler but he had less freedom of action than he liked to suppose. After Munich, Italy moved closer towards Germany. Count Galeazzo Ciano, Mussolini's son-in-law, who had been appointed Foreign Minister in 1936, had originally been opposed to close links with Germany. During 1938, he began to change his mind about this. Hitler and his Foreign Minister, Joachim von Ribbentrop, worked persistently to persuade Ciano in favour of an alliance. In May 1939, Italy signed the Pact of Steel with Germany.

Activity

Thinking point

Do some research on the Munich Conference of September 1938 and evaluate the significance of the role played by Mussolini. Make a list of the **three** most important consequences for Italy.

Key profiles

Count Galeazzo Ciano (1903–44)

Ciano was a rich playboy, married to Mussolini's daughter, Edda. He was Mussolini's Foreign Minister from 1936. Ciano supported the 1939 Pact of Steel with Germany, but became more and more anti-German after Italy's entry into the war in 1940. At the Fascist Grand Council meeting in July 1943, he voted with the majority against Mussolini. This led to his execution for treason in January 1944, after the Germans handed him over to the Salo Republic. (Edda never spoke to her father again.) After his death, Ciano's diaries became an important source for historians.

Joachim von Ribbentrop (1893–1946)

Ribbentrop was a businessman who joined the Nazi Party in 1932 and became useful to Hitler as a go-between during the rise to power, even though other leading Nazis detested him. Ribbentrop was Ambassador to Britain from 1936. In February 1938, he became Foreign Minister. He played a key role in the Munich conference and also negotiated the Nazi–Soviet Pact in August 1939. His influence declined during the war. In 1946, he was tried for war crimes at Nuremberg and executed.

The reason Mussolini wanted an alliance with Hitler is not because he wanted war. It is because he did not want war. Initially, Mussolini had ridiculed Hitler. Now he feared him. There was a certain affinity between Fascism and National Socialism but this was more to do with what they were against than what they were for. Mussolini chose Germany for two simple reasons, fear and greed. Britain wanted merely to stop an alliance between Hitler and Mussolini. This was fine as an aim but to achieve it Britain would have to offer Italy an alliance. This, Britain was not prepared to do. While Britain showed only limp interest, Hitler was full of seductive urgency. But Mussolini was still interested in his traditional policy of playing one side off against the other.

6 *N. Farrell, **Mussolini: A New Life**, 2003*

Fig. 9 *Hitler and Mussolini together following the signing of the Pact of Steel, May 1939*

The Pact of Steel

The relationship between Mussolini and Nazi Germany finally became a formal alliance in May 1939 when the Pact of Steel was signed. The Germans had been pushing for such an alliance for some time – they suggested it several times during 1938. Mussolini's attitude was much more cautious, wishing to keep options open. When the Pact of Steel was finally negotiated, it came as something of a surprise, especially to many leading Fascists, because there had been little detailed preparation beforehand.

On the German side, the negotiations leading to the Pact of Steel were logical and focused. Hitler knew he was going to war against Poland in the autumn of 1939. He wanted to cement an alliance with Italy in order to tie down British and French forces in the Mediterranean while his armies were fighting in the East (and to make absolutely certain that Mussolini would not suddenly switch sides). In April, Hitler sent Hermann Göring to Rome to convince Mussolini of the military strength of Germany and reassure him that he need not worry about going to war for another two or three years. Then it was arranged that Joachim von Ribbentrop would meet Ciano in Milan on 6 and 7 May to discuss a 'friendship' pact.

On the Italian side, the negotiations were muddled and improvised at the last moment. Mussolini was thinking in terms of being ready for war some time in 1943. He was still tempted by the idea of Italy holding the balance of power in Europe and not being committed to a formal alliance. He was hoping that the invasion of Albania, launched in April 1939, would demonstrate Italian strength. Late on 6 May, however, Mussolini made a sudden, apparently impulsive decision. He telephoned Ciano in Milan and told him to go ahead with a full alliance, which was more than the Germans had been asking for.

There was no detailed planning behind this and the actual terms of the Pact of Steel were drawn up by the German side, without any haggling over the details by Ciano. The agreement reached in Milan was then signed two weeks later on 22 May, in Berlin.

A closer look

Mussolini's foreign policy and the historians

Why Mussolini moved away from Britain and France and became the ally of Nazi Germany is not easy to explain. It may not even have been what Mussolini actually wanted, though this claim is a matter of dispute. Many historians, especially Denis Mack Smith in *Mussolini's Roman Empire,* put the blame squarely on the errors and muddled thinking of Mussolini himself. The pro-Mussolini biography by Nicholas Farrell, *Mussolini: A New Life,* blames British policymakers, above all Anthony Eden, for missing numerous opportunities to maintain good relations with Mussolini. According to Farrell, it was only when he became convinced there was no possibility of making a worthwhile deal with the British and the French that Mussolini decided it was necessary to side decisively with Germany.

In recent years, historians such as MacGregor Knox, Robert Mallett and John Gooch have strongly disagreed with this view of Mussolini as a 'rational opportunist'. They emphasise the vital role of ideology in shaping his foreign policies, and the great extent to which the links between Mussolini and the armed forces from the early 1920s onwards revealed long-term plans for deliberate wars of aggression. The title of Knox's book, *Mussolini Unleashed 1939–41,* reflects this view that Mussolini was ideologically driven and had a single-minded determination to launch war, even before 1935. In *Mussolini and his Generals,* Gooch argues that 'only the poor state of the Italian armed forces held him back'.

Deciding between the rival interpretations of Mussolini's foreign aims is difficult because Mussolini's words and actions were so often contradictory and deceptive, at times even to himself.

Mussolini had second thoughts almost immediately after the Pact of Steel had been signed. He sent a memorandum to von Ribbentrop a week later, stressing that Italy did not want any major war for the next three years – something he had omitted to include in the specific terms of the Pact. On the other hand, this memorandum still clearly showed Mussolini's aggressive intentions in the longer term; it was full of statements about Italian ambitions to achieve a dominant position in the Balkans.

The invasion of Albania

By 1939, Albania was already under virtually complete Italian control. Italy had exclusive rights for mining operations, oil exploration and fishing in the Adriatic. Italians controlled Albania's banks. The ruler of Albania, King Zog, depended on Italian 'loans' (there was no chance he could ever repay them) to carry on the business of government and administration. Italians held many key posts in the army, the civil service and the government. From 1938, Mussolini and Ciano began to make practical preparations for the complete annexation of Albania.

Key profile

King Zog of Albania (1895–1961)

Ahmet Zogu was President of Albania, with dictatorial powers, from 1925. He was crowned King of the Albanians in 1928 and reigned until 1939. During the 1930s, King Zog depended heavily on economic and military support from Italy; his efforts to resist Italian influence were not very effective. When Italian forces invaded Albania in April 1939, King Zog escaped into exile in England. Albania became an Italian protectorate until the end of the war.

In April 1939, Mussolini launched the invasion of Albania. One key motive for this was the idea that taking over Albania would 'compensate' Italy for the loss of influence over Austria after Hitler's Anschluss in March 1938. There were also economic motives. Fascist leaders, especially Ciano, convinced themselves that Albania was a potentially rich country, ripe for economic exploitation and for settling 2 million Italians there. In reality, Albania was already costing Italy far more money than any supposed profits that were gained. Italy was concerned to keep a monopoly influence in Albania and moved quickly to block attempts by King Zog to encourage foreign investment from Germany and Japan – but the drive to annex Albania was really about empire and prestige, not economics.

Activity

Revision exercise

Use the evidence in this chapter to write a paragraph evaluating the importance of economic factors for Mussolini's foreign policies between 1935 and 1939.

The military operations of the Italian forces were bungled and badly led (an Italian diplomat claimed sarcastically that, 'if the Albanians had possessed a reasonably efficient Fire Brigade, they could have driven us back into the sea)' but it was a one-sided war. Italy took complete control of Albania. King Zog went into exile and Victor Emmanuel became King of Albania as well as Italy. Mussolini's propaganda machine presented it as a great triumph, but the invasion of Albania actually showed how unprepared the Italian armed forces were for a major conflict.

Why did Italy remain non-belligerent in 1939?

Although Mussolini had signed the Pact of Steel in May 1939, clearly committing Italy to support Germany in any future war, Italy remained 'non-belligerent' after Hitler's invasion of Poland on 1 September until June 1940, when the German conquest of France was already nearly complete. Mussolini insisted that Italy's position was not neutrality. The term 'non-belligerent' indicated that Italy was clearly on Germany's side, even though not yet taking part in any fighting.

Italy's 'non-belligerence' in 1939–40 revealed that even the Pact of Steel had not finally ended Mussolini's indecision in foreign policy. There are several possible reasons why Mussolini decided to stay on the sidelines:

- Despite all his aggressive actions since 1935 and the serious disagreements with Britain and France, Mussolini still wanted to keep his options open. He always had mixed feelings about the German alliance, even after entering the war on Germany's side in 1940.
- Despite all his propaganda boasts about military greatness, he was afraid war might expose the fact that Italy was not militarily or economically ready for a major conflict.
- Mussolini had entered the Pact of Steel thinking in terms of making war in 1943 or even later. He had not realised how soon Hitler would attack Poland. When the war was imminent in the summer of 1939, Mussolini made desperate appeals to Hitler not to do it.
- Hitler did not really need Mussolini's help in Poland. For Germany, the value of the alliance with Italy was that Italian forces would tie down British and French forces and hinder any attempt they made to invade Germany, while Hitler's armies were busy in Poland.
- After the rapid defeat of Poland, the war in Europe entered the long lull in hostilities known as **the 'Phoney War'**. Mussolini was thus able to sit on the sidelines through the winter of 1939–40, waiting for Hitler's next move. Until almost the last moment in June 1940, Mussolini had the opportunity to stay out of Hitler's war – if he wanted to.

Key terms

The 'Phoney War': the nickname coined in Britain for the inaction in the European war between the conquest of Poland at the end of September 1939 and the launch of Hitler's invasion in the West in April 1940. There were almost no military operations during these months; for a time, Hitler was hopeful that Britain and France would actually make peace with him.

Activity

Revision exercise

Using the evidence in this chapter and that in Chapter 7, assemble a range of evidence to support the view that:

a. Mussolini allied himself to Nazi Germany because of his admiration for Hitler and Germany.
b. Mussolini allied himself to Nazi Germany because of the mistaken policies of Britain and France.

Learning outcomes

In this section, you have seen how Mussolini's foreign policy was informed by a personal desire for glory, plus ambitions for an Italian Empire and control of the 'Mare Nostrum'. His sense of destiny was fuelled by a series of foreign policy successes during the 1920s and 1930s, including a military triumph in the invasion of Abyssinia. Yet, you should also have gained an understanding of the weaknesses and indecision in Mussolini's foreign policy, and the problems within his military forces. Most importantly, you should see how Mussolini steadily drifted away from a potential alliance with Britain and France, into an actual alliance with Nazi Germany, expressed in the Pact of Steel.

Practice questions

(a) Explain why Mussolini signed the Pact of Steel in 1939. *(12 marks)*

Study tip An effective answer to this question would explain a range of reasons, both short and long term, not just as a list but with some comment and differentiation – perhaps analysing Mussolini's very ambivalent attitudes towards Germany, or the ways in which he was influenced by others in the fascist regime.

(b) 'Throughout the years 1923 to 1939, Mussolini's foreign policies were very successful.'
Explain why you agree or disagree with this view. *(24 marks)*

Study tip The key requirement here is a clear, balanced argument in response to the question. (Balanced, of course, need not mean even-handed, it just means you need to show awareness of alternative views.) Your argument might be that Mussolini was indeed very successful until the fatal error of joining the war in 1940; or that he was successful up to 1935 before everything fell apart after the invasion of Abyssinia; or that his foreign policies were always unrealistic and over-ambitious and never achieved any worthwhile or lasting success at all. Whatever your interpretation, it should be set out clearly and concisely and supported by selected specific examples. It would be a mistake to try to give a comprehensive account of all foreign policies.

5 War and the fall of Mussolini, 1940–45

9 Mussolini's war, 1940–43

Fig. 1 *A satirical cartoon shows Mussolini as Hitler's prisoner*

In this chapter you will learn about:

- Italy's international situation in 1939–40
- Italy's entry into the war in June 1940
- Italy's war effort in the Mediterranean and North Africa, 1940–43
- the impact of war and defeat on Italy.

Mussolini was fanatically determined to subject the Italian people to the anvil of war. 400 000 Italians died in war and Fascism sent one million people or more to their graves. The blood of all these people is on the hands of Mussolini, who ranks just after Hitler and Stalin in the list of European war criminals in the Second World War. He was driven to hitch Italy to the German war machine by his vainglorious lust for territorial expansion; he wanted an empire just when the age of imperialism was already passing.

1 R. Moseley, ***The Last Days of Mussolini***, 2006

Involvement in the Second World War was disastrous for Mussolini and for Italy. Italian forces suffered a string of military defeats. The Italian economy came under massive strain. Italy's war effort was increasingly dominated by Germany and public opinion turned against the war. In July 1943, allied armies landed in Sicily. On 25 July, King Victor Emmanuel III suddenly removed Mussolini from power but the war did not end. Italy became the battleground for two parallel wars, one fought by Germans and Italians against the allies, the other fought by Italians against Italians in a bitter civil war. All these disasters stemmed from the fatal decision to enter Hitler's war in June 1940 – a decision made by Mussolini only when French armies were close to final defeat and there seemed to be no danger of a long war.

Italy's international position in 1939

Superficially, Italy seemed to have achieved a secure position in the world by the end of 1939. Fascist aggression had succeeded in Abyssinia and Spain and enhanced Mussolini's prestige, even though it had made him enemies. The Western democracies appeared weak, committed to appeasement. The invasion of Albania in April 1939 had extended Italian influence across the Adriatic and provided Italy with a springboard for further expansion in the Balkans at the expense of Yugoslavia and Greece. The signing of the Pact of Steel in 1939 meant that Mussolini was closely allied to Hitler's Germany, but it was not yet impossible to escape involvement in Hitler's war.

Mussolini, like most people, expected the war Hitler launched in 1939 to be similar to the First World War. He thought another long-drawn stalemate like that of 1914–18 would give him plenty of time and enable him to keep his options open. Mussolini did not believe that Nazi Germany would be able to gain total victory over France and Britain (he was not sure he wanted this to happen anyway), but it was almost certain to weaken them considerably and allow him to carry through his ambitions in Africa and the Mediterranean.

Italy's international position was actually far weaker than it seemed. Mussolini had accepted Germany's Anschluss with Austria in 1938 only because there had been no way he could have prevented it. The Anschluss made Germany bigger and stronger. It also ruined one of Mussolini's key policies, to maximise Italian influence over Austria. Fear of Germany was an important factor in Mussolini's calculations. There were even private discussions between Mussolini and Ciano that Italy might one day be at war *against* Germany.

Italy's armed forces were nothing like as powerful or as ready for war as the fascist propaganda claimed, or as foreign powers believed. The Duce's military and economic advisers told him that Italy's armed forces were not yet militarily prepared for war; Mussolini himself told Hitler in 1939 that Italy would not be ready for war until 1943. This was why, when the European war began in September 1939, Italy remained 'non-belligerent'.

Finally, there was the problem that Mussolini had no coherent strategy and the armed forces were nowhere near ready to fight a major war. Mussolini told his generals to make preparations for war but they had no idea when, or which country they would be planning to fight against. As the 'Phoney War' continued into the early months of 1940, therefore, Mussolini's aims were unclear. Most of the time, he expected Italy would eventually join the war on Germany's side but he was unsure when the time would be right. Occasionally, he discussed the possibility of long-term neutrality, 'while the two lions tore each other to pieces'. Some leading Fascists like Dino Grandi urged him to make a last-minute change of policy and join with Britain and France.

Despite what was said in private by the experts Mussolini continued on occasion to act as though Italy were militarily and industrially ready for war. He did this even though he knew that only ten divisions were ready to fight. He ordered a strict supervision over the publication of photographs in the press so as to give the illusion of a well-drilled and well-prepared army, but nothing was done to set up adequate liaison with the German general staff and no plans were prepared for attacking Malta or Egypt. The armed forces were simply told to be ready for war against France, against Britain, or against Yugoslavia, or in North Africa, or indeed even against the Germans.

2 *D. Mack Smith,* ***From Mussolini's Roman Empire****, 1977*

Outwardly, Italy was in a strong international position and Mussolini still had the freedom of action to consider these possibilities but, privately, he knew the Italian armed forces were still weak, despite the massive military spending in the 1930s. There was institutional incompetence and divisive inter-service squabbling between the army, navy and air force. Efforts to modernise the Italian army in 1938 and 1939 may actually have weakened its fighting strength: the chief of staff, General Pariani, was a great believer in mechanised warfare, especially tanks, but this involved massive expenditure and re-training and the process of transformation was only half-complete. Mussolini knew the army would not be ready for a major war until 1943, perhaps not even then.

Key profile

General Alberto Pariani (1876–1955)

Pariani served in the First World War and was a staff officer in the 1920s. He was Italy's head of mission in Albania from 1927 to 1933. As army chief of staff in 1936 (he was also Mussolini's deputy as Secretary for War), Pariani was responsible for an ambitious plan to modernise the army, with an emphasis on tanks and motorised transport. During the war, he was commander of Italian forces in Albania. He was captured by the Germans in 1943. He was acquitted of war crimes in 1947.

The reasons why Italy entered the war in June 1940

On many occasions during the winter of 1939–40, Mussolini had indicated that Italy would eventually join the war on Germany's side but this had never been turned into an irrevocable decision. There was still great uncertainty about when, and even if, Italy would finally take the plunge. One part of Mussolini hoped that the war might come to an end after Hitler completed the conquest of Poland. He still could not make up his mind. Count Ciano wrote in his diaries: 'One minute the idea of intervention alongside the Germans attracts him; the next minute he openly hopes for their defeat.' Ciano's account may not be a totally reliable guide to Mussolini's views because Ciano himself strongly opposed joining Germany in the war – but it is clear that Mussolini was still far from certain exactly what to do and exactly when to do it.

At the end of March 1940, just before Hitler attacked in the West, Mussolini explained his thinking in a secret memorandum. He gave one copy to the King and another to Ciano (Source 3).

> Even if Italy changed attitude and passed over to the Franco-English side, it would not avoid war with Germany. There remains the other scenario, which is a war parallel to that of Germany to achieve our own objectives which are summed up as follows: liberty at sea and a window on the ocean.
>
> The problem, therefore, is not a question of knowing whether Italy will enter the war. It is only a question of knowing when and how. It is a question of delaying our entry into the war as long as possible, compatible with our honour and dignity –
>
> a to prepare in such a way that our intervention determines the outcome of the war;
>
> b because Italy cannot fight a long war, cannot spend hundreds of billions.

3 *Memorandum written by Mussolini, 31 March 1940. Quoted in N. Farrell,* ***Mussolini: A New Life****, 2004*

Mussolini's memorandum sounded more decisive than perhaps it really was. It did not mention the serious limitations of Italy's military preparedness. But it provides some insight into Mussolini's thinking and shows he did not always believe in his own propaganda boasts. A few days later, in April 1940, Hitler launched his *Blitzkrieg* on Western Europe and swept through Denmark, Holland and Belgium. Mussolini had no more time left; he had to make a decision.

Students searching for a balanced explanation of Mussolini's motives for entering the war in June 1940 need to consider three interlinked factors: ideology; fear; and greed.

Ideology

Mussolini's ideological obsession with war and violence was not only for show. He really wanted war to glorify Fascism. Without war, Mussolini believed, Italy would slide down into the second division of world powers. He really believed war was essential in order to harden the Italian people, to make them into a warrior race and so transform Italians into Fascists. Mussolini also believed in the fascist ideology of action. He told Ciano that: 'It is humiliating to stand by twiddling one's thumbs while others are making history; to make a people great it is necessary to take them into combat even if takes kicking them in the backside'. Mussolini was also a prisoner of his own propaganda. He had been pumping out the fascist ideology of war for so long that he had built up a psychology of expectancy. He could not easily back away from war at the last moment.

Fear

Mussolini was afraid of what might go wrong in 1940. He feared losing popularity if he missed out on a victorious war. He feared losing popularity if he joined the war and it went badly. He feared how powerful and dangerous Nazi Germany would become if Hitler won a decisive victory in the war. He feared not joining the war soon enough. He feared

Fig. 2 *A Mussolini portrait, characteristically displaying his medals*

joining the war too soon and exposing Italy to a long war that the armed forces and the economy would not be able to cope with. Many senior fascist leaders, such as Grandi, De Bono and Balbo, shared Mussolini's fears that Italy was not militarily ready for war. Mussolini held back from war until the speed of Hitler's victories on the Western Front pushed him forward. By 20 May, military advisers were informing Mussolini that France would soon surrender. Greed came to the fore.

Greed

Mussolini was motivated by opportunism as well as ideology. The defeat of Britain opened up possibilities to break free from British sea power and fulfil Italian ambitions in the Balkans, the Mediterranean and Africa. The defeat of France opened the opportunity to make easy territorial gains. Mussolini had a 'shopping list' of territorial demands he would make at the peace settlement after the war, so it was essential to earn a seat at the peace settlement by fighting the war against France for just long enough (and suffering just enough Italian casualties) to be able to pose as an essential contributor to the German victory. Mussolini was afraid of German power but he also wanted to use German power to gain his objectives. Greed for prestige and territory proved stronger than his fear of the consequences of going to war.

Mussolini had more or less made up his mind to enter the war by 13 May, but dithered over precisely where and when Italian forces would attack. He announced that he would not accept concessions from France, even if they offered him Corsica and Tunisia, because he wanted to have war and the prestige of victory. Italy finally declared war on 10 June. There was a storm of nationalist enthusiasm in the press but public opinion at large was not in favour of war. Mussolini hoped this would change when the excitement of victory arrived.

The Italian people were not the only ones who were not enthusiastic about Italy joining the war in France. Hitler was not in favour either. Earlier, in the winter of 1939–40, Hitler had strongly urged Mussolini to provide military support; in June, with Germany on the edge of victory, Italian intervention was more of a nuisance than a help. By this time, it was clear to Hitler that Mussolini wanted the Germans to provide Italy with victory on a plate.

> The Italy that went to war on 10 June, believing it would last only a few days or weeks, was an Italy not only materially unprepared but psychologically exhausted, tired of warlike speeches and inwardly convinced that the victory would be a victory of the Germans, a much more dangerous thing than defeat.

4 *Comments by the journalist and historian Indro Montanelli. Quoted in N. Farrell, **Mussolini: A New Life**, 2004*

The consequences of Mussolini's decision to enter the war were momentous, leading to the collapse of the fascist regime and to years of hardship, defeat and civil war in Italy. Another fascist dictator, Francisco Franco, was wiser (or perhaps just luckier) than Mussolini. Franco, too, came under pressure from Hitler to join the war in 1940, but Franco kept Spain out. Mussolini was overthrown in 1943 and was eventually captured and killed by anti-fascist partisans in 1945. Francisco Franco ruled Spain until 1975 and died peacefully, in his own bed.

Exploring the detail

Mussolini's 'shopping list'

Mussolini hoped that Italian entry into the war in 1940 would be rewarded by significant territorial gains from France. The first aim was to secure lands in south-west France that Italy had hoped to gain in 1870, especially Nice. The second aim was possession of the island of Corsica. The third aim was Italian domination over the French colonies in Tunisia. If (Mussolini thought it was when) Britain surrendered, Italy would take over further territories in Egypt and East Africa. Mussolini also expected to gain Malta, Crete and perhaps Cyprus.

Activity

Thinking point

Looking at Source 4 and using the evidence in this chapter, list **five** key reasons why Mussolini took Italy into the war in June 1940.

Key chronology

Hitler's Blitzkrieg, 1940

18 March	Meeting between Mussolini and Hitler at Brenner Pass
9 April	Invasion of Denmark and Norway
10 May	Invasion of Low Countries
25 May	Start of British evacuation at Dunkirk
10 June	Italian declaration of war
20 June	French surrender

Italy's war effort in the Mediterranean and North Africa, 1940–43

A closer look

Italy and the Second World War

The war that began in September 1939 was not really a world war at all. It was a European war that, much later, turned into a world war, involving the USSR, the United States and Japan. There were three important phases of the war.

Act One: September 1939 to November 1941, The War That Hitler Won

Hitler's Blitzkrieg victories began with the rapid conquest of Poland in September 1939. Britain and France declared war but did not attack Germany. The USSR, the United States and Japan were not involved. After the 'Phoney War' in the winter of 1939–40, Hitler launched his invasion in the West in April 1940; by the end of June the Germans occupied most of western Europe. Britain fought on alone. In October 1940, Mussolini launched his 'parallel war' in the Mediterranean and Africa. In 1941, Germany intervened in Italy's war and conquered Greece and Yugoslavia. In June 1941, Hitler began his invasion of the USSR and seemed on the edge of total victory by November.

Act Two: December 1941 to July 1943, World At War

Hitler's conquests were halted in December 1941. The USSR avoided defeat. The Japanese attack on Pearl Harbour brought the United States into the war. There was now a true world war between the Axis (Hitler, Mussolini and Japan) and the Grand Alliance (the USSR, the Americans and the British) in Russia, the Pacific, in the Atlantic and in the skies over Germany. Italy's 'parallel war' in the Balkans, the Mediterranean and North Africa became part of this world war. In the summer of 1943, the war turned decisively in favour of the allies and the Axis powers were forced on to the defensive. The allies invaded southern Italy; the country turned against Mussolini and the King dismissed him.

Act Three: August 1943 to August 1945, The Slow Death of the Axis

By July 1943, it was clear the Axis powers would ultimately be defeated but this defeat took at least a year longer than the allies hoped. Progress by the Americans in the Pacific, the allied invasion of western Europe and the Soviet advance from the East was painfully slow. It was the same in Italy, where the German forces were still stubbornly occupying northern Italy in early 1945. The war in Europe did not end until May; the war in the Far East was only ended in August 1945, after the use of atomic bombs on Japanese cities. By then, Mussolini was dead and Italy was moving from Fascism to democracy.

There were two distinct phases in Italy's war. In the first phase, up to May 1941, Mussolini attempted to run his own 'parallel war' separate from Germany's. This phase came to a sudden and humiliating end when Italian armies suffered a string of defeats and Hitler was forced into major military intervention in the Balkans and in North Africa. From then on, there was no real pretence of any independent Italian war effort. Italy became merely a subordinate ally in the German war.

Mussolini's war, 1940–41

Because Mussolini's entry into the war had been left until the last possible moment, there was barely enough time for Italian forces to do sufficient fighting (and suffer sufficient casualties) to justify Mussolini's military intervention. German forces reached Paris on 14 June, three days before Italian armies were even ordered into action and six days before they did any fighting. On 21 June, Mussolini met Hitler in Munich. The next day, the new French Chief of State, Marshal Pétain, signed an armistice with Hitler. Mussolini was not even invited to the signing of the armistice. Italy's war had lasted 100 hours.

Mussolini had hoped to gain Tunisia and Corsica, to occupy south-west France and to seize the French fleet but his only reward for the invasion of Menton, just over the French-Italian border on the Riviera (at the cost of 630 dead Italian soldiers) was the very small strip of territory his troops had occupied. Mussolini had made no serious contribution to the defeat of France and he made no serious gains from it either.

Afterwards, Mussolini blamed Hitler for failing to take the opportunity to seize control of the Mediterranean in the summer of 1940. It would have been relatively easy to take Malta from Britain and to occupy the whole coast of southern France and French North Africa. Hitler did not care much about the Mediterranean. He was happy to leave southern France under the control of Pétain's new French government at Vichy. As for Malta and the rest of the Mediterranean, the German view was that if Mussolini wanted them badly enough he could have sent Italian armies out to do the job on their own, instead of wasting resources on an unnecessary invasion of France.

Mussolini did not take advantage of the opportunity to attack Britain in the Mediterranean in the summer of 1940, when he might have been able to seize Egypt and the Suez Canal. Some historians consider that Italy might have acted more aggressively if Italo Balbo had taken charge of the war effort in North Africa, but Balbo was killed when his plane was shot down (by his own side) when landing at Tobruk on 28 June 1940. Balbo's replacement, Marshal Graziani, had no intention of 'taking risks'. Instead of acting independently, Italy spent months waiting for Hitler to win the Battle of Britain. It was only in September that Graziani began the invasion of Egypt; and this was soon overshadowed by Mussolini's decision to launch the invasion of Greece.

On 28 October, 70,000 Italian troops invaded Greece across the frontier with Albania. Why Mussolini chose to attack Greece, rather than more strategically important targets such as Malta, Crete or Egypt, is something of a puzzle. Greece had been low on his list of priorities until this point – Mussolini had actually said in late August that North Africa was more important for Italy than the Balkans. One possible explanation is that Germany had suddenly invaded Romania two weeks earlier. This infuriated Mussolini because, once again, Hitler had not told him in advance and because he regarded the Balkans as an Italian sphere of influence. Some historians claim that Mussolini was egged on by Ciano – the invasion of Greece has often been labelled 'Ciano's war'.

Cross-reference

Italo Balbo is profiled in Chapter 1 on page 10.

Graziani is profiled in Chapter 7 on page 90.

Key chronology

Italy at war, 1940–43

1940 June	Italy's entry into the war
1940 September	Small-scale invasion of Egypt
1940 October	Failure of Italian invasion of Greece
1940 November	Naval defeat at Taranto
1941 May	German invasion of Yugoslavia
1941 June	German takeover of war effort in North Africa
1943 July	Allied landings in Sicily; fall of Mussolini

Activity

Thinking point

Write a secret report from an Italian military expert in October 1940, warning the government about the possible adverse consequences of invading Greece.

Mussolini's plans depended upon a short, victorious war. Neither the Italian armed forces nor the economy was geared up for a long conflict. But the war went badly. Winter was already approaching when the invasion began. The invasion force was too small. The Italian generals in command were incompetent. On 11 November, while the land war was floundering, British naval forces badly damaged the Italian battle fleet in the Gulf of Taranto. Italian forces were pushed out of Greece back into Albania. Mussolini sacked his top general, Marshal Badoglio, and sent massive reinforcements but the war continued to go badly. In March 1941, Britain inflicted another crushing naval defeat at Cape Matapan off the south coast of Greece. Several Italian warships were sunk.

Cross-reference

Badoglio is profiled in Chapter 7 on page 90.

The situation in the North African war was just as bad. British forces in Egypt were badly outnumbered by Graziani's army but had superior air power. The Italians were first stopped and then pushed backwards. By the end of January 1941, 125,000 Italians had been taken prisoner. The British captured Tobruk and seemed certain to occupy the whole of Libya. Marshal Graziani resigned in February. There was a similar British counterattack in Abyssinia. Again, the Italians suffered defeats by smaller British forces. By April 1941, Italy had lost all the gains made in 1935–36. The Emperor Haile Selassie made a triumphant return from exile.

Mussolini's parallel war was turning into a disaster. In February 1941, a small but well-equipped German army, the Afrika Korps, commanded by General Erwin Rommel, arrived in Libya to rescue the situation. The Afrika Korps quickly stabilised the front in North Africa and started advancing eastwards into Egypt again. This was the beginning of the German takeover of Mussolini's war.

The Germans in control, 1941–43

Hitler was even more determined to intervene in Italy's war in the Balkans than in North Africa. He was desperate to sort out the situation in time to launch Operation Barbarossa, his invasion of Russia, scheduled for 15 May. German forces invaded Greece and Yugoslavia on 6 April. Yugoslavia surrendered on 18 May. Greece surrendered on 20 May. The Germans had succeeded within two weeks; Italy had got nowhere in six months.

Mussolini's 'parallel war' was finished. The Balkans, which Mussolini had always seen as an Italian sphere of influence, was under German domination.

Mussolini did make some gains from the German successes. Yugoslavia was divided up and Croatia became a semi-free puppet State led by Ante Pavelich, the leader of the fascist militia, the *Ustase*. Italy was able to exert a lot of influence over the Pavelich government and was also able to take control of the long Croatian coastline along the Adriatic. But it was clear who held the real power in the German-Italian alliance.

On 22 June, huge German armies stormed across the borders of the USSR. Operation Barbarossa had begun. Mussolini volunteered Italian forces to support Hitler's war in Russia. 62,000 Italian troops were sent to the Eastern Front but this was only a symbolic gesture. The Italian forces were tiny compared with the millions of German and Soviet soldiers involved. Later, in the summer of 1942, the size of the Italian army on the Eastern Front reached 230,000. Most of them were lost in the terrible defeat at Stalingrad by February 1943.

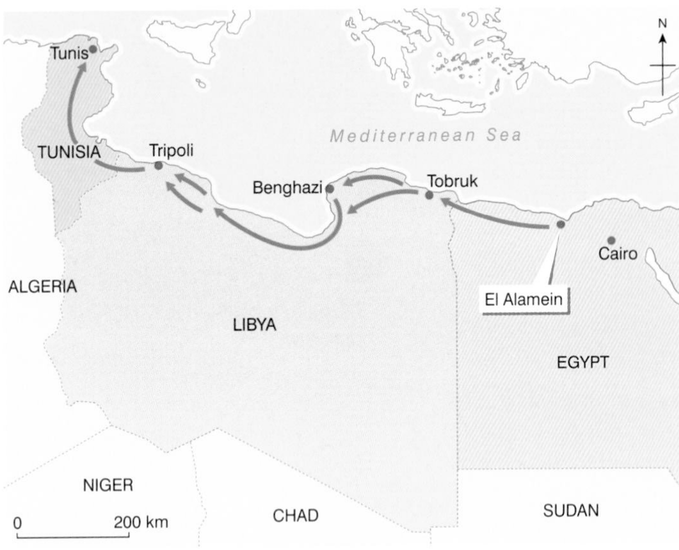

Fig. 3 *Map of allied advance from El Alamein, 1942–43*

In 1942, the war started to turn against the Axis. In April, there was a big effort to bomb Malta into surrender but this narrowly failed. Malta could easily have been conquered in 1940 but the opportunity had been missed. Failure to take Malta in 1942 made supplying Axis forces in North Africa by sea much more difficult. In June 1942, Rommel's advance through Egypt was halted at the First Battle of El Alamein. The hope of reaching the Suez Canal disappeared. In October, at the Second Battle of El Alamein, British forces broke through and started their final advance west. Two weeks later, American forces invaded French North Africa in Operation Torch. It was the beginning of the end for the Axis in the North African campaign.

In November 1942, Hitler ordered the occupation of the whole of France, brushing aside the Vichy government. The Italians were allowed to do what Mussolini had wanted to do in 1940 and occupied south-east France and the island of Corsica. But the war was going badly almost everywhere. In Yugoslavia, the partisans were becoming a major threat to the occupying armies. The German armies were bogged down in the siege of Stalingrad; they eventually surrendered in February 1943. Many people regarded this as the turning point of the war.

The military situation continued to deteriorate. Axis forces finally pulled out of North Africa in May. Everybody knew that the allied invasion of Italy would soon follow. The war was also going badly on the home front. During 1942, there were increasingly heavy bombing raids on northern Italian cities, especially Genoa, Milan and Turin. The Italian economy came under terrific strain and public opinion turned even more against the war.

Fig. 4 *Map of Italy at war, 1940–43*

The impact of war on the Italian economy, 1940–43

Italy was not prepared for total war in 1940. Mussolini had previously boasted about Italy having an army of '8 million bayonets' but, in practice, the armed forces amounted to just over 1 million. There were also serious deficiencies in equipment, especially the lack of modern tanks and artillery. To cope with a long war, Italy would have needed to mobilise all economic resources for the war effort. Other countries, such as Germany and Britain, placed great emphasis on running the war economy by central planning but Italy never really faced up to the economic requirements of 'total war'. Any advance economic planning had operated on the assumption that if war came, it would not last long. There was no serious economic reorganisation and no attempt to stockpile vital war materials before the war. As a result, Italy lagged far behind the other powers.

Table 1 *The war economy: Total GDP (Gross Domestic Product, i.e. value of the national economy in $ billions), 1939–45*

	1939	1940	1941	1942	1943	1944	1945
Italy	151	147	144	145	137	117	92
Germany	384	387	412	417	426	437	310
Britain	287	316	344	353	361	346	331
United States	869	943	1094	1235	1399	1499	1474

The proportion of Italy's GDP directed to war production never reached more than 25 per cent. This was hopelessly inadequate. In Germany, the figure was 64 per cent. As a result, Italian forces were badly equipped in terms of weapons, food and clothing. Wherever Italian soldiers fought alongside German units, they noticed how much better equipped the Germans were. One reason why larger Italian armies were often defeated

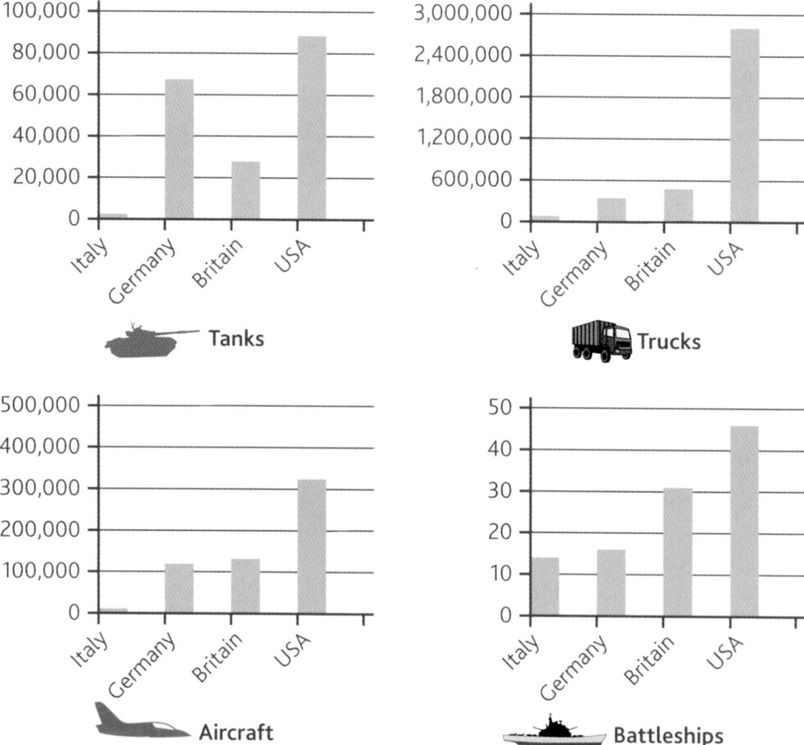

Fig. 5 *Arms production in the Second World War*

Exploring the detail

The Second Battle of El Alamein

The First Battle of El Alamein was fought on 1 July 1942 when British forces led by General Auckinleck halted the advance of Axis armies towards Cairo. Three months later, in November 1942, after a big build up of men and weaponry, the British Eighth Army led by General Bernard Montgomery defeated the German-Italian armies under Erwin Rommel and began driving them back to the West. This culminated in total withdrawal of Axis forces from North Africa in May 1943.

Activity

Talking point

How far was Mussolini master of his own destiny during 1940–42?

Activity

Source analysis

How might the statistics in Table 1 be used to support the view that the Italian war economy was mismanaged?

by smaller enemy forces in North Africa was that the other side had more and better weapons and equipment.

In theory, the fascist system should have been well suited to centralised direction of the economy, but this was not the case. Membership of the PNF increased, but the main motives behind this were the hopes of gaining perks and privileges as a party member or wangling exemptions from being called up by the army. The bureaucracy was inefficient and riddled with internal rivalries and corruption. This problem was made much worse by Mussolini's impetuous decision to appoint Aldo Vidussoni to the vital post of Secretary of the PNF in 1941. Vidussoni was inexperienced and out of his depth. The inefficiencies in the system got worse. One police report in 1941 noted the widespread belief that 'the war is the private business of the Fascists'.

Key profile

Aldo Vidussoni (1914–82)

Vidussoni trained as a lawyer and joined the PNF in 1936. He fought in the Abyssinian War and served with the Italian 'volunteers' in Spain, where he lost his right eye and his left arm. He then held important posts in the GUF. In December 1942, Vidussoni was appointed National Secretary of the PNF with special responsibility for propaganda. He was sacked in April 1943. He became a leader in the PRF (the Fascist Party of the Salo Republic) from September 1943. After the war, Vidussoni became an insurance salesman.

Steel production, vital for almost all aspects of the war effort, was incapable of meeting demands. There were serious shortages of raw materials because the normal flow of imports was cut off by the war and because the policy of 'autarchia' in the 1930s had not made Italy anywhere near self-sufficient. In 1942 and 1943, the economy also suffered from the loss of thousands of skilled workers who were transferred to work in German war factories. Of the leading powers in the war, only Italy failed to increase total production between 1940 and 1942. In 1941, German experts estimated that Italian industrial output was only 25 per cent of its actual capacity.

Cross-reference

Autarchia (autarky) is covered in Chapter 3 on page 49.

There was also a hopeless failure to keep the domestic economy functioning. The war years were a miserable experience for Italians, both in the cities and in the countryside. As early as December 1940 there were food shortages, with people complaining they could not obtain basic items such as olive oil, dried fish, rice and flour. Coal was also scarce. In January 1943, some rural areas faced a crisis in milk production because there was insufficient winter fodder for the cows. Food supplies were erratic and the system of rationing was mismanaged. The shortages got steadily worse through 1942 and 1943 as the tide of war turned against the Axis.

Allied bombing raids had a devastating impact. Industrial production, already low, was cut by 20 per cent. This was partly because of bomb damage to factories but the disruption to the workforce was an even bigger problem. Transport was badly affected. There were mass evacuations from the cities, often improvised and badly organised. Simply getting to and from places of work could take up half the day. Hiding in bomb shelters all night left workers too tired to work effectively. There was growing resentment against the war, against the Germans and against the regime. Propaganda put out by the regime to counter these trends had little effect.

Fig. 6 *Anti-fascist partisans, c.1944*

A closer look

The impact of wartime propaganda

One of the surprising things about Italy at war in 1940–43 was the failure of fascist propaganda. Philip Morgan claims that: 'Mussolini had the worst propaganda war of all the wartime leaders. Other leaders managed to inspire, reassure and reinvigorate their people with the right words, even in moments of defeat. This was beyond Mussolini.' Mussolini became cut off from ordinary people, which allowed rumours to spread. After bombing raids on Italian cities, Mussolini failed to make personal visits to inspect the damage and to keep up morale. Mussolini made only four big public speeches between June 1940 and July 1943. Even when he did make a big speech in December 1942 (his first for 18 months) it was a disaster. One woman wrote to her mother afterwards: 'the Duce's speech had demoralised me completely. I went home so depressed I could not eat anything.' Another comment at the time was that Mussolini was 'a dead man talking'.

In December 1942, Mussolini also made the disastrous decision to place responsibility for propaganda in the hands of Aldo Vidussoni, the new National Secretary of the PNF, Vidussoni *seemed* a good choice because he was 28 years old and so 'in tune' with the dynamic younger generation. He also had the right warrior image because he had fought in Abyssinia and in Spain, where he was badly wounded and awarded a medal for bravery. The trouble with Vidussoni was that he was an incompetent administrator who made numerous enemies within the fascist regime. Under his direction, the fascist propaganda machine functioned very badly.

Cross-reference

The growth of opposition to the regime is covered in Chapter 10 on pages 124–5.

In the early stages of the war, most Italians had broadly supported the regime but as the war continued to go badly they no longer believed the propaganda. People blamed Mussolini for the defeats, for the bombing raids, for the black market and the scarcity of food. There was war-weariness and defeatism. National morale started to crumble and Mussolini's popularity declined.

> The successful beginning of warlike activities by our troops induced the majority of the townspeople to judge the prosecution of military operations with excessive frivolity. Therefore, the recent painful episodes in Greece and on the Egyptian front have surprised public opinion all the more forcefully, in view of the strength of their illusions of an easy war.

5 *Report by a police superintendent in Forli, December 1940. Quoted in M. Knox, **Mussolini Unleashed 1939–1941: Politics & Strategy in Fascist Italy's Last War**, 1982*

> Many, many pessimists see Italy as merely the protectorate of Germany. They conclude that, if we needed three wars, the serious losses of the Navy and the merchant fleet, the sacrifice of our raw materials and gold reserves, together with the closing of all our foreign markets in order to give away our own political, economic and military independence, then there is nothing to be proud about in the policies that have been followed and the results that have been achieved up to now.

6 *Internal police report in Milan, 1941. Quoted in M. Knox, **Mussolini Unleashed 1939–1941: Politics & Strategy in Fascist Italy's Last War**, 1982*

> Not only do many people no longer believe in victory, they also hope for a quick end to the conflict, whatever the outcome may be. They are not even concerned about what happens afterwards.

7 *Report from the police chief in Turin, December 1942. Quoted in P. Morgan, **The Fall Of Mussolini**, 2007*

> The labour force can barely make ends meet, working in absolutely miserable conditions, rounding out their family budgets with the pathetic proceeds of work by the women, or by various expedients including the not-so-concealed prostitution of young girls. Without such expedients, conditions become absolutely unbearable.

8 *Report by a police superintendent in Venice on the situation of unskilled workers in the industrial complex at Porto Marghera in 1943. Quoted in M. Knox, **Mussolini Unleashed 1939–1941: Politics & Strategy in Fascist Italy's Last War**, 1982*

Activity

Source analysis

Examine the four police reports in Sources 5–8.

1. To what extent, and why, might these sources be regarded as useful and reliable evidence about national morale in wartime Italy?
2. To what extent do the sources agree or differ about the situation?
3. Using these sources and the evidence in this chapter, write a brief summary of the main reasons why Mussolini's popularity was declining by early 1943.

Summary questions

1. Why did Mussolini take Italy into the war in June 1940?
2. How important was the personal role of Mussolini in causing Italian military failures between 1940 and 1943?

10 The end of Fascism, 1943–45

In this chapter you will learn about:

- why Mussolini was removed from power in 1943
- why Italy continued to be ravaged by war and civil war after Mussolini's overthrow
- the rise and fall of the Salo Republic
- the role of resistance groups in the Civil War in Italy in 1944–45
- the reasons why the fascist regime collapsed.

Key chronology

1943: the turning point year

16 January	Allied demand for unconditional surrender
17 February	Surrender of Axis forces at Stalingrad
7 March	Strikes in Turin and northern cities
11 May	Withdrawal of Axis forces from North Africa
10 July	Allied invasion of Sicily
19 July	Allied bombing raid on Rome
25 July	Dismissal of Mussolini
3 September	Secret armistice with the allies
8 September	Armistice made public
12 September	Mussolini's escape from captivity
22 September	Massacre of Italian troops on Kefalonia
23 September	Proclamation of Salo Republic (ISR)
16 October	*Razzia* of Rome's Jews

Fig. 1 *Mussolini (second left) and Clara Petacci (third left) hang in a square in Milan, April 1945*

Why do you come to interview me, *Signora*? I am dead. Look at what remains of me. Go for a swim in the lake, sunbathe, enjoy your liberty and all the wonderful things life holds for you. Don't concern yourself with a ghost.

The only doors that will open for me are the doors of death. And that is just. I have erred and I must pay. I have never made a mistake when I followed my instinct, but always when I obeyed reason. I do not blame anyone. I do not reproach anyone but myself. I am responsible, just as much for the things I did well as for my weaknesses and decline. My star has set. I work and make an effort even though I know everything is a farce. My star has set.

1 *Comments by Mussolini to a journalist, Maddalena Mollier, when she interviewed him at his villa near Lake Garda in March 1945. Quoted in N. Farrell,* ***Mussolini: A New Life****, 2004*

Mussolini fell from power not once but twice: first in July 1943, when his own Fascist Grand Council turned against him and King Victor Emmanuel III dismissed him; and finally in April 1945, when he was captured and summarily executed by anti-fascist partisans. In the 20 months between these two downfalls, the people of Italy experienced upheaval and suffering under two parallel governments during two parallel wars. In the South, ruled by a new Italian government under Marshal Badoglio, allied forces advanced slowly against strong resistance from the German armies. In the North, Mussolini came back to power at the head of the German-dominated puppet State known as the Salo Republic, causing a vicious civil war of Italians against Italians as anti-fascist partisans attacked the fascist brigades and German occupiers.

These two wars were a tragedy for Italy. Hundreds of thousands died and millions faced hardship as the war dragged on. The first main cause of this continuing tragedy was the failure to secure a negotiated peace during the Forty-Five Days after the fall of Mussolini. The second cause was the failure of the allied armies to deliver a knockout blow to the German forces occupying northern Italy in 1944. As a result of the long-drawn out war and Civil War, bitter social and political divisions were stored up for the future.

Opposition to Mussolini and his removal from power in July 1943

The years of war opened the way for opposition against the regime. Some of this opposition was a direct reaction against the war and the hardships it created for ordinary people. Other forms of opposition were more deeply rooted. Anti-fascist groups who had always opposed the regime sensed the opportunity to start organising resistance activity as the public mood turned against Mussolini. People stopped thinking that Mussolini did not know how bad conditions were and that he would put things right if only he knew; they started to blame him personally for everything. All this gave an opportunity to the anti-fascist opposition.

Previously, the divisions between the various strands of opposition had played an important part in Mussolini gaining and keeping power, but by 1943 the growing anti-war feeling enabled diverse opposition groups to reach much more agreement and unity than they ever had before. There were four key anti-fascist groupings – Martin Clark labelled them Actionists, Communists, Socialists and Catholics (M. Clark, *Modern Italy 1871–1982*, 1984).

Cross-reference

The impact of the war on the home front between 1940 and early 1943 is covered in Chapter 9 on pages 119–122.

By 1943, wartime conditions in the industrial cities were causing resentment among the 6 million workers in war production. They were working longer shifts, under tighter controls, struggling with bombing raids, evacuations, rationing and food shortages. Prices were constantly rising and there was a growing black market. These pressures culminated in a massive wave of strikes by industrial workers in March 1943.

The strikes began in Turin at the beginning of March and spread across northern industrial areas, including Milan. Altogether, about 100,000 workers were involved. This was the first major strike in Fascist Italy since the Corporate State had been set up. The workers were careful not to go too far. The strikes were usually in the form of brief, 'sit-down strikes', designed to make a point but not bring factories to a standstill, or to cost the workers too much in punishments or loss of wages. Even so, the strikes were a massive threat to the fascist system.

Cross-reference

The PCI is covered in more detail in Chapter 1 on page 19.

The strikes also became politically motivated and organised by activists from the PCI. The Communists had been driven underground for many years and were small in numbers, but they were very effective in focusing people's grievances, even though they were only a small fraction of the workers involved. In the Fiat works in Turin, 21,000 workers took part in the strikes but only 80 of them were Communists.

The strikes were not direct political opposition to the regime. The main demands were for more food, better conditions and an end to the war. There was no direct link between the industrial unrest and the fall of Mussolini. However, the protests were indeed politically important. They showed that many Italians hated the war and the way it had been run. The strikes showed that many people were losing faith in Fascism and losing faith in Mussolini.

Posters appeared proclaiming the anti-war message.

Fig. 2 *Italian anti-war slogans*

Another factor causing opposition was the ever-increasing dominance of Italy's war effort by the Germans. People wanted to know why 200,000 Italian soldiers had to be lost at Stalingrad, fighting Hitler's war on the Eastern Front. They wanted to know why thousands of skilled workers were shifted from Italy to work in factories in Germany. Many of the Italians who witnessed it objected to the harsh treatment inflicted by the Germans on the people in occupied Greece and Yugoslavia. Like the anti-war feeling, anti-German feeling led to criticism of Mussolini. This encouraged dissidents within the fascist movement to start plotting against him.

By mid-July 1943, Italy was close to defeat. Axis forces had pulled out of North Africa. Allied armies had landed in Sicily and were advancing northwards. Mussolini did not hesitate to blame others. He blamed the Italian generals for failing to carry out his orders. He blamed Hitler (at least in private) for wasting men and resources in the Russian campaign when he should, in Mussolini's view, have concentrated all available forces to win the war in Western Europe.

Most other people preferred to blame Mussolini. He was the man who had dominated Italian politics so completely since the 1920s. He was the man who had taken Italy into Hitler's war and who had commanded Italy's war effort. Now, many people reasoned, the best hope was for a quick end to the war by deserting the alliance with Nazi Germany in order to make the best peace deal possible with the allies. For those who wanted to pursue this course, Mussolini was no longer the solution to Italy's problem – he *was* the problem.

A closer look

Bringing down Mussolini?

The extent and importance of internal opposition to the fascist regime is still controversial. After Mussolini's fall, the Italian Communists claimed that industrial unrest and political activity on behalf of the workers had played a key role in bringing down Fascism. Many historians have disputed this, arguing that internal opposition had little or no impact on events in July 1943 and that communist influence in Italy only became significant much later, when the Salo Republic was already falling apart in the winter of 1944–45.

It is true that the wave of industrial strikes starting in Turin in March 1943 showed the depth of anger and disillusionment at the harsh wartime conditions and the impact of heavy bombing raids. It is also true that one reason the strikes spread was the influence of Communist Party activists who steered workers' grievances over pay and conditions towards anti-war and anti-fascist protest. On the other hand, the police and the Fascist Party officials handled the strikes quite skilfully. The key organisers of the strikes were arrested. Concessions were made to the workers on higher wages and back pay. Although the strikes showed dissatisfaction with the regime, there was no popular revolution. Police reports on the public mood in the first half of 1943 indicated that people were tired, apathetic and 'switched off', but not on the edge of aggressive rebellion.

Activity

Thinking point

After the war was over, why did the Italian Communist Party place such importance on the role of the left opposition to Mussolini before July 1943?

Cross-reference

Grandi's role in the early years of Fascism is covered in Chapter 1 on pages 11–12.

Fig. 3 *Count Galeazzo Ciano was Italian Minister of Foreign Affairs and Benito Mussolini's son-in-law*

Cross-reference

Giuseppe Bottai is profiled in Chapter 6 on page 73.

Did you know?

Mussolini never forgave Ciano for joining in the plot to remove him in July 1943. When Mussolini got back into power as leader of the Salo Republic in September, one of the top priorities of the new regime was the trial and execution of Ciano and other 'traitors' who had voted against the Duce at the Fascist Grand Council.

Cross-reference

The Salo Republic is covered later in this chapter on pages 131–4.

His regime may have been seriously weakened by industrial unrest but Mussolini was not overthrown by a popular uprising. There was little organised anti-fascist opposition to his regime until after he had been dismissed from power. Mussolini's downfall was brought about by a 'coup from above' – a decision by the half-forgotten King of Italy, Victor Emmanuel, to remove the dictator who had overshadowed the monarchy for so long. What prompted the King to take this step was a revolt against Mussolini from his own generals and from dissidents within his own Fascist Grand Council.

The Fascist Grand Council

Despite its imposing title, the Fascist Grand Council mostly existed to rubber-stamp Mussolini's decisions. Its members were mostly hand-picked by Mussolini who rarely, if ever, challenged him. Mussolini had not bothered to call a meeting of the Fascist Grand Council since the beginning of the war. The reason why he called a meeting of the Fascist Grand Council for 24 July was his belief that he could reinforce his authority by bullying the fascist leaders into declaring their support. By calling the meeting, however, Mussolini placed a constitutional weapon in the hands of his opponents. One of the key personalities ready to use this weapon was Dino Grandi, once very powerful in the fascist movement but virtually sidelined since 1939 (Source 2).

> Finally! Finally! After more than three years Mussolini has remembered that the Grand Council exists. So it is at the Grand Council that I shall attack and give definitive battle. I shall do my duty and am resolved to go the whole way. The moment has come to act, even if the King will not do so. I shall act. It's not possible to go on like this, not even for one more day.

2 *From the diaries of Dino Grandi, July 1943. Quoted in J. Steinberg,* ***All Or Nothing: The Axis and the Holocaust****, 1991*

Grandi started plotting with another discontented Fascist, Giuseppe Bottai, and Mussolini's son-in-law, Ciano. They worked on the undecided members of the Council to gain acceptance of Grandi's resolution that the Council had no confidence in Mussolini: 'The Grand Council announces the immediate restoration of all State functions, giving back to the King, the Grand Council, the Government, Parliament and the Corporations all the tasks and responsibilities laid down by our constitutional laws.'

When the Grand Council met on Saturday 24 July, many of the rebels were afraid of what Mussolini might do; several members went armed with pistols, one took a hand grenade. However, Mussolini seemed taken by surprise and had not taken any extra precautions, even though rumours had been flying around Rome for 48 hours beforehand. After a blustering speech by Mussolini and tense discussions around the table, Grandi's resolution was passed by 19 votes to 7. One of those who voted against Mussolini was his son-in-law, Galeazzo Ciano. Mussolini was slow to recognise the danger he was in. He seemed to assume that the resolution was all hot air and that things would carry on as usual.

Mussolini and the King

On the afternoon of Sunday 25 July, Mussolini went to see the King. Il Duce was still over-confident. He had bullied and humiliated Victor Emmanuel ever since coming to power more than 29 years earlier and he could not believe that the King would be a serious challenge. Mussolini gave a long report on the military situation, as if he were still in control of affairs. The King then interrupted him to say that the war was irrevocably lost and that he had decided to dismiss Mussolini and to replace him as prime minister with Marshal Badoglio. A stunned Mussolini was arrested, bundled into an ambulance and taken away as a prisoner.

Dino Grandi wrote in his diary that Sunday night (Source 3).

> An incessant demonstration in Rome begins and goes on until late at night. 'Viva Italia!' they shout, 'Viva Badoglio!' They curse Fascism and Mussolini. The crowd tries to storm the Fascist Party headquarters.

3 *From the diaries of Dino Grandi July 1943. Quoted in J. Steinberg,* ***All Or Nothing: The Axis and the Holocaust****, 1991*

Grandi and the other fascist leaders were premature to celebrate. They had supposed that Fascism would carry on without Mussolini but there was a violent reaction against the whole regime. People burned fascist uniforms and gave streets new anti-fascist names. The dismissal of Mussolini was popular with many people because they believed it would bring a quick end to the war. Hitler could see this, too. He immediately launched plans for the German occupation of Italy, for the arrest of the King and Marshal Badoglio and for setting Mussolini free again.

Activity

Group activity

Working in two groups, analyse the evidence in this chapter and assemble a range of factors to prove:

a. why several leading Fascists plotted against Mussolini in July 1943
b. why Mussolini was taken by surprise when they did.

Italy without Mussolini and the continuation of war

The Forty-Five Days from Mussolini's dismissal on 25 July to the announcement of Italy's surrender on 8 September had a crucial impact on Italy. The King and Badoglio hoped for a swift, painless exit from the war but had made only sketchy plans to negotiate peace with the allies. They did not move quickly or decisively enough. Hitler did. Most of northern Italy came under complete German control. Mussolini was released from captivity and restored to power. The Italian people had to endure nearly two more years of war and Civil War.

The King and Badoglio feared the consequences of declaring an immediate end to the war. They wanted to get out of the war without losing their own power and without having to fight against the Germans. Grandi had advised the King that the only solution was to immediately change sides and to declare war on Nazi Germany, but Badoglio was terrified of provoking a strong German reaction by making such a move. He hoped for Italy to become neutral in the war, with allied and German armies pulling out, leaving Italy alone.

tutti gli italiani in quest'ora grave e decisiva per i destini della Nazione;

dichiara

che a tale scopo è necessario l'immediato ripristino di tutte le funzioni statali, attribuendo alla Corona, al Gran Consiglio, al Governo, al Parlamento, alle Corporazioni i compiti e le responsabilità stabilite dalle nostre leggi statutarie e costituzionali;

invita

il Governo a pregare la Maestà del Re, verso il quale si rivolge fedele e fiducioso il cuore di tutta la Nazione, affinchè Egli voglia per l'onore e per la salvezza della Patria assumere con l'effettivo comando delle forze armate di terra, di mare e dell'aria, secondo l'articolo 5 dello Statuto del Regno, quella suprema iniziativa di decisione che le nostre istituzioni a Lui attribuiscono e che sono sempre state in tutta la nostra storia nazionale il retaggio glorioso della nostra Augusta Dinastia di Savoia.

Fig. 4 *Fascist Grand Council resolution against Mussolini, July 1943*

Key chronology

The 'Forty-Five Days', July to September 1943

24 July	Fascist Grand Council Meeting
25 July	Mussolini dismissed and arrested
	Marshal Badoglio made head of government
26 July	Outbreak of peace demonstrations across Italy
27 July	Rome placed under German military control
3 August	Shooting of 23 demonstrators in Bari by Italian troops
19 August	Major strikes in Turin
3 September	Secret armistice agreement with allies
8 September	Public announcement of the armistice
9 September	Flight of King Victor Emmanuel III from Rome

This was hopelessly unrealistic because the Germans were determined to occupy Italy anyway, whatever the new Italian government did or did not do. There was no chance of Hitler allowing Italy to leave the war without a fight. During the Forty-Five Days, therefore, the Badoglio government moved too slowly and sent out confused messages, both to the allies and to the Italian people. In the meantime, Hitler rushed extra troops into Italy and stationed German units alongside Italian forces to guard against the danger of Italy making a separate peace.

On 8 September, news leaked out that an armistice had been agreed. A radio announcement was rushed out to proclaim the end of hostilities: 'The Italian government, acknowledging the impossibility of continuing the unequal struggle against the overwhelming power of our opponents, and with the aim of sparing the nation from further and more serious harm, has requested an armistice. This request has been met. Consequently, all hostilities against Anglo-American forces by Italian forces must stop. Italian forces, however, will resist attacks coming from any other source.'

The government broadcast was deliberately vague – it said next to nothing about what should be done about fighting against the Germans, something that was almost inevitable. The Badoglio government was still clinging to the impossible dream of getting the Germans out of Italy without having to fight them. Italian armies were based far and wide – in France, Croatia, Greece and the Greek islands. They received no clear orders. This resulted in dangerous tensions between Italian and German forces, as the Germans were determined to prevent Italian forces from surrendering or changing sides. The most explosive example of the chaos and uncertainty was the massacre of 8,500 Italian troops by German forces on the island of Kefalonia in the last week of September.

A closer look

Kefalonia, September 1943

After the German conquest of Greece in May 1941, the country was divided up into zones of occupation. Italian forces occupied most of the Greek islands, including Kefalonia, where there was a garrison of 12,000 troops of the Acqui Division. In the summer of 1943, the Germans deployed military units alongside the Italians, because they feared Italy might be about to make a separate peace with the allies. When the Badoglio government publicly announced the armistice on 8 September 1943, the situation on Kefalonia became very tense. The Italian commander, General Gandin, faced a choice between joining with the Germans, surrendering to them, or fighting against them.

Most of Gandin's troops wanted to resist German demands to hand over their weapons. On 15 September, the Germans gave Gandin an ultimatum to disarm. When the ultimatum expired, the Germans resorted to force. There were several days of fighting, decided by the Germans' superior air power. The Italians surrendered on 22 September.

Even before this, the Germans had begun mass killings of Italian soldiers. General Gandin and his officers were shot for 'treason'. The massacre continued for a week. About 5,000 soldiers were shot. In a separate incident, 3,000 Italian soldiers who were being shipped to POW camps died when their ship sank after hitting a mine in the Adriatic. There were similar, smaller massacres on the islands of Corfu and Kos. The story of the massacre on Kefalonia forms the historical background to an excellent novel, *Captain Corelli's Mandolin*, by Louis De Bernières. In 1999, the book was made into a feature film starring Nicholas Cage in the lead role.

On the morning of 9 September, King Victor Emmanuel III and his staff evacuated Rome and left it to the Germans. General Kesselring moved very swiftly to station German military units in Rome. There were some instances of resistance against the Germans and several casualties, but within 48 hours the city was under German control. Rome would not be liberated until almost a year later, in June 1944.

Key profile

Field Marshal Albert Kesselring (1885–1960)

Kesselring was Commander in Chief South from November 1941, in overall control of German forces in North Africa and Italy. He started his army career in 1904, fought in the First World War and was chief of staff of the Luftwaffe from 1936. As Commander in Chief South, Kesselring was responsible for quickly seizing Rome after the armistice of 8 September 1943 and for masterminding the long and stubborn defensive operations that delayed the advancing allied armies in Italy throughout 1943 and 1944. After the war, Kesselring was sentenced to death for war crimes but was later released.

Activity

Revision exercise

Using the evidence in this chapter and in Chapter 9, list **five** main reasons to support the argument that:

a the continuation of the war in Italy after September 1943 was due to the avoidable mistakes of Badoglio and the King

b circumstances made it impossible for the Italian government to negotiate its way out of the war in 1943.

Fig. 5 *Mussolini is released from captivity by the Germans, 1943*

On 12 September 1943, the hopes of an early end to Italy's war were hit by Mussolini's escape from captivity. After his arrest on 25 July, Mussolini had been moved to various secure locations until he ended up at a hotel in a ski resort in the Gran Sasso mountains, north-east of Rome. This supposedly secret location was detected by the Germans who launched Operation Oak, a daring airborne raid by gliders and light aircraft, led by Otto Skorzeny. Mussolini was 'liberated' from Gran Sasso and flown to a hero's welcome in Vienna. The escape was a propaganda coup for the Germans and for Mussolini, who was effusively grateful to Hitler.

Mussolini, however, was not really free. He was going to be used by Nazi Germany as a political puppet. Mussolini was taken back to Italy where he became leader of the new Italian Social Republic (Salo Republic) with its 'capital' in small towns on the western shore of Lake Garda. He hoped he would be able to rebuild fascist rule, at least in northern Italy, but it soon became clear that the Germans had no intention of allowing Mussolini to be independent.

From September 1943, therefore, there were two different Italies. From Rome northwards, was the Italy still under German occupation, no longer allied to Germany on a supposedly equal basis but regarded suspiciously as a potential enemy to Germany and thus needing to be closely controlled. This was the situation facing Mussolini and his Italian Social Republic. South of Rome, recently liberated by the allies, was the 'Kingdom of the South', moving tentatively towards pro-Western democracy.

A closer look

Fig. 6 *Map of the 'Two Italies': the 'Kingdom of the South' and the Salo Republic, 1944*

The 'Kingdom of the South'

By the time of the armistice on 8 September, most of Italy south of Rome had been liberated and so came under the control of the provisional government established by King Victor Emmanuel III after the dismissal of Mussolini. Its first leader, Marshal Badoglio, was seen as too closely associated with the fascist regime; in 1944, the King replaced him with Ivanoe Bonomi, an old-style Liberal who was not tainted by Fascism. The Bonomi government had little real authority, however, because it was the allies who had ultimate control over the situation, especially in terms of the economy.

The slow progress of the war meant that ordinary Italians continued to live in terrible conditions and were still affected by bombing raids. For many people, smuggling and the black market were the only means of survival. There was a lot of corruption. This was made worse by the decision of the American secret service (the OSS) to use Italian-American criminal elements to link up with the Mafia in Italy. One of the few achievements of Mussolini's rule had been to suppress the Mafia in Italy – now the Mafia was back in business through official American backing.

Naples was liberated in October 1943. Rome was liberated much later, in June 1944. Although there was a lot of pro-allied enthusiasm at first, economic conditions got worse and many ordinary people regarded the allied troops as just another army of occupation. The retreating Germans inflicted a lot of damage and committed many atrocities. They also carried away with them a lot of machinery and industrial goods. There was no quick relief from the misery of the war and very many Italians became disillusioned and apathetic. There was little prospect of a smooth transition to a stable post-war Italy.

Cross-reference

Ivanoe Bonomi is profiled in Chapter 1 on page 9.

Did you know?

The 1946 feature film *Rome: Open City* directed by Roberto Rossellini gives a vivid picture of the lives of ordinary Italians in the ruined State of Italy during 1944 and 1945.

The Salo Republic

The Italian Social Republic (*Repubblica Sociale Italiana* or RSI) is commonly known as the 'Salo Republic' after the small lakeside resort on the western shore of Lake Garda, where some of the government agencies were based. However, the name is misleading. There was no real centre of authority for the RSI, as its various government departments were scattered over a wide area. Salo was in no sense a real centre of government and authority. Mussolini himself lived at Gardone, some miles north of Salo. Many key sections of the government were in Milan, several hours away by road. Mussolini had wanted his government to be based in Milan but the Germans blocked this proposal, on the grounds that there was too great a danger from allied air raids on Milan. The real reason was that they wanted to prevent Mussolini from having a significant power base – it suited them to have Mussolini sidelined at Lake Garda with his government ministers dispersed around northern Italy.

The Salo Republic lasted for 600 days. It had all the trappings of a sovereign State. Rome was declared the 'official' capital, although in reality it was completely outside the authority of the RSI. Mussolini was Head of State and Foreign Minister of a republic that refused to recognise the King of Italy. There was a full set of government departments headed by cabinet ministers, who were mostly loyal old-style Fascists. Among the key figures who ran the RSI government were General Rodolfo Graziani, the Defence Minister; Guido Buffarini Guidi, the Interior Minister; and Alessandro Pavolino, boss of the Republican Fascist Party, the replacement for the PNF.

REPUBBLICA SOCIALE ITALIANA

STEMMA DELLO STATO

SIGILLO DELLO STATO

Stemma della Repubblica Sociale Italiana proclamata il 18 ottobre 1943

Fig. 7 *The coat of arms of the RSI*

Key profiles

Guido Buffarini Guidi (1895–1945)

Buffarini was an ex-soldier who joined the PNF in 1921. In the early 1920s, he was a leader in the MVSN (Blackshirt militia) and he held various government posts in the 1930s. On 25 July 1943, he was one of the few to vote in favour of Mussolini at the Fascist Grand Council. As a reward, he was given the post of Minister of the Interior under the Salo Republic, but was dismissed early in 1945 due to allegations of corruption. He was captured by partisans in April 1945 and sentenced to death by a military tribunal.

Alessandro Pavolino (1903–45)

Pavolino was a journalist and fascist politician. He was leader of a fascist squad in the March on Rome in 1922 and was a youth leader in the 1920s. From 1929 to 1934, he was the local leader of the PNF in Florence. In 1943, he was made head of the re-formed Republican Fascist Party of the Salo Republic (PFR) and stayed in that post until April 1945, when he was captured and executed alongside Mussolini and Clara Petacci.

The RSI had an army, a navy and even an air force fighting alongside the German armed forces. Recruiting soldiers for General Graziani's army was difficult, but by July 1944 there were four divisions totalling more than 50,000 men. In addition, there was the fascist police force, the Republican National Guard (GNR) and various fascist militias, such as the so-called Black Brigades. These paramilitary groups played a key role in fighting the Civil War against the partisans.

The militias were often fanatical Fascists, rather like the squadristi of the early days of Fascism. Mussolini claimed that the Salo Republic represented a return to the ideology of 'true Fascism' (though it is striking that the RSI, a fascist State led by the founder of Fascist Italy, Benito Mussolini, did not include the word 'Fascist' in its title). Mussolini was keen to stress the socialist principles that he maintained had always been a key element in Fascism. He spent a lot of time stressing the importance of breaking away from big business and adopting radical 'anti-bourgeois' social policies.

Fascism has been liberated from all those frills which slowed down its forward march and from the too many compromises which circumstances obliged it to accept. Fascism has returned to its revolutionary origins in all sectors, especially the social one.

4

An article written by Mussolini in November 1943. Quoted in N. Farrell, ***Mussolini: A New Life****, 2004*

The creation of the Fascist Republic (the RSI) marked the return of Fascists who were more fanatically Fascist than Mussolini himself. The Fascists of the last hour were the Fascists of the first hour, many of them believers in the violent paramilitary Fascism of the early 1920s; now they were middle-aged men with paunches, squeezing themselves back into party uniform. Some, of course, had never really been away, like Farinacci and Pavolino.

5

P. Morgan, ***The Fall of Mussolini****, 2007*

The RSI was a state riddled with contradictions, corruption and incompetence, while also being an organisation willing to condone and conduct violence of the most barbarous kind. Fascist Italians became direct perpetrators of the Final Solution. Some 7500 Jews were collected, generally by Italians, and despatched to their fate in the East. Six hundred and ten lived.

6

R. J. B. Bosworth, ***Mussolini's Italy: Life Under the Dictatorship****, 2002*

Activity

Thinking point

Read carefully Sources 4–6 and look at the other evidence in this chapter.

a How far do these sources agree or differ in their view of the Salo Republic?

b Which one do you find the most convincing?

In reality, the RSI was far from being a real government and there was little chance of Mussolini putting his policies into action. There were many reasons for this:

- The RSI only controlled part of Italy, and even controlling that reduced area depended on the German armies holding back the advance of the allied armies. Keeping normal economic life going was very difficult.
- Mussolini was virtually a puppet ruler under close German supervision. He had no freedom of movement and his villa was under SS guard. His actual powers were very limited and he rarely made public appearances. He kept himself busy, regularly meeting 'important' visitors, but this was merely going through the motions.
- Mussolini was no longer the dynamic leader he had been in the 1920s and 1930s. He was ageing and frequently unwell. (He suffered from chronic stomach problems, partly because of his habit of consuming vast quantities of warm milk every day.) He was prone to bouts of pessimism, as Source 1 (page 123) shows.
- Even within the shrinking borders of the RSI, there were many Italians opposed to Mussolini's rule. Many people wanted a quick end to the war and saw Mussolini as the reason why it was continuing. There was a gradual increase in the numbers of partisans. By the middle of 1944, the fascist militias and their German allies were having to fight a vicious civil war against the communist partisans.

Fig. 8 *'Bandits and Rebels – here is your end', a poster of the Salo Republic*

Key profile

Clara Petacci

Clara Petacci (often known as Claretta) was the last and most loyal of Benito Mussolini's many mistresses. She was the daughter of a prominent doctor in Rome and was of a much higher social class than Mussolini's wife Dona Rachele, who was extremely jealous of Petacci during the time of the Salo Republic. In 1945, Clara refused the chance to escape from Italy and stayed with Mussolini until they were captured and executed near Lake Como.

Did you know?

Mussolini also had troubled family relationships. When Dona Rachele discovered that Mussolini's mistress, Clara Petacci, was living in a villa close to Mussolini, she made a tremendous scene, trying to climb over the gates of the villa before the SS guards reluctantly let her in. She then threatened Petacci with a revolver. Mussolini's son, Vittorio, continued to be an embarrassment by his corruption and flashy behaviour. Mussolini's daughter, Edda, became completely estranged from her father after Count Ciano, Edda's husband and Mussolini's son-in-law, was executed for treason in January 1944.

A closer look

Victims of the German occupation of Italy, 1943–45

After the armistice was proclaimed on 8 September 1943, the German army quickly consolidated its hold on Rome and northern Italy. The SS controlled security, including deportations of Italian Jews. Mussolini had passed race laws in 1938 but persecution of Italian Jews was mild until 1943. Then, in the razzia of

16 November, 8,000 Jews in Rome were rounded up for deportation. Most went to the death camps, though some were protected by neighbours, or by the Church. It is still a matter of bitter debate whether Pope Pius XII and the Church should be condemned as guilty of collaborating with the Nazis and condoning anti-Semitic atrocities, or applauded for working quietly behind the scenes to save as many Jews as they could. In the Salo Republic, there were also round ups of Jews, organised by Giovanni Preziosi, a fanatical anti-Semite who was Inspector of Race from March 1944, though other fascist officials occasionally intervened to overrule Preziosi.

The Germans also carried out brutal reprisals against the partisans. The worst was the Ardeatine Caves massacre, near Rome, on 24 March 1944, when 335 Italian hostages, 77 of them Jewish, were killed on the orders of the SS police chief in Rome, Herbert Kappler. Hitler personally demanded the killings in revenge for an attack by partisans the day before, in which 28 German policemen had been killed. It was not only a German crime; Kappler got a lot of assistance from the Italian police chief in Rome, who rounded up the hostages for him.

It is estimated that German forces and the fascist militias killed 9,500 Italian partisans during 1943–45. Mussolini denounced the Germans for 'stupidity' in using extreme violence (though he took no action to stop them) and there was also increased anti-German feeling among ordinary Italians. Germany controlled most of the political and economic activities of the Salo Republic until the end of the war. The government of the RSI had very limited freedom of action. Its economy was totally subordinated to the German war effort and many skilled workers were conscripted for work in factories in Germany.

The Salo Republic was always living on borrowed time. Sooner or later, the Germans would eventually be defeated and the RSI could not survive without the presence of German armies. The end of Salo, and defeat of the Germans, was accelerated by the rise of resistance movements and partisan fighters, especially on the left.

Key profile

Pope Pius XII (1876–1958)

Pius XII (Cardinal Eugenio Pacelli), sometimes known as 'Hitler's Pope', became the subject of huge controversy after 1945 because of his perceived failure to speak out against anti-Jewish atrocities, such as the round up of Roman Jews in October 1943. Pacelli was a diplomatic expert, who spent many years in Germany. He negotiated the Concordat between the papacy and Nazi Germany in 1933. He was elected pope in 1939. His defenders claim Pius XII's diplomacy behind the scenes secured protection for many Jews. His critics have accused him of virtual collusion with German, Austrian, Croatian and Italian war criminals.

Activity

Talking point

To what extent was Mussolini personally responsible for the violence inflicted on Jews and anti-fascists in 1943–45?

The left resistance movements

During the 20 years of Mussolini's rule from 1922, resistance from the left had been suppressed so effectively that it was almost non-existent.

By 1943, however, the social conditions of wartime Italy provided an opportunity for anti-fascist opposition to gain support. The left was able to make a political comeback. Some of the left resistance was led by men who had been in exile in the United States or in the USSR, but there was also a home-grown element.

There were several different strands of opposition on the left and many divisions between the various factions, but it did prove possible for them to cooperate at times, even though there was never a single united resistance. The CLNAI (Committee of National Liberation for Northern Italy) was formed in January 1944 as an umbrella organisation coordinating anti-fascist resistance in German-occupied Italy. The main groups were:

- *Actionists.* Moderate, middle-class opposition centred on intellectuals and left Liberals and led by Ivanoe Bonomi. They started to become politically active in 1940 and formed the Party of Action in 1943. About 25,000 of the partisans in 1944–45 were loyal to the Actionists.
- *Socialists.* Remnants of the old Socialist Party became involved in the resistance but they represented only a small proportion of the active partisan fighters.
- *Catholics.* Catholic opposition was centred on the newly-formed Christian Democrats (DC), drawing support from people who had previously supported the PPI, or belonged to Azione Cattolica. There were about 20,000 Catholic partisans. The Catholic resistance was not exactly on the left but was willing to cooperate with the left more than it ever had in the past.
- *Communists.* The best-organised resistance came from the Communists, who controlled more than 30,000 partisans. The impact of the Communists was increased by a change in policy by Stalin, whose traditional policy had been to forbid Communists to cooperate with 'bourgeois' parties. In March 1944, Stalin sent the Italian communist leader, Palmiro Togliatti, who had spent long years in exile (some of the time in Moscow), to Naples with instructions to collaborate with the provisional government and the other anti-fascist opposition groups.

Ecco i "Liberatori"!

Fig. 9 *'Here are the "liberators"!' An Italian fascist poster from the Second World War showing the Statue of Liberty as an angel of death, and Italian cities on fire after a bombing*

Key profile

Palmiro Togliatti (1893–1964)

Togliatti was a founder member of the Italian Communist Party (PCI) in 1919 and was leader of the PCI from 1927 until his death in 1964. Most of his career was spent in exile outside Italy. He was trained alongside other foreign Communists in Moscow and played a key role in the intervention in the Spanish Civil War. Togliatti went back to Italy in 1944 and led the PCI into the so-called 'Salerno Turn', which rejected armed struggle in favour of cooperation with democratic parties. The PCI took part in the first post-war governments until 1947, with Togliatti as Minister for Justice.

The PCI wanted to ensure that there would be strong communist influence in the post-war government of Italy. It also wanted to take the lead in the resistance against the Salo Republic in order to gain legitimacy. The PCI made a big effort to recruit partisans for the guerrilla warfare in the North. This took a long time to get going but was more effective and on a larger scale as time went on.

Did you know?

The communist resistance strategy in Italy was very similar to that in France and Yugoslavia. In each case, there was a determined effort to maximise resistance activities and to establish a communist monopoly over the leadership of the resistance. The success of Josip Tito, the leader of the partisans in Yugoslavia, provided a model for the Italian Communists to follow.

The resistance was a communist success story, although they were never able to monopolise the whole resistance movement. The Italian partisans were localised, with allegiance to many different parties. The partisans could not win pitched battles against the fascist militias in the North, but they were very effective in mobile hit-and-run warfare, such as sabotage, assassinations and ambushes. There were atrocities by both sides; whole village populations sometimes massacred as collective punishment. The larger partisan forces operated in the countryside but there were also urban guerrillas, such as the communist GAP (Patriotic Action Group).

The effectiveness of the resistance is often disputed. Certainly, the Communists after the war were guilty of exaggerating the scale of their activities, or at least of claiming they had made a big impact much earlier than they actually did. It was in the second half of 1944 that the resistance really gained momentum and many people joined the partisans very late in the war, when it was clear to see who the winning side was.

Fig. 10 *The execution of Achille Starace, 1945*

The resistance had more than nuisance value. Partisan activities in northern Italy tied down huge numbers of German soldiers and fascist militiamen by blocking their ability to move around and by forcing them into action in places they did not want to be. About 5,000 German soldiers were killed by partisans and another 25,000 wounded. The partisans also scored a propaganda triumph for anti-Fascism. One important effect of this was to 'legitimise' the PCI. A myth grew up around the heroic resistance by Italians liberating their country from Fascism. In reality, of course, it was not the 80,000 lightly-armed partisan fighters who defeated the German army. It was the massive force of the regular allied armies.

Fig. 11 *The allied advance through Italy, 1943–45*

Mussolini's capture and death

By April 1945, the Third Reich was facing its final defeat and the German occupation of Italy was coming to an end. Long before this, Mussolini had become only a pale shadow of the charismatic dictator he had once been. Even dictators grow old. By 1945, Benito Mussolini was 61 years old. It was 22 years since the March on Rome. In that time, Mussolini had aged and lost much of his energy and freshness. So had many of his loyal fascist supporters. When Mussolini made his increasingly rare speeches on the radio, he was not able to exercise the same magnetic power as in the early days. The Italy he ruled over was shrinking – so was Mussolini himself.

On 9 April, the allies launched their final offensive on the Italian front. (A few days later, American and Soviet forces met in the heart of Germany at Torgau-on-the-Elbe.) It was time for Mussolini to give up and leave. Sometimes he was fatalistic, convinced he would be captured and killed. The Germans expected him to commit suicide. Sometimes Mussolini expressed hopes of somehow escaping to the North, perhaps to Switzerland. On 25 April, Mussolini set off in the direction of Lake Como, in a long convoy of motor vehicles. He tried to persuade Clara Petacci to stay behind but she insisted on coming with him.

There was no real plan and it is not certain exactly where Mussolini was hoping to get to. He eventually joined a convoy of German military trucks on its way north. By chance, the convoy was stopped by a small group of partisans. They quickly saw through Mussolini's disguise as a drunken German soldier. Mussolini was arrested, taken down to the lakeside village of Dongo. The next day, 28 April, the local partisan leader, Valerio, ordered the immediate execution of Mussolini, together with Clara Petacci and some of the other fascist leaders who had been caught, including Alessandro Pavolino. The bodies were then taken to Milan, where they were placed on public view, hung upside down at a petrol station in a small city square.

Cross-reference

Clara Petacci is profiled earlier in this chapter on page 133.

Activity

Thinking point

Why do you think Mussolini was summarily executed rather than put on public trial?

Did you know?

Adolf Hitler was appalled at the news of the sordid treatment of Mussolini after his death. Hitler was very afraid of being treated in the same way. When Hitler committed suicide, together with Eva Braun, in Berlin on 2 May, he left strict orders that the bodies were to be burned beyond recognition.

Why the fascist regime collapsed

The main reason why Fascism collapsed in 1945 is the obvious one: it was in 1945 that the Axis was finally defeated. The retreat of the German armies meant that the Salo Republic could no longer survive. The end of Mussolini in 1945, however, was not the first collapse of Fascism. The removal of Mussolini from power in July 1943 was more significant. Again, there is an obvious explanation – that Fascism collapsed because Italian involvement in the Second World War had gone disastrously wrong – but there were other important reasons. The collapse of Fascism was due to a complex mixture of foreign and domestic issues.

The inter-relationship of foreign and domestic issues

Between 1940 and 1945, the fate of Italy was decided by domestic and foreign issues that were inextricably linked. Once Italy had entered the war in 1940, Mussolini found that he was increasingly losing control over the internal situation in Italy. From 1943 until the end of the war, allied armies invaded and occupied southern Italy; German armies dominated the situation in northern Italy. After the war ended in 1945, it was obvious that the post-war government of Italy would be along lines laid down by the victorious allies. The following list indicates how some, though by no means all, of the events that happened to Italy and to the Italian people was determined by the inter-relationship of foreign and domestic issues:

- If Italy had stayed out of the war in 1940 (or if the war had been the short victorious war Mussolini hoped for), Italy might have avoided the enormous economic strains and political upheavals that resulted from the war.
- Italy's attempt to fight a separate, 'parallel' war completely failed. From April 1941, the direction of the Italian war effort was dominated by Mussolini's German allies.
- The Italian economy, though it had not achieved the successes claimed by fascist propaganda, was doing comparatively well by the end of the 1930s. It became badly overstretched from 1940 as a result of Mussolini's unrealistic foreign ambitions.
- Mussolini lost a lot of popularity because of the consequences of his alliance with Germany. People resented the commitment of 200,000 Italian troops to fight on the Eastern Front at Stalingrad. They resented the fact that many skilled workers were taken out of Italy in the later years of the war to work in German factories.

- The Forty-Five Days from July to September 1943 showed how decisive foreign issues were. Italy might have escaped two years of the miseries of war if it had been possible to negotiate a separate peace and a swift exit from the war. This did not happen, partly because of the failures by Italian political leaders and partly because of the actions of the allies and, especially, of the Germans.
- Between 1943 and 1945, the lives of Italians in the 'Kingdom of the South' were shaped by the actions of the allied armies. Being fed properly, being in a job, even being alive, depended on whether you were in the way of the fighting armies, or hit by bombing raids, or adversely affected by rising prices and the black market. The Italian provisional government in the South could only act in ways the allies permitted.
- Between 1943 and 1945, the lives of Italians in northern Italy were shaped by the German occupation and by the partisan Civil War. The Salo Republic was led by Mussolini and his fascist government, but the RSI only existed because the Germans liberated Mussolini from captivity and put him back in power. The RSI only existed as long as German armies remained in northern Italy.
- After the defeat of the Axis in May 1945, the future of post-war Italy was at least as much in the hands of foreign powers as of Italians. The economy was desperately in need of foreign aid. The transition to democracy in post-war Italy was going to be influenced by the policies and actions of the victorious allies.

Fig. 12 *Allied forces liberating the town of Pachino in Sicily*

Activity

Talking point

Working in groups, assemble evidence and arguments for and against the view that: 'The collapse of Fascism in 1943–45 was mainly due to external factors beyond Mussolini's control.'

The legacy of Fascism by 1945

Mussolini certainly promised to change Italy. In many ways, he succeeded, both by design and in ways that he had never intended. Some of these changes were for the better, at least temporarily, but many were disastrously for the worse.

In one sense, the legacy of Fascism by 1945 was obvious. Fascism, or at least Mussolini's version of Fascism, had led Italy into war in 1940. The war had turned out badly. By May 1945, the Italian people had suffered five years of military defeats, economic hardships and occupation by foreign powers. Fascist Italy was in ruins, Mussolini was dead and his regime and its ideology were totally discredited. The legacy of Fascism could be summed up as a mixture of failure and evil.

There was perhaps more to it than that. The consequences of Mussolini's rule in Italy were undeniably more harmful than beneficial, but it is possible to make a retrospective assessment of Mussolini's achievements (some of them unintentional) as well as his evident crimes and failures (Figure 13).

POSITIVE	NEGATIVE
✓ Mussolini's fascist rule stabilised Italy after the post-war crisis of 1919–22.	✗ Mussolini's fascist rule involved systematic State violence and the crushing of civil liberties and the freedom of the press.
✓ Mussolini successfully dominated Italian politics for more than 20 years.	✗ The actual achievements of Fascism were minimal compared with the promises and the propaganda.
✓ He achieved historic and lasting reconciliation between Church and State.	✗ The Corporate State promised to overcome class divisions but was actually a right-wing conspiracy against the working classes.
✓ He modernised Italy's infrastructure and communications network.	✗ Mussolini alienated the Western democracies when it would have been relatively easy to make agreements with them.
✓ His social and economic policies reduced some of the inequalities in Italy and narrowed the gap between North and South.	✗ The alliance with Hitler and the decision to enter Hitler's war were fatal, avoidable errors. Mussolini followed the fascist ideology of war but completely failed to produce the military machine to carry it through.
✓ He ameliorated the effects of Nazi race policies and saved many Jews from the Holocaust.	✗ He badly mismanaged Italy's war effort both at home and abroad, causing massive military losses and terrible hardships on the home front.
✓ By discrediting Fascism so completely by 1945, he paved the way (unintentionally) for the transition to democracy after 1945.	✗ His failure to get out of the war in 1943 and his return to power in the RSI caused a vicious civil war and deepened the divisions in Italy.

Fig. 13 *Positives and negatives of Mussolini's rule*

Activity

Thinking point

Write an obituary of Mussolini to be published in a British newspaper after receiving news of his death in Milan.

Learning outcomes

In this section, you have looked at Italy's role in the Second World War and at the political and economic impact of the war upon Italy. In 1940, Fascist Italy had the outward appearance of success and international importance. Fascist ideology held sway; Socialism, Liberalism and democracy were in retreat. You have seen how Mussolini's decision to join Hitler's war brought Italy to defeat and caused the collapse of the fascist regime in 1943; and how the continuation of the war until 1945 deepened the political divisions within Italy.

Practice questions

In 1943–45, the main aim of the Communists had to be the liberation of Italy, not a socialist revolution. Togliatti made this explicit in the instructions he wrote for the party in June 1944: 'Remember always that the insurrection we want has not got the aim of imposing social and political transformations in a socialist or communist sense. Its aim is rather national liberation and the destruction of Fascism. All the other problems will be resolved by the people tomorrow, once Italy is liberated, by the means of a free popular vote and the election of a Constituent Assembly.'

A *P. Ginsborg,* ***A History of Contemporary Italy 1943–1988****, 1990*

[Palmiro] Togliatti had been a member of the Comintern which directed International Communism. On 27 March Stalin's Italian arrived by ship in Naples. His first move, on Stalin's orders, was to direct his Italian comrades, for the sake of national unity, to withdraw their objections to the abolition of the monarchy until after the liberation. His aim – and that of Stalin – was cynically simple: to ensure that the Communists formed part of whichever government replaced Badoglio. He did not interest himself in the Partisan struggle, which he rightly regarded as of minor importance. The Allies would liberate Italy, not the partisans. Togliatti and Stalin were thinking from the start of after the Liberation when the Allies had gone home.

B *N. Farrell,* ***Mussolini: A New Life****, 2004*

[This extract should be seen in the context of the earlier liberation of southern Italy by Allied armies without any involvement of partisan forces]

The situation was very different north of Rome. Here anti-fascists had to remain underground after the July 1943 coup. In these areas the Resistance played an active part in helping to liberate Italy, though the main fighting was done by the Allied armies. Numbering over 100 000 regulars by early 1945, the partisans launched a series of attacks on the Germans and the supporters of the Salo Republic. The communists especially fought a brutal war with Mussolini's remaining followers, which almost certainly increased the ferocity of the fascist response.

C *R. Eatwell,* ***Fascism: A History****, 1995*

(a) Use Sources A and B and your own knowledge. Explain how far the views in Source B differ from those in Source A in relation to the aims of the Communists in Italy in 1944. *(12 marks)*

Study tip It is important to make a direct comparison between the two sources, thinking about the overall message of each source rather than paraphrasing the literal meaning of the words in each source line by line. There are clearly many similarities here – Source A comes mostly direct from Togliatti, while Source B is explaining and commenting on Togliatti's views – but it is important to analyse the differences. Farrell clearly takes a very negative view of the role of the partisans – his tone and emphasis are very different from Source A. You should also use your own knowledge of the context of 1944–5 to explain and comment on the reasons why the sources have different viewpoints. (For example, do you believe Farrell is correct?)

(b) Use Sources A, B and C and your own knowledge. How important was the contribution of anti-fascist partisans to the liberation of Italy between September 1943 and April 1945? *(24 marks)*

Study tip It is essential to use the sources in your answer, but it would be a good idea to use your own knowledge to set out your answer to the question first. Then you can selectively use the sources to back up your argument. There are several relevant points and comments in Source A and, especially, Source B, but you will find the most plentiful evidence in Source C. A balanced answer would weigh the importance of the role of the partisans in the Civil War against a range of other factors, such as the dominant influence of foreign powers, or the inbuilt weaknesses of Mussolini's Salo Republic after September 1943.

6 Conclusion

Fig. 1 *'The destructiveness of Fascism': fascist squadrons, armed with cudgels, burning the newspaper* Il Paese *on a Roman street, during Mussolini's rise to power*

Italy after Fascism

When the Second World War in Europe finally ended, Italy had been badly damaged by war and Civil War. The national economy had virtually broken down. Almost 1 million soldiers had been killed. Millions of Italians had gone hungry, endured bombing raids, become homeless or unemployed. There was corruption and the growth of the black market. There was inflation; by 1945, the cost of living was 23 times higher than in 1938. The situation of poor agricultural labourers in the South was desperate. There was high unemployment, which persisted after 1945. Around 1.6 million were still unemployed in 1947.

Mussolini's promise to build a new Roman Empire had led to complete failure. All Mussolini's foreign conquests were lost and Italy was occupied

Exploring the detail

Look at the key profiles scattered throughout this book and you will see how the careers of many leading Fascists followed a similar pattern: they were 'Fascists of the first hour' who joined the Fascist Party in 1919–20, took part in the March on Rome, lived through the ups and downs of Fascist Italy and then died in 1944–45 – executed for 'treason' like Ciano and De Bono, killed by partisans, like Pavolino and Mussolini himself, committed suicide like Preziosi.

by foreign armies. The peace treaty between Italy and the Allies, signed in Paris in February 1947, stripped Italy of all its colonies apart from Somalia. Eritrea was given to Ethiopia. Libya was handed over to British rule and became independent in 1952. Fiume was handed to Yugoslavia and France took possession of territories on Italy's Alpine frontier. Far from achieving a new Roman Empire, Mussolini had left Italy a smaller, defeated nation with no empire at all.

Within Italy there was a dangerous political vacuum and bitter political divisions. Rebuilding the Italian State out of the ruins of Mussolini's Italy was bound to be a difficult and lengthy process. Between the end of the war and 1947, it gradually became clear who were the losers and who were the winners.

For the foreseeable future, Fascism in Italy was discredited. Mussolini was both disgraced and dead. So were almost all of the leading fascist personalities. There were some remnants of Fascism. Some old Fascists stayed loyal to Il Duce's memory. (There was a brief sensation when a small group of Fascists 'stole' Mussolini's body from its unmarked grave in Milan and hid it in a church in Pavia.) A new neo-fascist party, the MSI, was formed but got very little support. There was no prospect of any revival of Fascism.

Another loser was the monarchy. Despite the unification in the 19th century, many Italians had never really accepted the monarchy. From 1922 to 1943, King Victor Emmanuel III had been sidelined by Mussolini, who became the real figurehead of the Italian nation. With Mussolini as Head of State, it was hard to see any reason for Victor Emmanuel's existence. The King made a brief political comeback when he dismissed Mussolini in 1943, but was not able to restore his authority. Italy became a republic in 1946.

Surprisingly, the Communists were losers, too. They did well in the first post-war elections and the PCI leader, Palmiro Togliatti, had a key role in the new government as Minister of Defence. In the crisis that followed the war, there were genuine fears that Italy would be taken over by the Communists, like the states of East Central Europe. This was one of the main reasons for the American decision to pour foreign aid into Italy. From 1947, it was clear that Italy would be on the side of the West in the Cold War. The PCI was excluded from the government and remained in frustrated opposition for decades.

The winners in post-war Italian politics were the groups Mussolini thought he had destroyed in the 1920s. The extremes of Fascism and Communism were out; liberal democracy made a comeback. So did the political influence of Catholicism. The capitalist system was put back in place, with big business controlling the industrial economy again. Between 1950 and 1957, Italy became a founder member of the EEC (European Economic Community) – which, ironically, made Italy once again an ally of Germany.

The political leaders of the new Italy all claimed that they represented the values and achievements of the resistance. The numbers of partisans eventually reached nearly 3 million by April 1945, but the majority of these joined only at the last moment, when victory was certain. The effective fighting forces in the Civil War totalled between 80,000 and 100,000. About 10,000 were killed, 21,000 badly wounded and more than 9,000 deported to Germany. The partisans did contribute to winning the last phase of the war but the Italian resistance was never as united as it pretended to be, nor was it as important in overthrowing Mussolini as was claimed; but the 'Resistance Myth' was very useful for giving credibility to the post-war political parties.

Italy's first post-war government, led by Ferruccio Parri, was a coalition of Actionists, Liberals, the PCI and the Socialists. Parri's government gave a misleading impression of unity. Beneath the surface, there was a wide gap between the left and the right. After five months, a new government was formed, led by Alcide De Gasperi and dominated by the real political winners of post-Fascist Italy – the Christian Democrats.

The DC (*Democrazia Cristiana*, or Christian Democrats) appealed to business, the middle classes and Catholics. The DC was founded partly on the old PPI led by Don Sturzo between 1919 and 1922, and on the Catholic trade unions. De Gasperi and other DC party leaders had close links to the Church and the DC was strongly supported by the Vatican newspaper, *L'Osservatore Romano*. The Catholic Church succeeded brilliantly in convincing people that it had all along been anti-fascist; the many examples of collaboration with Mussolini's regime were forgotten. From 1947–48 until the 1990s, Italian politics was virtually a DC monopoly.

One reason for the dominance of the DC was the influence of the United States. American influence had always been strong in Italy. Before 1914, millions of Italians had emigrated to the United States. There was a lot of contact between Italian-Americans and families back in Italy. The presence of allied armies during 1943–45 had also 'Americanised' much of Italy, especially in cities like Naples. After 1945, Italy, like most of western Europe, was enthusiastic about American popular culture. This Americanisation was strengthened by the Cold War, with American troops stationed in Europe, American economic aid flowing in and American political influence directed towards making Italy 'safe for democracy'.

Mussolini and Fascism, therefore, faded away with remarkable speed. Italy ceased to be either fascist or in any way exceptional. In most respects, Italy became a normal western democracy. The memory of Mussolini and Fascism did not completely disappear. There were still half-buried bitter memories of the divisions and Civil War of 1944–45; and lingering fascist loyalties in the MSI and in the old generation of fascist followers. However, they were only ghosts of the past. In the 50 years after his death, it became clear that Mussolini, the man who had promised to change everything, had not really changed Italy much at all.

Glossary

A

Acerbo Law: the electoral law of 1923, allowing the victorious Fascist National List to claim two-thirds of the seats in parliament after the 1924 election.

Adowa: humiliating defeat of Italian forces in Abyssinia in 1896.

Alpini: elite mountain troops.

ANI: Italian Nationalist Association.

***Anschluss*:** union between Germany and Austria, which had been specifically forbidden by the Treaty of Versailles in 1919. Hitler, himself of Austrian origin, eagerly supported the idea of *Anschluss*, along with many nationalists both in Germany and Austria.

anti-clericalism: opposition to the Church having influence on politics and society outside the religious sphere.

anti-Comintern pacts: agreements between Fascist Italy, Nazi Germany and Imperial Japan in the late 1930s, based on joint hostility to Communism and the USSR.

AOI (*Africa Orientale Italiana*, Italian East Africa): the empire established after the conquests of the Abyssinian War in 1935–36.

***arditi*:** elite military units (storm troopers).

***autarchia* (autarky):** the policy of economic self-sufficiency, maximising domestic production and avoiding dependence on foreign imports. Autarky was linked to the ideology of Nationalism and being prepared for war.

ʿventine Secession: the name given ˀ the boycott of parliament by the ʳal and democratic opposition ꜱ in 1924. This action was ˀ on the practice in the ˀman Republic of 'going ˀne Hill', hence the Secession.

***Azione Cattolica* (Catholic Action):** Catholic lay organisation, sometimes in opposition to fascist organisations.

B

balance of payments: the relationship between the total economic value of income, from exports, compared with the total economic costs of imports. A balance of payments surplus is the sign of a healthy economy; a balance of payments deficit can push governments into economic crisis.

BN (*Brigate Nere*): the 'Black Brigades', volunteer militia groups formed to defend the Salo Republic.

Camorra: organised crime in southern Italy, centred on Naples.

Caporetto: the great battles between Italian and Austrian armies in the Dolomite Mountains in 1917–18, often known as the 'White War'.

***Carabinieri*:** Italy's national police force.

cartelisation: the encouragement of the growth of big conglomerate economic enterprises (cartels) through mergers and takeovers, in order to remove competition and to monopolise key industries.

CGL (General Confederation of Labour): the national organisation of trade unions set up under the Corporate State.

***Cheka*:** the secret police department of the fascist militia, the MVSN. The leader of the Cheka was Amerigo Dumini. The Cheka took its name from the secret police of the Bolshevik regime in Russia, set up by Lenin in 1921.

CNLAI (Committee of National Liberation for Northern Italy): organisation formed to coordinate the various resistance groups fighting to liberate Italy in 1943–45.

***Confindustria*:** was the Italian Employers Federation founded in 1910. After 1922, Confindustria gave financial support to Mussolini in return for fascist actions against workers and trade unions. From 1925, Confindustria was an important part of the Corporate State.

Corporate State: Mussolini's policy (often known as the 'third way') to coordinate Italian society and the economy, overcoming the conflicts between industrialists and workers.

***Corriere della Sera* (Evening Courier):** major national newspaper, published in Milan since 1876.

coup d'état: overturning a government and seizing power by the use of force.

culture: all forms of the arts and entertainment (art, architecture, cinema, radio, literature, theatre and music), both 'high' culture for the elites and 'popular' culture for the masses. Like all other dictatorships, Mussolini's regime exploited and manipulated culture for propaganda purposes.

D

DC (*Democrazia Cristiana*, Christian Democrats): formed in 1944 as Catholic, democratic and anti-Communist party. The DC dominated post-war Italian politics until 1994.

demographic: demography is the scientific study of changes affecting population patterns, such as birth and death rates, where people live, or the age profile of the population.

diktat: the idea of the Treaty of Versailles as a 'dictated peace', imposed upon the Germans without any negotiations.

Dodecanese Islands: islands in the Mediterranean, including Rhodes and Kos.

E

economic sanctions: a form of diplomatic blackmail. By cutting off imports of vital goods and raw materials, sanctions are intended to force a change in policy and behaviour by the country being targeted by sanctions. The idea of sanctions was popular in the 1930s as a way of taking action but avoiding war.

EIAR: the Italian Radio Company.

fasces: bundles of wooden rods that were the symbol of authority in Ancient Rome and adopted as the fascist emblem from 1919.

***Fasci di combattimento* (*Fasci d'azione rivoluzionaria*):** uniformed fascist militia groups.

Fascistisation: (in Italian, *l'Inquadramento*, or 'totalitarian regimentation') aimed at the complete coordination of society according to the principles of fascist ideology.

FIOM: metallurgical workers union.

Fiume: sea port on the Adriatic coast that was made a free city after the collapse of Austria-Hungary. Possession of Fiume was disputed between Italy and Yugoslavia until Mussolini gained it for Italy in January 1924.

Garibaldi Brigades: communist partisans fighting against fascist militias and German forces in 1943–45.

'*Gerarchia*' (Hierarchy): the senior leaders of Mussolini's fascist movement were often referred to as 'gerarchs' (hierarchs).

***Giovinezza!*:** popular marching song that was the 'signature tune' of fascist youth groups and the armed forces.

GUF (*Gioventu Universitaria Fascisti*): Fascist University Youth.

ideology: the ideas, values and beliefs of a political movement, as opposed to its specific practical policies.

***Il Popolo d'Italia* (People of Italy):** fascist newspaper founded by Mussolini in 1914. It ceased publication in 1943.

infrastructure: the framework of a modern industrial economy – roads, railways, telecommunications, power stations, public utilities, etc.

IRI: Institute for the Reconstruction of Industry, set up in 1933.

Lateran Pacts: historic compromise of 1929, reconciling Church and State in Italy after bitter dispute lasting 59 years since unification.

lay organisation: run by and on behalf of 'lay' people (that is, people who have not been ordained into the priesthood).

Liberal Italy: the name commonly given to the new united Italy from 1870 to 1922. Liberal Italy was a parliamentary democracy, ruled by a constitutional monarchy.

Littoriali Games: organised sporting activities for Italian youth groups. The Games were a propaganda method of coordinating youth and bringing attention to the 'Littoriali' project to reclaim marshlands and develop new cities on the coast west of Rome.

***L'Osservatore Romano* (Roman Observer):** official newspaper of the papacy and the Catholic Church in Italy.

M

March on Rome: symbolic demonstration of power and mass support for Fascism in 1922, calculated to panic the Italian government into accepting Mussolini.

Marxism: the ideology of Socialism and Communism, first set out by Karl Marx and Friedrich Engels in the *Communist Manifesto* of 1849.

MSI (Italian Social Movement): neo-fascist party established after the end of the Second World War.

MVSN (Voluntary Militia for National Security): paramilitary organisation of uniformed fascist militia.

oligarchy: the monopolisation of political power by social and political groups. In an oligarchy, power is rotated or shared (and there may be the outward trappings of democracy) but is actually controlled by a narrow group for their own interests.

ONB (*Opera Nazionale Balilla*): fascist boy scouts.

OND (*Opera Nazionale Dopolavoro*): National After Work Association.

OVRA (Organisation for Vigilance and Repression against Anti-Fascism): the secret state police in Fascist Italy.

papal encyclical: a letter containing official pronouncements from the Pope, circulated round the worldwide Catholic Church.

PCI (*Partito Communista Italiano*, Italian Communist Party): volunteer armies fighting against the Salo Republic and German forces in northern Italy in 1943–45.

PFR (Fascist Party of the Republic): the re-formed Fascist Party of the Salo Republic, replacing the PNF.

PNF (*Partito Nationale Fascista*): National Fascist Party.

PNM (National Monarchist Party): party supporting the Italian monarchy against Republicanism.

***podesta*:** fascist local official, replacing the post of mayor.

PPI (*Partito Popolare Italiano – Popolari*, Italian Popular Party): Catholic political party headed by Don Sturzo.

protective tariffs: duties imposed on imported goods to make them more expensive and thus 'protect' goods produced in the home country.

PSI (*Partito Socialista Italiano*): the Italian Socialist Party.

***Quadrumvirs*:** the leaders of the four columns of the March on Rome: Italo Balbo; Michele

Bianchi; Emilio De Bono; and Cesare Maria De Vecchi. The term was taken from the *Quadrumvirate* who had been joint leaders of the Republic in Ancient Rome.

R

'Radiant May': the mass national enthusiasm in response to Italy's entry into the war in 1915.

radicalisation: imposing more radical and extreme policies in accordance with ideological aims.

***ras*:** title of the important leaders of fascist action squads.

real wages: the value of wages after prices have been taken into account – a pay rise may actually be the same as a pay cut if prices rise by a greater amount. The best measurement of real wages is the calculation of how many hours work would be required in order to pay for necessities like food and rent.

***Risorgimento*:** the 19th-century movement for national independence and unification of Italy, led by Mazzini, Garibaldi and Cavour, culminating in the emergence of Liberal Italy by 1870.

RSI (*Repubblica Sociale Italiana*): North Italian Social Republic, often known as the Salo Republic.

S

***squadristi*:** squads of uniformed fascist militia.

Stresa Front: agreement between Italy, Britain and France, signed in 1935.

syndicalism: the organisation of trade unions for political purposes.

T

The 'Phoney War': the nickname coined in Britain for the inaction in the European war between the conquest of Poland at the end of September 1939 and the launch of Hitler's invasion in the West in April 1940. There were almost no military operations during these months; for a time, Hitler was hopeful that Britain and France would actually make peace with him.

Totalitarian state: a state in which political power is totally controlled by one party and in which all individuals are totally merged into one coordinated mass society.

Totalitarianism: the belief that all aspects of society must be coordinated by the State and that all individuals in society should become one single, united mass dedicated to the same ideological goals and loyal to the leader.

Treaty of Lausanne: peace agreement to finalise the borders between Greece and Turkey in 1923. This treaty re-negotiated the agreement made at Sevres in 1920.

Treaty of Rapallo: treaty agreed between Italy and Yugoslavia in November 1920, fixing the new borders between the two countries and making Fiume a free city.

U

***Unione Spirituale Dannunziana*:** the Spiritual League of admirers of Gabriele D'Annunzio.

***Ustase*:** Croatian fascist militia, headed by Ante Pavelich.

Vidoni Pact: pact between workers organisations and employers, signed at the Palazzo Vidoni in 1925.

Bibliography

General

Students

Evans, D. (2005) *Teach Yourself Mussolini's Italy*, Hodder.

Hite, J. and Hinton, C. (1998) *Fascist Italy*, Hodder Murray.

Robson, M. (2006) *Italy: The Rise of Fascism 1915–1945*, Hodder.

Teachers and extension

Blinkhorn, M. (1984) *Mussolini and Fascist Italy*, Methuen.

Bosworth, R. J. B. (2006) *Mussolini's Italy: Life under the Dictatorship*, Penguin.

Bosworth, R. J. B. (2002) *Mussolini*, Hodder Arnold.

Clark, M. (2005) *Mussolini*, Pearson.

Clark, M. (1984) *Modern Italy 1871–1982*, Longman.

Duggan, C. (2007) *The Force of Destiny: Italy Since 1796*, Penguin.

Duggan, C. (1994) *A Concise History of Italy*, Cambridge University Press.

Farrell, N. (2004) *Mussolini: A New Life*, Phoenix.

Knight, P. (2003) *Mussolini & Fascism*, Routledge.

Mack Smith, D. (1981) *Mussolini*, Weidenfeld & Nicolson.

Morgan, P. (2004) *Italian Fascism 1915–1945*, Macmillan.

Mussolini, B. (1928) *My Autobiography*, Mayflower Press.

Overy, R. (1998) *Times Atlas of 20th Century History*.

Pearce, R. (1997) *Fascism & Nazism*, Hodder & Stoughton.

Pollard, J. (1998) *The Fascist Experience in Italy*, Routledge.

Seldes, G. (1936) *Sawdust Caesar*, Arthur Barker Ltd.

Whittam, J. (1995) *Fascist Italy*, Manchester University Press.

Section 1 Establishing the fascist regime, 1922–29

Students

Laver, J. and Wolfson, R. (1999) *Years of Change: Europe 1890–1945*, Hodder.

Townley, E. (2002) *Mussolini and Italy 1922–1940*, Heinemann.

Teachers and extension

Lyttleton, A. (2004) *The Seizure of Power – Fascism in Italy 1919–29*, Routledge.

Pollard, J. (1985) *The Vatican and Italian Fascism*, Cambridge.

Sassoon, D. (2007) *Mussolini and the Rise of Fascism*, HarperCollins.

Williamson, D. (1997) *Mussolini: From Socialist to Fascist*, Hodder.

Section 2 The Corporate State

Students

Townley, E. (2002) *Mussolini & Italy 1922–1940*, Heinemann.

Teachers and extension

Bosworth, R. J. B. (2006) *Mussolini's Italy: Life under the Dictatorship*, Penguin.

De Grand, A. (2000) *Italian Fascism*, University of Nebraska.

Whittam, J. (1995) *Fascist Italy*, Manchester University Press.

Section 3 Fascist ideology and social change

Students

Hite, J. and Hinton, C. (1998) *Fascist Italy*, Hodder Murray.

Teachers and extension

De Grazia, V. (1993) *How Fascism Ruled Women: Italy 1922–1945*, California University Press.

Eatwell, R. (1995) *Fascism: A History*, Chatto & Windus.

Falasca-Zamponi, S. (2000) *Fascist Spectacle*, California University Press.

Griffin, R. (1991) *The Nature of Fascism*, Routledge.

Thompson, D. (1991) *State Control in Fascist Italy*, Manchester University Press.

Wiskemann, E. (1969) *Fascism in Italy*, Macmillan.

Other sources

Ambler, E. (1938) *Cause for Alarm*, Penguin.

Hayward Gallery exhibition catalogue (1995) *Art and Power.*

Section 4 Italian foreign policy, 1923–39

Students

Robson, M. (2006) *Italy: The Rise of Fascism 1915–1945*, Hodder.

Teachers and extension

Gooch, J. (2008) *Mussolini and his Generals*, Cambridge University Press.

Grenville, J. A. S. (1994) *The Collins History of the 20th Century*, HarperCollins.

Mack Smith, D. (1977) *Mussolini's Roman Empire*, Penguin.

Mallett, R. (2003) *Mussolini and the Origins of the Second World War 1933–1940*, Palgrave Macmillan.

Overy, R. and Wheatcroft, A. (1990) *The Road To War: Italy*, Random House.

Section 5 War and the fall of Mussolini, 1940–45

Students

Clark, M. (2005) *Mussolini*, Pearson.

Teachers and extension

Deakin, F. W. (1981) *The Brutal Friendship*, Penguin.

Ginsborg, P. (1990) *A History of Contemporary Italy 1943–1988*, Penguin.

Knox, M. (1982) *Mussolini Unleashed 1939–1941: Politics & Strategy in Fascist Italy's Last War*, Cambridge University Press.

Morgan, P. (2007) *The Fall of Mussolini*, Oxford.

Moseley, R. (2006) *The Last Days of Mussolini*, Macmillan.

Steinberg, J. (1991) *All or Nothing: The Axis and the Holocaust*, Routledge.

Taylor, A. J. P. (1978) *The Warlords*, Penguin.

Film/DVD

1900 (dir. Bernardo Bertolucci) 1993.

The Garden of the Finzi-Continis (dir. Vittorio De Sica) 1971.

Italian Fascism in Colour, 2007.

Rome, Open City (dir. Roberrto Rossellini) 1945.

Men of Our Time: Mussolini (narrated by A. J. P. Taylor) 1970.

Mussolini: Italy's Nightmare, 1995.

The Road to War: Italy. (BBC) 1989.

Novel

Newby, E. (1996) *Love and War in the Appennines*, Picador.

Websites

Useful source material is provided on the following websites:

Spartacus Educational – a good general documentary resource:
www.spartacus.schoolnet.co.uk

BBC 'On This Day' site – lively in-depth accounts of important events:
http://news.bbc.co.uk/onthisday/

Mussolini in pictures:
http://home.comcast.net/~lowe9101/mussolini/

Extensive materials on the rise of Fascism:
www.thecorner.org/hist/total/f-italy.htm

Acknowledgements

The author and publisher would like to thank the following for permission to reproduce material:

Source texts:

p12 (2) Short extract from *Italian Fascism* by Giampiero Carocci (Pelican 1975) © Giampiero Carocci, 1975. Reprinted with permission of Penguin Books; pp12 (3), 44 (4) short extracts from *The Fascist Experience In Italy* by John Pollard, Routledge 1998. Reprinted with permission of Taylor and Francis Books (UK); p24 short extract from *The Dark Valley* by Piers Brandon, Vintage 2002; p34 short extract from *Fascist Italy* by John Wittam, published by Manchester University Press, 1991. Reprinted with permission of Manchester University Press; pp38 (Source C), 45 (6) short extracts from *Italian Fascism: Its Origins And Development* by Alexander J. De Grant by permission of the University of Nebraska Press © 1982, 1989, 2000; p42 short extract from *Mussolini* by Martin Clark, Prentice Hall, 2005. Reprinted with permission of Pearson Education Ltd; pp65, 140 (Source C) short extracts from *Fascism: A History* by Roger Eatwell, published by Pimlico and Penguin © 1996 by Roger Eatwell. Reprinted with permission of The Random House Group Ltd and Penguin, a division of Penguin Group (USA) Inc; p70 short extract from *How Fascism Ruled Women: Italy 1922-1945* by Victoria De Grazia, University of California Press, 1992 © 1992 by the Regents of the University of California. Reprinted with permission; p71 short extract from *Italy: The Rise of Fascism, 1915-1945* by Mark Robson, Hodder Education, 2006. Reprinted with permission of Hodder Education; p72 short extract from *State Control in Fascist Italy* by Doug Thompson, MUP 1991 © Doug Thompson. Reprinted with permission of the author; p82 short extract from *Italian Fascism and Female Body: Sport, Submissive Women and Strong Mothers* by Gigliola Gori, Routledge 2004. Reprinted with permission of Cengage Learning Services Limited; pp84, 88, 112 short extracts from *Mussolini's Roman Empire* by Denis Mack Smith published by Penguin 1977 © Denis Mack Smith. Reprinted with permission of the author; p92 short extract from *Mussolini's Italy* by Max Gallo. Translated from French by Charles Lam Markmann. Copyright © 1964 by Librairie Academique Perrin. English translation copyright © 1973 by Macmillan Publishing Co, Inc. All rights reserved; p95 short extract from *Mussolini's Roman Empire* by G. T. Garratt, published by Penguin 1938; p103 short extract from *Modern Italy* by Martin Clark, Longman 1984. Reprinted with permission of Pearson Education Ltd; pp105, 140 (B) short extracts from *Mussolini: A New Life* by Nicholas Farrell, Weidenfeld & Nicholson 2003. Reprinted with permission of The Orion Publishing Group Limited; p110 short extract from *The Last Days of Mussolini* by Ray Moseley, Sutton Publishing 2006. Reprinted with permission of the publisher; p132 (5) short extract from *Fall of Mussolini* by Philip Morgan, OUP 2007. Reprinted with permission of Oxford University Press; (6) short extract from *Mussolini* by R. J. B. Bosworth, Hodder Arnold 2002. Reprinted with permission of Bloomsbury Academic, an imprint of A&C Black Publishers Limited; p140 (A) short extract from *A History of Contemporary Italy: Society and Politics 1943-1988* © Paul Ginsborg by permission of United Agents Ltd (www.unitedagents.co.uk) on behalf of the author.

Photographs:

Edimedia Archive pp4, 10, 12, 13, 20, 29, 31, 33 (top), 34, 37, 44, 45, 54, 56, 58, 59, 64, 65, 71, 74, 76, 80, 84, 85, 90 (top), 93, 95, 96, 98, 99, 106, 113, 123, 126, 128, 131, 133, 135, 136; G. Apostolo p102; Photos12 pp8, 21, 39, 62, 94, 97, 110, 138, The Fry Collection pp61, 63; The Print Collector p82; Topfoto pp68, 141, 90 (bottom); World History Archive pp24, 27, 33 (bottom) 50, 130.

Photo Research by *www.mediaselectors.com*.

Researchers: Alexander Goldberg & Jason Newman

Every effort has been made to contact the copyright holders and we apologise if any have been overlooked. Should copyright have been unwittingly infringed in this book, the owners should contact the publishers, who will make the corrections at reprint.

Index

Key terms are in **bold**